A PEOPLE'S HISTORY OF
TOTTENHAM
HOTSPUR
FOOTBALL CLUB

A PEOPLE'S HISTORY OF

TOTTENHAM HOTSPUR

FOOTBALL CLUB

HOW SPURS FANS SHAPED THE IDENTITY OF ONE OF THE WORLD'S MOST FAMOUS CLUBS

MARTIN CLOAKE
AND ALAN FISHER

First published by Pitch Publishing, 2016

Pitch Publishing
A2 Yeoman Gate
Yeoman Way
Worthing
Sussex
BN13 3QZ
www.pitchpublishing.co.uk

© 2016, Martin Cloake and Alan Fisher

ISBN 978-1-78531-188-8

Typesetting and origination by Pitch Publishing

Printed by Bell & Bain, Glasgow, Scotland

Contents

Acknowledgements

MANY people over many years have influenced our approach to this book and helped shape our thoughts. The fans who gave up their time are all named as this people's history unfolds, but there are many more who we have met over the years who have influenced what we've produced but who are not named. Any omissions are purely down to the passage of time and the number of people we've met.

Producing a book such as this requires not only effort by the authors, but help from a large number of people. We'd like to thank Adam Powley, Katrina Law, Stuart Mutler, John Williams, Flav Bateman, Julie Welch, Mark Damazer, Andrea Warman, Simon Schama, Rob White, Tom Fisher, Paul Irons, Charles Atterton, Dan and Chris Whymark, readers of Tottenham On My Mind. At Pitch Publishing, Paul and Jane Camillin have provided vital support and a belief that this book could happen. Thanks also to Duncan Olner and Dean Rockett.

Finally, thanks to our families, friends and fellow fans who put up with us while we were writing this.

Foreword

I CAN place, with almost frightening accuracy, the exact moment I became a Spurs fan.

It was Saturday, 6 May 1961, a few days before my eighth birthday, the day Spurs won the Double. To be honest, I knew a bit, but not all that much about football, or Spurs, for that matter until then but I knew they had done something very special because the man on the telly said they had become the first team in the 20th century to win the league and the FA Cup in the same season.

Even my dad, who was more into boxing than football but was watching the cup final with me, was impressed, and told me that this was something that Arsenal, who, he assured me, were Spurs' biggest rivals, had never done, and somehow, don't ask me why now, that just clinched it. The seed was sown and it's been nurtured for more than half a century. Of course, not yet being eight, I had no idea what I had let myself in for but there has never been a second's regret that this is my club.

Ask any Spurs fan what being a Spurs fan means to them and this is, more or less, the answer: "I love it, I love the way we play, I loved Jimmy Greaves, Dave Mackay, Glenn Hoddle, Ossie, Ricky, Gazza, Bale. I love Harry Kane and Dele Alli right now, but it's been agony, it's been heart-breaking, so many false dawns, some days of glory, but years of envy, of frustration, of finishing behind Arsenal, never winning at the Bridge. But we are Spurs, it'll be alright, its all about the glory, we are special." Or as my mate, the world-weary Chris says, "It's a hideous addiction. So much frustration." But, as he also admits: "It could have been a lot worse, we could have ended up supporting Rochdale, no slight intended, but you know what I mean."

We do indeed and in writing this book, Martin and Alan have set out to find exactly what it does mean to support Spurs and how that has shaped the club by talking to fans across the generations to bring together this *People's History of Tottenham Hotspur Football Club*.

I first went to White Hart Lane in August 1964 (2-0 v Sheffield United, Greaves and Saul), and have since seen almost 800 matches there and I am going to miss the old place when it's gone, but at the same time can't wait to see the new stadium completed.

I've sat or stood with Neil, Louis, Shaun, Ryan, Nuts, Ken, Martyn, Kevin, Jimmy, Richard, William, Siobhan, Hannah, Melissa, Andy, Alex, Steve, Eddie, Simon, Chris, Gill, Andrew and all the others: Upper and Lower, East and West, Park Lane and Paxton, and even played there once in 2002 for a press team, despite doing my hammy in the warm-up. I was on crutches for a month afterwards but I've still got the turf that I scraped off my boots in a sealed jar at home.

I was there the April day we beat Arsenal 5-0, the night we beat Anderlecht on penalties, the 9-0 v Bristol Rovers, the 9-1 v Wigan, the night Maradona and Hoddle did their party tricks in Ossie's testimonial and the day Hoddle scored his last goal against Oxford.

A hideous addiction? No, more of a lifelong love affair. Read the stories from the fans in these pages. You'll know exactly what I mean.

Mike Collett
Lifelong Spurs fan, Football Editor of Reuters,
the international news agency, and author of the
Complete Record of the FA Cup

Introduction

WHEN Tottenham Hotspur announced an interest in moving from Tottenham to Stratford in 2010, it seemed a very modern football development. At Stratford was the Olympic Stadium, new, well-connected to the transport system, helpfully funded by the taxpayer. Tottenham was down at heel and badly connected and White Hart Lane was falling behind rival stadiums able to generate significantly more money every matchday.

Of course, there were objections – but weren't there always? Football fans are very fond of citing tradition, but in a world of competing global brands, what did a few miles across the same city matter? Success is everything, and the days of achieving success through the strength of local support or the machinations of a clever manager were long gone. Now, success comes from money, so making as much money as possible increases the chances of success. Tottenham Hotspur, Stratford Hotspur, Schmotspur Hotspur – the harsh realities of modern football meant that hard heads, not bleeding hearts, were needed.

But Tottenham Hotspur never did go to Stratford. There are some, very well-connected, people who insist the club never intended to go – it was just a negotiating ploy to get Haringey Council to roll over. Others say that, even if it was originally a ploy, Spurs would have jumped at Stratford if it had been offered. And, of course, it was entirely possible that the story was as it appeared on the surface – that the board of Tottenham Hotspur saw a move to Stratford as the future. The truth, until the club's chairman Daniel Levy decides to write his life story, will never be known. But the whole affair revealed something remarkable.

Despite all of football's efforts to present its top teams as global brands, to break with the past and instead submit to a future in which the measure of your support will be defined only in proportion to your willingness to consume the product, a significant number of Tottenham Hotspur fans said their team was more than just a brand. As they campaigned noisily they talked of community and identity. And perhaps more remarkable still, people who lived and worked near the ground but were rarely seen inside it also spoke of community and identity as they joined those urging the club to stay in the area it had been in for over 150 years.

Tottenham Hotspur meant something more than the name of a global brand, and what's more a number of communities recognised and valued this. The local community was one, and the fact that it valued the presence of Tottenham Hotspur so strongly came as a surprise to many.

The area of Tottenham, once an airy, leafy suburb, has become symbolic of inner-city decay. It has never recovered from the closure of the Gestetner factory in 1979, and languished for decades while other areas blighted by de-industrialisation and the various social and economic convulsions of late 20th century capitalism were reinvented. The fact that it's one of those solid Labour-voting areas that the Tories punish and Labour takes for granted probably hasn't helped. It has a high black and ethnic minority population, fuelling prejudice and the feeling that it is a place apart. And it has periodically spoken its mind in the strongest terms, with some of the fiercest civil disturbances witnessed in mainland Britain. It is non-conformist, opinionated, independent. Gentrification has barely touched Tottenham High Street and the warren of terraced houses and estates surrounding it. It looks tatty and dated and life is hard for those who live there, meaning many must make hard choices about how to get by.

Into this area, roughly once a fortnight, sometimes three times in a week, come 36,000 outsiders. They are mainly better off than the people who live in Tottenham, and often suspicious of and worried by the area. They drink, eat, drop litter, crowd the buses, clog the roads, swear, sing and sometimes fight. If tensions are high, police swell the numbers, sometimes marching large gangs of snarling men through the streets while attempting to stop other groups of snarling men getting to grips with them. Roads are closed, parking restricted, inconvenience at best and damage at worst is to be expected. All of these people are attracted by a business that sits in the middle of but somehow apart from the area that surrounds it. The business turns over millions of pounds a year, on a par with a decent-sized supermarket branch but far beyond what any of the struggling independent outfits on the High Road can dream of. It buys and sells players for millions, pays them millions, returns large profits and is owned by a tax exile.

If ever there was an alien presence, it is Tottenham Hotspur Football Club. The community turns over rapidly. Many who lived there when the players could be seen regularly in the local streets and pubs and businesses and lived in the Edwardian and Victorian terraces rather than the plush avenues of London's outer rim are long gone. New communities with other pasts and other ties have replaced them. They have no historic reason to embrace the club, and little reason to identify with it in modern times.

But in the uproar that followed the news that Tottenham Hotspur FC was considering a move to Stratford in east London, that local community talked of "our club", of pride and identity. And they wanted it to stay.

For Tottenham's fans, the considerations were different. Many regularly cursed the lousy transport links – although the stadium is served by ten bus routes and five train stations, the bottlenecks caused by the numbers coming to games are notorious. Few lived in

Tottenham. If you could afford a ticket, you almost certainly could afford to live somewhere better. The old, traditional communities had moved out; partly a result of the pattern of London living which saw affluence ripple ever outwards; the inevitable consequence of years of neglect. Add to this the club's fame and its permanent presence in the shiny global Premier League gaining it supporters not only from far beyond the N17 postcode but from across the globe, and it would have been easy to assume that Tottenham the area was far from being a prime consideration for supporters.

But overwhelmingly – although not unanimously – Tottenham's fans said community and identity meant not only the One Hotspur the club marketed, but Tottenham Hotspur from Tottenham.

Few could have predicted that would be the case. And, as some commentators observed at the time, it was hard to know what people really meant when they spoke of community and identity. What was certain was that these concepts mattered, despite the attempts of the modern game to marginalise them. We wanted to find out why, and how.

Both of us are long-time Spurs fans. Our link with the area is through family, although we moved away years ago. We've travelled to watch the team all over Europe, meeting and getting to know the community of committed Spurs fans, for years. And we've both always had more than a passing interest in the history of the club. The idea of writing a people's history of the club we support has been in our minds for some time. The events of 2010 rattled those thoughts around and threw them into the mix with all of the discussions and protests and assertions of those days, days in which the club's board and the fans opposing its plans to move accused each other of trying to destroy the club.

That Spurs built a reputation upon playing attractive football is a truth that has become a cliché. But the club's reputation was also built upon being the side of the emerging suburbs, a north London team that could take on and beat the best of the dominant industrial north of England, plucky independents who were badly treated by the game's authorities. Formed by Tottenham schoolboys under a municipal gas lamp on Tottenham High Road, the club added Tottenham to its original name of Hotspur to distinguish itself from another London Hotspur. Dubbed the Flower of the South, the suburban amateurs won the Southern League in style and banged upon the door of the northern-dominated Football League.

The FA, then as now, did not take kindly to those who tried to change the established order. Spurs were treated harshly in a dispute over a payment to a player, leading to closure of the ground. The perceived injustice attracted support and crowds grew. The Southern League win underlined the club's credentials, but two years later the biggest crowd ever at that time to gather for a British football match, over 114,815, swamped Crystal Palace Park in Sydenham, south London, to watch Spurs take on Sheffield United in the FA Cup Final. United represented the industrial, professional, dominant north. Spurs were the coming force. The match was drawn, but only due to the referee's incorrect line call – the first official to be caught out by moving picture film. Yet more injustice, yet more support, and when Spurs won the replay – becoming the first and remaining the only non-league team to win the cup – there were wild celebrations in the streets of Tottenham.

Already, the personality was being formed – that thing we call Tottenham. It is more than the colour of a jersey, more than a single achievement, an honours list or current potential. It is a collection of experiences, of shared history, of a past and a present understood and interpreted. It is a community, many-stranded, often fractious, but always Tottenham. In this book, we aim to try and articulate an idea of what Tottenham is. Not Tottenham Hotspur the club, because that is clear enough, but Tottenham Hotspur the idea, the thing that is held dear by so many for so many different reasons.

We believe this is important because the game is, increasingly, attempting to redefine our own history in order to sell it back to us. At Hull City and Cardiff City, owners are attempting to annex what they have inherited, discarding that which they have used to gain influence in the first place. At Coventry City, a club has been ripped from its community. In Milton Keynes, the festering sore of franchised football remains – although there too a complex discussion about community and identity is emerging. At Leeds United and Northampton Town and all across the country, the battle for a culture and a game created by ordinary people is being fought.

Telling such a story, articulating such an idea, is a challenge. By definition, folk histories are particular perspectives, so the story as seen by one person or one set of people will be very different from that identified with by another. For that reason this book is not The, but A, people's history. We have researched and drawn on a wide range of sources but, inevitably, at a club of this size with 133 years of history, there will be strands of the story we haven't covered, and perspectives on those we have included missing. We've tried to give a sense of that in how we've organised the book. We begin by telling the story from the club's formation to the Second World War, drawing mainly on published sources to tell the story of how the club and its support created a unique identity. We look at how the development of London and particularly the suburbs helped fuel that identity, and we try to give an idea of what Tottenham Hotspur meant to the people who made the club their own.

As the story continues, we take a less linear approach. As well as published material, we were able to draw on original research and experience, talking to fans who lived through the times about their experiences and hearing them explain their idea of Tottenham Hotspur. As the club and its support became bigger, so the strands of folk history mutiply and fragment, spinning and spiralling ever outwards. The linear tale becomes a vista of snapshots, a series of experiences running concurrently, sometimes almost entirely unconnected but for that single strand – Tottenham Hotspur. In this part of the story, it is the emerging themes that we focus on, following their development rather than a strict timeline. As the club's standing grows, its support is drawn from a wider pool as a national reputation becomes international. New generations of fans begin to form their own bonds with the club, and the influence of disposable incomes and youth culture are felt. There's a growing sense of supporters defining themselves as well as their club, something which feeds into an independence of thought and a sense that the club and its fans are not always the same thing. And we see a more pronounced emergence of communities, rather than a single community, of Spurs fans.

Since 1992, football – at the top level especially – has undergone enormous change. The Premier League, an idea enthusiastically pushed by Tottenham Hotspur but which the club has so far failed to capitalise on as it envisaged, is now that most modern of things, a global brand. And a hugely successful one at that. With that have come increasing strains between the people's game and the people. The danger that the game will confuse the results of its popularity with the reasons for its popularity is ever-present. This modern people's history is still being written and so, in the final part of the book, we provide our own take on this unfolding chapter as well as drawing on the views of other supporters.

Football forms a significant part of culture. In Britain it has a unique history and connection to community and identity. The most high-profile, richest brand in world sport is something that was created by the hearts and dreams and aspirations of ordinary people. It matters to people because it really is the people's game, created by the people and invested with its importance by people – their efforts, their dreams, their disappointments.

As we neared completion of this book, the question of whether we had taken on an impossible task kept plaguing us. For every take on a people's history, there would be another. Our view of some events and our interpretation of others would be completely different to the views and interpretations of other fans. And what of the perspectives not included? How could we be sure that every perspective had been included? Of course, we couldn't, which leads us to make the point again that this can only be A people's history. Perhaps a result of us writing this book will be to prompt others to come forward and tell their story. The more people who put their history in the public domain, the more accurate the picture will be. This book will merely be the start of the process, but what is important is that ordinary people who have shaped the character of one of the world's great football clubs get the chance to tell a story that others want to tell for them, for their own reasons.

Every club can tell the story of what makes it unique, of why it is more than just a brand.

This is one such story.

1

A crowd walked across the muddy fields to watch the Hotspur play

IN 1882 Tottenham was a thriving, vibrant community intent on developing an identity in keeping with its fast-growing prosperity and status. The transformation from rustic village to urban hinterland that began in the early years of the century generated irresistible momentum in the 1850s, the reverberations of which were tangible. Housing, industry and infrastructure mushroomed alongside exponential population growth to change the character of the area irrevocably. As local industry and business flourished, so the area developed a corresponding sense of civic pride. The burgeoning middle classes enthusiastically embraced late-Victorian values of hard work, self-reliance and abstinence.

People had farmed the Tottenham area since medieval times. For centuries it remained unchanged in bucolic splendour, noted by travellers as a restful place to stop, relax, maybe fish by the River Lea, on the journey from London north along the High Road to the leafy pastures of Enfield, Hertfordshire and beyond.

However, for regular travellers it became hard work with poorly maintained roads and highwaymen lurking in the shadows. Gradual improvements by the Turnpike Trust turned the road from a glorified cart-track into a highway fit for the new age, although improvements barely kept pace with the upsurge in traffic. Tottenham was ideally placed to carry the vast increase of business and commercial traffic south into London and north to Hertford, Cambridge and the north.

By 1830 there were daily coach services from London to the north, stopping to pick up passengers at the Ship Inn in the High Road, still a pub about ten minutes' walk from White Hart Lane. Half-hourly coach services and then the introduction of the horse-drawn omnibus enabled professional residents of Tottenham to commute to and from the City. The completion of the Seven Sisters Road in 1833 opened up routes to west London. Trams arrived in 1870.

Although the railway came near the village in 1840, it was little used by passengers. The Liverpool Street to Enfield line, finished in 1872 with stations at White Hart Lane, Bruce Grove and Seven Sisters, transformed the area within a few years. The coaches and buses were used mainly by the professional middle classes. The railway opened Tottenham up to clerks, tradesmen and artisans, attracted by cheaper rents, a better environment and weekly fares of one shilling to and from central London. Tottenham was an attractive place to live in mid-Victorian times. Rural but within reach of the city, it also had abundant natural resources to interest industry.

The railway had a profound and lasting effect on the population, which rose from 9,120 in 1851 to 71,343 in 40 years, an increase of nearly 800%. Tottenham was a place of migration, the urban middle and lower middle classes moving out from London to the suburbs where they mixed with rural folk from all over the country attracted by the prospect of finding work in the city.

"Wealthy landowners moved out, the workmen, labourers, clerks and teachers moved in, and Tottenham shifted to a predominantly lower middle and working class area," according to Christine Protz in her history of the Tottenham area.

There was a housing boom, with a mixture of tightly packed and often jerry-built terraces marching up from South Tottenham to Park Lane at which point they met the semi-detached houses and detached villas of Northumberland Park and Philip Lane, where residents considered themselves socially superior to the terrace-dwelling tradesmen, artisans and factory workers. This is typical London where social status was marked in subtle ways clearly decipherable to local people as classes lived cheek by jowl. Tottenham as a village disappeared for 150 years, at least until the name if not the reality was rediscovered by estate agents and builders luring another generation to the area with the same prospect of lower house prices.

Gradually the population became less reliant on London as a source of employment and income. The work came to Tottenham as industry settled in the area, bringing jobs and prosperity. White Hart Lane was the setting for two large potteries. Off the High Road was Warne's rubber factory, an important local employer. Brewing was another significant local industry, taking advantage of the good local water supplies. The extensive Bell Brewery near the present ground was taken over by Whitbread. Brewer Charrington was another local firm with land in the area.

Later, at the turn of the century, Harris Lebus, the son of a Jewish immigrant, opened a furniture factory close to Tottenham Hale that at one point employed more than 1,000 people. Another Jewish immigrant, David Gestetner, moved to Tottenham from the East End in 1906, his office equipment business remaining a major local employer even after it became a multi-national organisation. The area has never fully recovered from the closure of Gestetner's factory in the late 1970s. Many of the workers were Jewish migrants from Europe who settled around Tottenham Hale, known locally for a time as 'Little Russia'.

With these developments came the problems associated with rapid population growth: poor sanitary and health conditions. What little public services were around were bursting at the seams. The Parish of Tottenham could significantly improve the supply of drinking water in the early part of the century by erecting a fountain opposite the Bell and Hare public house. That was no longer enough.

Fledging local government improved the sanitation and water supply as the century drew to a close. Local subscriptions established the Tottenham and Edmonton Dispensary in 1864 to provide access to a doctor for working people. Rebuilt in 1910, the facade is to be retained as part of the new stadium development. There were hospitals too, on the site of the old Prince of Wales Hospital in Tottenham Green, and St Ann's Hospital. The considerable local Jewish community helped to fund the Jewish Home and Hospital for Incurables, built on the High Road in 1889.

With the expansion came a sense of civic pride. People had migrated to Tottenham but many wanted to settle and make it a place fit to bring up their families. Local amenities were opened with fanfare and celebration. The annual carnival was well-attended and brought people out into the streets. The middle class saw it as their duty to put something back into the community and enthusiastically sponsored libraries, hospitals and schools. Involvement in these projects was also good advertising for local businesses, who also saw civic duties as good public relations as well as bequeathing social status.

One feature of the Tottenham area as early as the 1600s was the number of schools established in the area, boarding schools at first catering for the middle classes, then a grammar school and several schools with a more varied curriculum opened and run by Quaker dissenters.

In the mid-19th century, a number of day schools for the middle classes were established and the long-standing grammar school continued to operate on its site in Somerset Road, reformed and reopened in 1877 as a fee-paying secondary school. Nearby a Mr Cameron ran St John's School, a Presbyterian institution.

Boys from the Grammar and St John's came together to play cricket for the Hotspur Club, so named in honour of Sir Henry Percy from the Northumberland family, an heroic rebel better known as Harry Hotspur. The family owned land in north London, including what is now called Northumberland Park, home to many of the middle-class boys whose sport embodied the virtues of teamwork and physical exercise.

These boys grew up amidst this environment of rapid change and advancement, knowing nothing else but this spirit of enterprise and self-reliance. Their families were ambitious for them. They were encouraged to think for themselves, to earn their status, to be grateful for their relatively privileged upbringing but knowing that, like their parents, they had to work to better themselves rather than assume privilege as of right. From their parents they learned the value of education, knowledge and hard work, of working together, of friendship, and that their town and a sense of local pride were important.

These were the boys, and they were boys not men, who gathered one evening under the second lamppost along the High Road south of the present ground to form Hotspur Football Club. Faced with winter boredom and ungodly idleness when the cricket season came to an end, they created their own solution.

This club was also Hotspur and they chose to play football under association rules. Impromptu committee meetings took place under a street lamp in Northumberland Park. They planned their future and picked the team by candlelight meetings in half-built houses in Willoughby Lane, which runs between the present ground and the railway line through Northumberland Park.

Of the 15 members who appear in the 1881 census, when the club was formed, nine were no older than 13, three no older than 15 and two were 12 or under. The oldest was 16. It makes their determination all the more remarkable. The majority of the boys came from what are best described as skilled technical or entrepreneurial middle-class families. Most had servants at home. The 1881 Census records the father's occupation for 10 of the boys as follows:

> Retired silk manufacturer
> Yarn and fibre merchant
> Printer
> Watch and clock maker
> Plumber and decorator master
> Meteorological Officer Civil Service
> Boot Manufacturer
> Pensioner Gunmaker
> Artist and Sign-writer of Names Over Shops
> Commercial clerk

There's little about their mothers, recorded only as 'Wife', except for Mrs Anderson who lives on "income from railway stock". This was sufficient to maintain four children aged between 12 and seven, plus a servant. Seven of the boys lived in households with a servant, most in the large detached properties, or 'villas' as they were styled by the builders, of Northumberland Park. Two of the lads were already working, the others were at school.

To them this was adventure, as much *Boys' Own* and *Secret Seven* as football. This not-quite-secret society served to develop bonds of solidarity. By the end of the season there were 17 or 18 friends available for selection. It became a closed shop: all were playing members so they were not keen on letting others in. They needed that friendship and solidarity because in their first year they had only their own resources to rely on.

Funds were raised by subscription: sixpence a year. The cricket club helped out a little but otherwise they made the best of what they had. These meagre funds were enough for wood for goal and flag posts, tape (no crossbars in those days), stationery and stamps. Only later did they have enough for a ball. In the meantime, the first ball came from the elder brother of two club members and the goalposts were made by their father.

They played their first matches on public parkland in Tottenham Marshes where they had to claim and mark out their own pitch afresh every time they played. Not quite jumpers for goalposts but only one step above. One early match was abandoned with Hotspur a goal up when the ball burst.

Records are scant enough of the early days of the embryonic Hotspur club, let alone who came to watch, if anyone. However, it seems reasonable to assume that like today's Sunday schoolboy games, a few friends, players not selected that day, brothers and fathers (but unlikely to be mothers) shivered in the mud and wind on the open marshes, fetched the ball when it was booted onto adjacent pitches and carried the posts back to the clubhouse in search of a warming cup of tea.

Mr Casey, the father of club vice-captain Ham Casey and treasurer L.R. Casey, was in all likelihood there, with the boys' older brother who graciously donated their first ball. Bumberry, Davies, Fisher, Howlett, Iverson, Lovell or Tyrell, who joined later in the year, paying double subs for the privilege, probably came to watch before signing up. Friends from school and the cricket club perhaps.

We will never know for sure, but these and others lost in the mists of history were unknowingly the progenitors of an august tradition that has lasted 134 years to the present day. They devoted their precious, hard-earned leisure time to watch the Hotspur.

These values of self-reliance, determination, enterprise, creativity and civic pride were fundamental to the creation of the Hotspur and characterised the club's development – and not just in the next few years. A legacy of creativity and innovation ripples through the club's history. That resilience in those precarious formative years stood the club in good stead and enabled it to survive in a competitive world, marking out territory for the future with more permanence than the lines on the park pitch and contributing first to survival then to stability and success. There were other local teams, other groups of boys banding together and seeking to make a mark. Park FC, Stars, the Radicals or local rivals Latymer. These were the other Tottenham clubs in the early 1880s, playing on the marshes and nearby. There's only one Hotspur, still here while these others have disappeared, leaving their imprint in football history only because some of their players joined the side that fast became the team to play for – Hotspur.

The drive and determination that characterised the formative years of Hotspur football club were further tested and strengthened in adversity. In the first couple of years, the boys played firstly games between themselves. Then, on the first Saturday of October 1883, came the first recorded friendly against another club when Hotspur defeated Brownlow Rovers 9-0 on the marshes. Life was still precarious – the return was abandoned ten minutes from time with Hotspur a goal up when the ball burst. Funds were so short for some amateur sides at the time that a single ball had to last out the season.

One measure of the club's burgeoning reputation was its growing fixture list, bearing in mind they were playing friendlies, not league football. As ever, some games were less friendly than others. Already Edmonton rivals Latymer were conspiring to do down the upstarts. In one fixture they fielded 12 men for the entire first half without being discovered and their second XI played the same trick. A disputed nil-nil draw drew an editorial from the *Herald*: "If these clubs cannot agree, but send contradictory reports, we shall have no alternative but to reject them altogether."

During the 1884/85 season, high jinks at the YMCA meant the boys were undesirables. Gathering in a basement room, they could not resist the urge to kick a ball around. The light broke and the ball went up a chimney, to emerge covered in soot. With impeccable comedy timing, one of the YMCA councillors, having been disturbed in their deliberations in the room above, entered the room and the ball hit him squarely in the face.

This indignity, coupled with accusations of card-playing and pinching the mulberries from the tree in the back garden, was a step too far. Their benefactor, local Bible class teacher John Ripsher, stepped in and with the help of the local vicar found them new premises at 1 Dorset Villas in Northumberland Park, where they remained for two years until Ripsher found better headquarters at the Red House on the High Road.

The middle-class lads from Northumberland Park had rivals in the shape of the High Street Gang, working-class boys from the Lancasterian school, known as Barker's Bulldogs, and the Park Lane school, Simmonds' Greyhounds. This was less about football and more about local rivalry, fierce at times. The Bulldogs caught one luckless Saint, a St John's boy, on his way to school and threw him through a plate glass window.

These Hotspur boys had to have their airs and graces beaten out of them. Greville Wagstaffe-Simmons in his *The History of Tottenham Hotspur Football Club 1882–1947* is in no doubt that this had its roots in class rather than any other allegiance. This was, he solemnly says, "unreasonable hostility, not perhaps so much to football as to the supposed higher social standing of the lads who played it". Organised football in the Tottenham area at least, was not a working-class sport. A few Hotspur members were indeed put off but it seems to have made the others all the more determined.

The games themselves offered little respite. On the marshes it was every man for himself. This was public parkland and some unscrupulous teams simply took over a pitch that had been claimed by others to save themselves the time and trouble of marking out the lines. The Hotspur boys had to stand up for themselves and fight for the right to play.

Trouble came from other sources. Wagstaffe-Simmons records with sniffy disapproval that "there was a gang at that time who watched without cost to themselves the games played on the Marshes and they indulged their bent to use language which was not of a Parliamentary kind. Remonstrances only challenged further abuse. Uncomplimentary epithets were hurled at home players and visitors. The hooligan of those days acted upon the presumption that he had the right to use expletives in abundance about anything and everything of which he did not approve, and there was much in the football of the Marshes that did not appeal to his ignorant taste."

Hotspur suffered too. Just before Christmas 1883, Hotspur played Latymer, an Edmonton team, in what was to become the local derby of the 1880s. The *Herald* reported that they were given a hostile reception: "The visitors suffered much annoyance from the spectators, who, unchecked by the home team, were often coarsely personal in their remarks."

This provoked a stern reply from vice-captain Billy Harston via the newspaper's letters page: "I feel it is my duty to write to you in reference to the one-sided report appearing in your columns. I am surprised that the decision of an experienced umpire should be publicly disputed, as he acted for both elevens. It is utterly impossible to keep a public ground free from such coarse personal remarks and it is not pleasant for a local or any other club to be thus stigmatised by such reports."

Football crowds abusing the players. Friction provoked by a controversial refereeing decision in a derby game. Hooligan behaviour with an edge of violence surrounding the game. Biased media reporting. Truly there is nothing new under the sun. Yet the importance of these accounts, describing the events and atmosphere that incubated the fledging Hotspur club in 1883 and 1884, is that they reveal the existence of a crowd and demonstrate the emergence of a club with a personality, a reputation which that crowd embraced. Rowdy, raucous and uncontrolled that crowd may have been with no allegiance save to have a good time, and we have no idea of numbers, but a crowd walked from Tottenham across the muddy fields to watch the Hotspur play.

You can still follow in their footsteps. Go down to Northumberland Park station, then cross over the level crossing. The road forms a crescent to the right leading to the marshes and around there, between the railway and the River Lea, a crowd gathered around the touchlines of what came to be the Hotspur pitch.

Under this scrutiny, the players did not buckle. On the contrary, their determination to carry on and play seems to have won them grudging respect even on the wilds of the marshes. They must have made an impression because as time went on, their right to their chosen pitch was accepted and they could play on unchallenged. Their devotion to the game and steely regard to carry on, not to mention their ability to play attractive football, gradually won the locals over.

In April 1885 Hotspur cancelled their final fixture and went as a group to watch the FA Cup Final at Kennington Oval between Blackburn Rovers and Queen's Park. This Victorian team-building exercise evidently had a great impact on these impressionable young men, who were so influenced by Blackburn's cultured passing game, with a then revolutionary idea of one of the centre-forwards dropping deep to link defence and attack, that they resolved not just to emulate the style of their new heroes but also to change the club colours from navy blue to the light blue and white halves of the Rovers. Replica shirts were sold in those colours in 2007 to mark the club's 125th anniversary. The letter H remained proud near the boys' hearts. No doubt their dreams took them far beyond Tottenham Marshes.

At the start of the 1884/85 season, to cement local links and to distinguish themselves from another club named London Hotspur, the boys resolved to rename the club. From then on, it became Tottenham Hotspur.

The team quickly developed a reputation for playing good football in a style that fans wanted to see and in so doing established a tradition, some would say an imperative, that resonates with Spurs supporters down the generations.

In 1883/84, Spurs played 11 matches, winning nine. The following season, this total more than doubled. They finished with a record of played 30, won 18, drawn 5. They were also able regularly to field a second XI. Income (from subscriptions, there were no gate receipts) was £5 0s 1d, expenditure £4 11s 1d. Spurs were making a profit of a shilling a year. The club passed a vote of thanks to Mr Martin, stationmaster at Northumberland Park station, for storing the goalposts during the week.

Some players already stood out. Jim Randall was the skipper, drawn to the Hotspur from the Radicals. Jack Jull was a resolute full-back while upfield the left-wing duo of Harston and Buckle distinguished themselves with their pace and combination play. Harston was the ball-player, Buckle fast and direct. Inside them was Cottrell, a great dribbler who laughed with joy as he weaved his way past man after man. Behind them was a parsimonious defence, conceding few goals.

Spurs' style and prowess attracted the attention of able players in the area. Recruits joined from Star while Park FC disbanded in the face of competition. Players now changed in the Milford Tavern in Park Lane between the current ground and Northumberland Park station, a pub popular pre-match until it recently closed.

The Hotspur attracted the attention of local people too. Crowds grew from a handful of spectators to over a hundred. In October 1885, 400 people came to the marshes to watch Spurs' first competitive match, a 5-2 victory against St Albans in the first round of the London Association Cup. Stalwarts Mason and Harston were carried shoulder-high from the field at the final whistle. The day did not end well for Harston however – during the game someone had pinched his overcoat from the changing room.

There were no admission prices but for the first time local people were invited to participate in club activities, at a price. The first concert in aid of the club took place at the Park Lane Drill Hall. It was "crowded out" and made a substantial profit of £15 6s 3 1/2d. The committee resolved to "have rope and stakes around the ground". Spurs were marking out their territory. Crowd control was a factor for the first time. Their first annual dinner raised further funds and the club was renamed Tottenham Hotspur Athletic Club.

The marshes was the scene of another momentous event in Tottenham's history, the first match against Arsenal, although in those days it did not carry any local significance because the then Royal Arsenal travelled from Woolwich in south-east London. Nothing changes: a contemporary report states that the Arsenal scored "a lucky goal within 10 minutes". Luck remained on their side. Spurs fought back well to lead 2-1 but the game was abandoned because it was too dark to play on.

The real rivalry only began 20 years later when Arsenal migrated north of the river to invade Spurs' territory but the fixture demonstrates that opponents were prepared to travel to play Spurs because of their status. This was a friendly as Spurs had not joined a league, and as the club searched for opponents it travelled as far north as Luton for away games. Even in these early days of the club, the area's good transport links enabled its horizons to expand. Spurs were also considered good enough to play representative district sides made up of the best players in Edmonton.

Soon it became clear that Hotspur had outgrown the marshes. The people came to watch the team. Tens became hundreds became thousands. Not only that, they became partisan. No longer did local people come just to watch a good game of football. Around this period, a transformation took place: fans became supporters. They came to get behind their team to help them overcome their opponents, and not always in a positive way.

Writing in 1900 in the *Football News*, a popular national magazine, former player P.J. Moss was another to make reference to the nature of the crowd during this period:

"In some of the games played on the Marshes, with absolutely no gate-money, it is no exaggeration to say that 4,000 spectators surrounded the field of play. These were not always considerate of the feelings of visiting teams, and I well remember some East End Cup-ties in which visitors were freely pelted with mud, rotten turnips, and other vegetable refuse."

Four thousand people standing several deep around a park pitch, no admission, no stands, no police, only touchline ropes to keep the crowd back – all these elements combined to create a raucous, partisan and anarchic atmosphere at the big games of the period. The fans who were there felt the stirrings of that sense of identity and thrill of being part of the crowd that so captivates supporters throughout the world.

From those simple beginnings under a lamppost on Tottenham High Road, something far bigger was emerging. The players remained at the centre, but around this nucleus other matter was circulating ever more rapidly – reputation, identity, values. The gathering crowd was attracted by those forces but what was becoming clear was that it also contributed to the sense of what Tottenham Hotspur was. Two distinct identities, linked but operating independently – one an increasingly formal sporting institution, the other an informal, anarchic, ebbing and flowing organism. Across the country, as the people embraced their game, they created a culture that was wrapped around it. And as each identity developed, so did the tensions that would characterise the relationship for years to come. For the club and for the fans, what was being created meant increasingly serious business.

2

Enclosure changed the game forever

T HE tale of the rise of Tottenham Hotspur is a remarkable one. Barely ten years after its formation, Tottenham Hotspur was the "Flower of the South", the pre-eminent southern professional football club. Within 15 years it had won the FA Cup. It's an extraordinary rise, scarcely believable even as the stuff of fiction in modern times, let alone reality.

Then, as now, what happened on the pitch wasn't enough. Every club needs to be well-organised off the field with sound finances and doughty leadership with a vision for the future. Without significant off-the-field changes, the club would not have breathed freely beyond incubation. The fact that it has implemented those changes and developed into something that would be scarcely recognisable to those founding members is also remarkable when you consider the fact it has all happened while the club has remained within 100 yards of the site of its foundation.

It was the emergence of the crowd that gave impetus to the club's growth, that changed what began as a boys' leisure pursuit into a sporting institution. Ironic, really, when you consider some of the complaints of fans who set themselves against modern football and the business behemoth it has become. Because the emergence of the crowd, if you take a romantic look at the pure sporting origins of the game, brought with it the end of innocence. As crowds grew, so did the need to enclose the space in which the sport was played. Enclosure changed the game forever, turning it into a business and formalising the relationship between watchers and watched while also laying the seeds of alienation between the two.

It is here that evidence of a theme that has run through British football history can be identified – major changes in spectator experience and safety take place only as a response to potential or actual disaster. The potential problems of public disorder and safety caused by thousands of people on open parkland were one factor in the choice of the Tottenham Hotspur club committee to move to a private ground. The other was the other major driver for change in football – money. No ambitious club could afford to miss out on gate receipts.

Never ones to stray far from their roots, the members settled on a ground off Northumberland Park, used by a tennis club in the summer so the turf was of the high quality that suited Spurs' good football. Another club, Foxes FC, played on an adjacent pitch.

This may not seem much but at the time it represented a significant step upwards in terms of ambition and status. There were risks. One anonymous writer at the time, obviously close to the club, expressed the feeling of some that Hotspur were getting above themselves: "People said we should soon go to ruin, the public would go to see us free, but when it came to paying, would not."

Also, for the first time the club had fixed costs to cover in the form of rent of £17 per annum. However, Spurs were made of sterner stuff. The same author gives a sense of the club's spirit at that time: "But we had the right men to guide us, and [players and leading members] Robert Buckle, F. Hatton, J.Jull, and H.D. Casey with their backs to the wall, stood firm, and we entered our new home."

The first game at the new ground took place on 13 October 1888, a reserve match versus, depending on which account you read, Stratford St John's in the London Junior Cup or Orion Gymnasium. The members must have been pleased and not a little relieved after counting gate receipts of 17 shillings.

In the next few seasons, Tottenham Hotspur continued to play attractive football against sides of varying quality. The supporters were prepared to pay for the privilege of watching them at the usual price of 3d a game. In season 1890/91, Spurs had a good run in the London Cup, beating Queens Park Rangers in a second round replay before a crowd of 350 before being knocked out in round five by Millwall.

By the early 1890s, Tottenham were now sole tenants of their ground. Cup games brought out the crowds, 3,000 spectators paying 6d each for the visit of Casuals in the 1892/93 season while a charity match versus a district representative side drew 4,000.

This season was notable as the first when Spurs had joined a league, the Southern Alliance. Although the club attracted better players, core stalwarts from the early days remained: Jull the captain, Casey and Harston as players then secretary/treasurer. Thus there was a great deal of continuity with players and backroom staff staying close to home.

Spurs introduced primitive ground improvements. The 'stand' was a rickety old wagon left behind by the field's previous tenant while behind one goal was an old tin shed, known as Dunn's shed after a cup tie with Old Etonians who brought many of their 1882 cup-winning side to Spurs in 1888, among them forward A. Dunn, whose ferocious shooting repeatedly peppered the hapless tin shed. No goal-nets in those days.

However, the club provided wooden trestles upon which to stand in wet weather, which ranked high in the order of ground improvements in those days. Later for the start of the 1893/94 season, a new entrance to an enclosure was constructed on the east side of the ground, for which an extra charge of 2d was made. Apart from the old wagon, this appears to be the first time any distinction was made between different groups of spectators. Presumably the enclosure gave a better view on the side of the pitch and protected those able to afford the extra a measure of exclusivity from the masses in more crowded areas.

These enclosures were common in English football grounds until the early 1980s. The authors recall going to Anfield, Old Trafford and Highbury in that period, where there was less pushing and shoving and certainly no hooliganism. At White Hart Lane, the enclosure was the standing area in the old lower West Stand.

Some people would always try to avoid paying. No turnstiles to slip under in those days but as the *Herald* reported: "A number of people were able to obtain a cheap view of the matches through the enterprise of an individual owning some land which overlooks the ground and who improvised a platform, charging people a modest 2d to see."

Perhaps it is a backhanded compliment to the Hotspur that people should go to such lengths to watch the side. Certainly local people were taking notice. The fixture card for 1889 lists local MP Joseph Howard as patron while Morton Cadman, destined to play an important role in the club's future, joined the committee. The dressing rooms were now in the Northumberland Arms in Northumberland Park, rebranded in 2007 as the Bill Nicholson, and having flirted briefly with red shirts, when they changed, the players donned navy blue and white.

As Spurs prepared for greater things, one key figure is noticeable by his absence. There is no mention in the contemporary accounts of John Ripsher. And yet without him, the Hotspur club would have been stillborn. When the Hotspur lads wanted to get organised, they looked for someone with some standing in the local community. A contemporary history written by an anonymous club member describes Ripsher as "something in the City". The writer continues: "He was a favourite with the lads, and although a bachelor, had a fatherly affection for these young hopefuls." Ripsher ran a Bible class at All Hallows Parish Church, whose warden was the father of two of the club's players, the Thompson boys. He was also a leading member of the local YMCA, whose facilities could come in handy.

Doubtless Ripsher saw it as his civic and moral duty to support community activities, in keeping with many other middle-class churchgoers. Sport had its detractors but broadly was seen as a healthy, legitimate activity for young men's minds and bodies, inculcating the right values of comradeship, team spirit and self-reliance. So he agreed to help out this new club and in August 1883 presided over a meeting in the front basement kitchen of the YMCA Institute in Tottenham High Road. Our historian was there too. He concludes: "In spite of the fact that the table was rather rickety, many of the chairs had no backs and the ceiling was badly discoloured, the lads conspired to form a football club."

Ripsher's formal title was president and treasurer but he has been described as the club's "real father and founder". It's clear he brought much-needed organisation to the administration of the club that enabled it to grow on sound foundations. He sorted out the subs, the balance sheet and the fixture list. Colours were agreed – navy blue with a scarlet shield on the left breast bearing the letter 'H'. He made sure the boys could use the YMCA as a base. When the boys could not find a ball to play with on the Friday, Ripsher would tell them, "the Lord will find a way" and on the Saturday would turn up with two under his arm. He defended them to the elders of the church, unconditionally sticking with them when they were in trouble. He negotiated a move, first to 1 Dorset Villas in Northumberland Park then to better premises in the Red House, which stood in front of the ground in the High Road for many years. Ripsher's biographer Peter Lupton credits him with "establishing a reputation for fair play and good sportsmanship that made them the most popular club in England". Our debt to him is incalculable.

Although he remained club president until resigning in 1894, his services were no longer actively required. His unassuming steadfastness no longer had a place in the thrusting, go-ahead Tottenham of the last decade of the 19th century. As the club grew, Ripsher melted into the shadows. He moved to Dover to live with his sister and her husband, working as a clerk in a steam laundry and then an iron foundry. His health declined, as did the fortunes of his family. In 1906 he was admitted to the workhouse, and it was in those terrible surroundings that he died in September 1907. Buried in a pauper's grave, he lay forgotten until author Peter Lupton rediscovered his grave in 2007. The Tottenham Tribute Trust, set up by fans in the modern era to raise funds for former players who had fallen on hard times, raised a headstone, inscribed with the club's crest and the fitting motto *audere est facere*, to dare is to do. Ripsher saw it as his duty to dare and a century on, Spurs fans had not forgotten, leading the effort to finally give him the tribute his service to our club deserved.

His legacy remains in the spirit of enterprise he encouraged in the boys who met under the lamppost and then felt sufficiently determined and empowered to see the club into the new century and beyond. Cruelly ironic, then, that it was that very enterprise that pushed him into the shadows.

Ripsher had instilled a spirit of sportsmanship and fair play that was attracting support, but an incident in which Spurs were seen as wronged parties and as standing up for the side of right against the authorities helped broaden that support. The episode known as the Payne's Boots Affair not only united the club with the community of which it became an increasingly important part, it also catapulted Spurs into the national football consciousness for the first time. The club never looked back.

In October 1893 the Fulham reserve left-winger Ernie Payne decided to accept Spurs' offer of regular football. Both clubs were strictly amateur so no transfer fees or contract offers were involved. Payne's first game for Spurs took place on 21 October. The story goes that when he arrived at Fulham on the morning of the match to collect his kit, he discovered that it had all been stolen. Spurs provided shirt and shorts but had no boots for him so they gave him 10s to buy a pair, which he duly did and took his place in the side for that afternoon's fixture.

No doubt peeved at the loss of their player, albeit one they had not selected all season, Fulham complained to the London Football Association that Spurs had poached Payne and, worse, were guilty of professionalism. The London FA responded swiftly and punitively. The charge of poaching was dismissed but the FA judged that the payment for the boots breached the rules against professionalism and was an unfair inducement to come to north London. Spurs were suspended for a fortnight and Payne for a week.

Payne did the decent thing and returned the cash while Spurs appealed to no avail. The sentences were not severe – Spurs missed a couple of games and that was that. However, the case gained national notoriety because it highlighted the blurred lines between amateurism and the growing professional game in its northern and midland heartlands. The football press and public felt the club had been unfairly treated over a trumped-up charge. The positive publicity meant that the club was swamped with invitations to play. The following month, 6,000 people saw them lose 1-0 away to Southampton. Spurs had a national profile and saw their opportunity to make the most of it.

We've seen that the club had become an important part of the community and that its good football brought in the crowds. The spirit and togetherness within the club was strong too. The early history of the English game, *Association Football and the Men Who Made It*, records that "the good fellowship which characterised the early stages of the club's history still exists, despite… rise to fame… there is no club in the country in which there is better feeling between the players and the directors".

However, to make the next step up, Spurs looked to the classic football model of a local entrepreneur who wanted to invest in the club in order to enhance his personal social standing and the fortunes of his business.

John Ripsher was replaced as president by a very different figure who represented and understood the new world of enterprise and commerce. John Oliver was a furniture manufacturer who saw the opportunity to invest in a popular side with plenty of potential and a national profile. As the former president of the Southern Alliance, he knew his way around the game and it seems likely he understood the prospects of many of the region's clubs before choosing Spurs as the right investment.

Giving one's time and other philanthropic deeds for the local community was in late-Victorian times not only an expression of civic pride but also a favourite way of increasing social standing, especially for the business classes. Football was only part of Oliver's portfolio but it was useful advertising as well as an act that enhanced his personal status.

His involvement brought other skills and expertise that hitherto they had lacked. His business acumen transformed the club behind the scenes while his contacts in the game assisted applications for league status and no doubt in player wheeling and dealing. He knew how the professional game worked. He gave players a job in his Old Street furniture factory, a powerful and legal inducement to sign. He made sure the club was indebted to him by lending it the money to build a new grandstand. It could not have been very solid because the roof soon blew off in a gale; fortunately no one was injured. It was soon rebuilt to provide the first seats and the only covered accommodation for a hundred or so supporters.

To sustain the club's progress in the long term, Oliver advocated turning professional. At the time, this provoked vigorous debate within the club and in the community. The language is strikingly similar to contemporary debate around the influence of money in sport. The *Herald* of 20 December 1895 reflects on the issues. The writer is a sceptic: "I am not altogether an advocate of professionalism as I think it tends to make sport a business."

However, he reports that there had been problems on the field as Spurs were obviously struggling with the demands of a busy fixture list at a higher level. The club had no cover for a few injuries, resulting in bad displays which were "a source of much grumbling on the part of spectators". During the debate, it was stated that if nothing was done about the quality and depth of the squad, gates would fall by 50%.

Oliver prepared well. When the members gathered at the Eagle pub on a Monday night, it emerged that the committee had met several days before to agree the resolution in favour of professionalism. Oliver both chaired the meeting and spoke strongly in favour. Some members protested about such secrecy but Oliver had shrewdly got the club stalwarts on board, those who had been part of the club from the early days. The majority of current players were in favour.

Interestingly in terms of what was to follow, in response to a question from the floor, Oliver overcame one argument by stating he had no intention to form a company. He was in a powerful position: the club had debts of £65, £60 of which was owed to him for the stand. After a hearty, sustained debate, in the final vote only one was cast against although several abstained. On 20 December 1895, Tottenham Hotspur became a professional football club.

It is hard to gauge the supporters' reaction to these developments because of the lack of records. However, it is safe to assume that the vast majority would have had little objection to better quality league football against opponents from further afield who they would otherwise have been able only to read about on the back pages.

In April 1896 the famous Aston Villa, one of the very top teams at the time, came to Tottenham. Sniffily they rejected the humble dressing rooms as being beneath their status, instead hiring a large room in the Northumberland Arms to change in. This great attraction drew a club record 6,000 gate, to a ground without stands for the masses.

In the summer, Spurs joined the Southern League, going straight into the top division because of their reputation and also no doubt because they could generate large gates for the time.

Oliver could grease the wheels. Playing now in chocolate and gold, a combination resuscitated for a season in 2007 as a sold-out third strip, the first season was one of consolidation, then they invested more heavily in players. The long-standing links with Scottish players began when no less than nine were signed in autumn 1897. Internationals arrived from Burnley. Spurs finished third in the league. In 1899/1900 they won it, their first major trophy.

Despite Spurs' higher profile and a loyal local following, the committee running the club were disappointed that a year on, professionalism had not boosted attendances by as much as they expected. Therefore they sought alternative sources of income. Early in 1898, the committee took advice from Charles Roberts, who later became the only chairman of Tottenham Hotspur – or indeed any British club – to have once pitched for the Brooklyn baseball team. As a result, they resolved to become a limited company. With shades of modern takeovers, the company took on the assets and the debts for an agreed sum.

Some 8,000 shares at £1 each were issued. The news was greeted positively by the *Herald*, which believed that "if the limited company is floated all right, the greatest team in Britain is promised for Tottenham". It is unlikely that the share issue would have produced much of a reaction amongst the vast majority of supporters. Rising living standards amongst working people plus a precious Saturday afternoon off work meant a growing proportion of the local male populace could afford 6d at the turnstile but the notion of owning shares had no place in their world where the margin between a reasonable standard of living and subsistence was terrifyingly narrow. The ill-health or death of the breadwinner or unemployment could tip a family into destitution.

Nevertheless the instigation of the limited company was a chance to broaden the base of ownership and influence of local people, if not quite to become a democracy. However, with echoes of Spurs' floatation on the Stock Market 90 years later, the idea of supporter involvement in the club through a share issue proved illusory. The shares were not popular, despite a series of public meetings throughout the 1898/99 season designed to drum up business. In the end, only 1,558 shares were sold to 296 people, and two-thirds of those people lived outside the district. Spurs were £501 in the red by the end of the season, provoking the resignation of Oliver. Never again would local people and supporters have a chance for significant involvement in the running of the club.

1898 was a momentous year for the club in another sense. On Good Friday, a ground record 14,000 spectators came to see Woolwich Arsenal. It's hard to conceive how they all fitted in to what remained little more than the equivalent of a modern sports club ground. The refreshment bar collapsed during the game after 80 people climbed onto the roof. Fortunately no one was seriously injured. The impact of potential disaster in the crowd and on the balance sheet provoked some sharp, fast thinking by the board. Spurs had to move to a bigger ground.

When Roberts, now chairman, came to talk to the landlord of the White Hart in the High Road about the vacant ground behind his pub, the publican disconcertingly had never heard of the Hotspur. However, he knew about the potential business that clubs drew to an area because he used to be a licensee near Millwall.

He was keen but it was up to Charrington, the brewers. It saw profit in the land too – from houses, not football. In the end, the brewers sought a guaranteed attendance of 1,000 per first-team match, 500 for reserves. It was not much of a deal. Spurs averaged 4,000 a game. From the beginning of the 1899 season, White Hart Lane became the club's home ground. Notts County, the oldest club in existence, had the honour of being Spurs' first opponents. A crowd of 5,000 paid £115 to celebrate a 4-1 victory.

The turf was perfect – the land used to be a nursery – but huge concrete foundations had to be blown out of the ground. Bits were still turning up 50 years later when the pitch was relaid. Groundsman John Over was used to preparing Test match wickets at the Oval. The Lane soon had the reputation of being the best playing surface in the country, without which Spurs could not have played the flowing passing football that sealed the success which lay just around the corner. Ground improvements continued. In 1906 capacity increased from 35,000 to 40,000. By 1908 the club made £4,000 profit.

Tottenham Hotspur had a reputation, a stadium and a growing band of supporters. Its location at the outer edges of the capital city would also prove to be key. The ability to be in the right place at the right time is treasured in football. The efforts of the Casey brothers, John Ripsher and the rest already detailed played their part in ensuring the club formed under the lamppost in 1882 would not flicker briefly and fade from sight, sure enough, but on their own those efforts almost certainly would not have been enough. For that club to establish itself as something of lasting significance, greater forces exercised their influence.

Those greater forces were not the ones that John Ripsher the churchman would have credited. Instead, more material influences would come together to create the conditions from which a giant of the game would grow. Fuelling the rise of Tottenham Hotspur was the energy of a new force – the suburbs. It was the suburbs that made London different, and so when we talk of identity and of roots and of community, we need to understand what the suburbs were and how they came about. Because Tottenham Hotspur become the team of the suburbs, the Flower of the South rising as the teams from the industrial centres of the north that forged the English game's early powers began to decline.

As Stephen Inwood observes in his forensic *History of London*: "Nothing struck visitors to Victorian London more forcibly than the enormous extent of its suburbs. Other great European cities were different. Paris and Rome, for instance, remained compact, within fairly clear boundaries, while London spread... and surrounded itself with 'suburb clinging to suburb, like onions fifty on a rope'."

London's area grew twice as fast as its population during the 19th century, with the focus of population growth shifting markedly outwards after 1851. London's outer suburban ring had 400,000 inhabitants in 1861; by 1911 it had 2.7 million, 37% of the total metropolitan population. By the 1860s, the area of London had extended to reach Upper Holloway, Hackney, Peckham and Hammersmith, stretching the outer borders of the city by three or four miles on either side from the boundaries shown in Ralph Horwood's 1813 map of London. By 1901, ordnance survey maps show London's boundaries reaching Tottenham and Wood Green, Acton and Brentford, East Ham and Barking Creek, and Penge and Croydon. Between 1861 and 1911, population growth of over 30% was recorded in 67 English towns or boroughs. Of those 67, 30 were London suburbs. By the 1880s, the four fastest-growing English towns were Leyton, with a growth rate of 133%, Willesden (122%), Tottenham (95%) and West Ham (59%).

The people who came and settled in the suburbs were overwhelmingly the emerging middle classes. They were not rich enough to afford a second home in the country, an ambition that continues to assert its allure to this day, but they were well-off enough to be able to afford the daily train or bus fare into the central London offices where they worked. As wages rose, working hours became shorter and fares dropped – halcyon days indeed when viewed from the vantage point of an age in which all those trends have been reversed, which we are told is progress – so the lower middle classes and even some working-class Londoners fetched up in the suburbs. When Charles Booth gathered his data on London's population, he found that 80% of the city's commercial clerks, lawyers, schoolteachers, architects and merchants lived in the suburbs.

What is interesting about the suburbs too is that they are almost entirely a product of the people. Inwood observes that the great and the good criticised the suburbs for "their dull uniformity, their narrow-minded respectability, their failure to be either real town or real country". But when ordinary people, by dint of better wages and shorter working hours, and helped by an improved transport system, were able to choose where they lived, they overwhelmingly chose the suburbs. It represents, perhaps, a peculiarly English tendency for ordinary people to bloody-mindedly stick to what we have created, rather than embrace what we are told is good for us.

And all that goes some way towards explaining why Tottenham Hotspur found itself in the right place at the right time. The energy generated by suburban growth needed application; newly-formed communities seek symbols with which to identify and which in turn bond them closer together. It is human nature to want to define who we are, and the club in the heart of one of the four fastest-growing areas of population in the country would help the suburban masses to do just that. It is against this background that the importance of the Payne's Boots Affair can be judged, because what is even better than having a local symbol to identify with is having a wronged local symbol to identify with. Tottenham Hotspur had been wronged by 'them', who were always telling 'us' what to do. And people weren't having it. They were Tottenham Hotspur, and they would do what they want.

The suburbs represented a move from industrial to commercial Britain, from working class to middle class. What this meant overwhelmingly was the rise of the south and the decline of the north. It had been the great northern industrial towns, Preston, Manchester, Burnley, Sheffield, Liverpool, Blackburn, that had dominated football in its early years. The division over professionalism was, in part, rooted in the fault lines between north and south, between gentlemen and players, that ran through Britain. But now the south was rising, its clubs embracing the techniques on and off the field that helped to move it on from outdated Corinthianism. All it needed was for one of the southern teams to beat the northerners at their own game.

Having gone professional in 1895, Spurs continued to build their reputation and to draw a fiercely committed mass support from the bloody-minded suburbanites who lived in the area the club was now making famous. By 1896, Spurs were competing in the prestigious Southern League, and by 1899 the first of the four visionary managers whose efforts would embed a style that would define the club forever was in charge, one John Cameron. Throughout the 1899/1900 season, Spurs battled it out with the south coast powers of Southampton and Portsmouth for the league title.

On 28 April 1900, the Spurs were away at New Brompton in Kent, little more than a tiny hamlet. The place was swamped by Spurs fans eager to see their team secure the win they needed to secure the title. Spurs won 2-1 and the massed ranks of travelling supporters burst onto the pitch and swept their heroes shoulder high into the dressing rooms. Back in Tottenham, many thousands more flooded into the streets to welcome the team back. The players and the travelling supporters were joined by the Tottenham Town Band as they walked from the station back to the ground.

A London team, a suburban team, had won a major trophy and the world would never be the same again. The press dubbed Spurs the Flower of the South and the *Tottenham Herald* penned the verse;

> *I care not for things political,*
> *Or which party's out or in,*
> *The only thing I care about,*
> *Is will Tottenham Hotspurs win.*

The civic pride in the team that, in those days, regularly had an 's' appended to its name, is unmistakable. Tottenham Hotspur had put Tottenham on the map. And eyes now turned to the FA Cup.

The FA Cup was, even then, a trophy infused with legend and symbolism. It was the first association football competition to be established anywhere in the world. It was the brainchild of Charles Alcock, the secretary of the Football Association, who based the competition on an inter-house tournament at Harrow School, which he had attended as a pupil. The first competition was held in 1871/72, and the first final held at Kennington Oval. Wanderers, a team of former public schoolboys from London, won that first final, and in subsequent years the trophy was retained by teams of wealthy amateurs from the south. Then, in 1883, Blackburn Olympic beat Old Etonians to take the trophy north, where it stayed for two decades.

In 1900, as Spurs were winning their first trophy, Southampton reached the FA Cup Final and were strongly fancied to bring the cup back south. But they lost 4-0 to Bury. Now attention turned to the Flower of the South. Would the Spurs be strong enough to break the grip of the north, to really announce the arrival of the south and become the first professional side, the first southern team not drawn from the ranks of the toffs, to win the most coveted trophy in world football? When Spurs reached the final in 1901, interest reached fever pitch. A crowd of 114,815 descended upon Crystal Palace park in Sydenham, south-east London, a location that sat on the southern edge of the bowl of the city as an almost direct reflection of Tottenham's position on the north, to find out. It was the largest crowd ever to watch a football match anywhere in the world, and one that was 36,000 higher than the previous record for an FA Cup final. An evocative passage in John Cottrell's 1971 book *A Century of Great Soccer Drama* sets the scene.

"On this freakishly incandescent April Day, a mass migration moved from the north of London to the south. By trams, pony-traps, and trains packed with bodies to the luggage racks, they travelled in their tens of thousands, many wearing bowlers and trilbies with 'Play Up Hotspurs' emblazoned in blue on white bands. At London Bridge and Victoria stations, these North London hordes mingled with a different breed, long-distance travellers from Yorkshire whose favoured headgear was cloth caps decorated with red-and-white rosettes. The northerners and the southerners sported different colours and they guzzled different beer – bitter for the blue-and-whites, stout for the rest. But their destination was the same: Crystal Palace, for the biggest Cup Final attraction of all time – Tottenham Hotspur versus Sheffield United, Spurs against Blades."

The interest was unprecedented. But for all the regional pride that was at stake, there was a great irony. The Spurs side, in which southern hopes were so passionately invested, comprised an Irishman, two Welshmen, three Englishmen of northern extraction, and five Scots.

The game ended in anti-climax, but not without drama. The final score was 2-2, but furious Spurs fans spoke for days afterwards of the goal that never was. United's second goal was awarded after Spurs keeper George Clawley beat down a shot from the Blades' Walter Bennett which bounced down and out of play. It did not cross the line, but the referee ruled it did. Unfortunately for the official, a Mr Arthur Kingscott from Derby, the 'no-goal' was seen not only by a good proportion of the crowd assembled at Crystal Palace, but by a small crew experimenting with a device that captured moving pictures for display. The cine-camera pictures of the ball not crossing the line were shown widely at the pay-screenings that were gaining popularity at the time, and Kingscott's mistake was plain to see. An incorrect ruling on a ball crossing the goal line in an important match against a team called United – it could never happen today.

It was, of course, more injustice that served to bind Spurs and its supporters. Insult was piled upon insult when the replay was announced for a midweek evening at Bolton's Burnden Park, and then the train companies refused requests for cheap tickets. The fact that so many were both willing and able to make the journey on a midweek evening is a remarkable demonstration of supporter commitment though, and a decent proportion of the 30,000 crowd were from London. The game was described as one of the best of all time by the correspondent from *The Times*, and it finished up 3-1 to Spurs.

Once again, Tottenham's jubilant fans spilled onto the pitch, their celebrations delaying the presentation of the trophy. The wife of club director Morton Cadman tied blue and white ribbons to the handles of the cup in the melee, establishing a tradition that endures to this day. Team and supporters arrived back at South Tottenham station at 1am to be greeted by wild scenes of celebration, likened to those that followed the relief of Mafeking in the Boer War. There were fireworks and bands and 30,000 people celebrating in the streets and singing and cheering and marching with the team back to the ground. Over 40,000 people celebrated in the streets, the band struck up *See the Conquering Hero Comes* and the fans marched with the team back to the ground. It took well over an hour to travel a mile and a half from the station.

The *Daily Chronicle* reported that: "The news became known throughout London shortly after five, and immediately there set in a vast and enthusiastic pilgrimage to the North. From all quarters the people streamed and when the evening fell, Tottenham High Road between the South Station and the White Hart Hotel was filled with a solid and almost immovable mass of men and women."

The *Yorkshire Post* waxed lyrical at the amazing scenes: "From an early hour in the evening the air rang with the cry 'Spurs!' 'Spurs!' 'Spurs!' in every variety of joyous inflection of which the human voice is capable. Now it rose in a crescendo roar of triumph, and again sank to a soothing murmur. In one mood Tottenham was proud of its Spurs, and defiant, as it had a right to be, of the whole football world; in another it was caressingly affectionate."

The crowd sang as they waited. Flags were displayed from windows, trumpets were blown and fireworks let off. An "In Memoriam" card was circulated amongst the waiting throng with the epitaph: "In doleful memory of poor Sheffield United, buried by Tottenham Hotspur."

This was a victory for Tottenham, not just the Hotspur, and the whole town shared the joy. The *Herald* announced that at 9pm on 29 April the club would show "Animated Pictures" of the final and replay at White Hart Lane. The Tottenham Brass Band were to be there plus "many other pictures of local interest will also be shewn (sic) by the Prestwich Manufacturing Company of Tottenham". Price 6d, 3d for boys, presumably allowed on this special occasion to stay up late. The series of Ogden's Cigarette cards of the players, team and cup would rekindle the memories in the months and years to come. The south had risen.

So too had Tottenham Hotspur. The first and still the only non-league side to win the FA Cup. The team that broke the grip of the north, that signalled the rise of the south, that fired the imagination and gave an emerging part of a great city a sense of identity and pride the like of which it had never had before.

The story of 1901 became folklore and the story was passed on. Spurs fan David John, speaking in 2015 about his family, said: "They lived in Tottenham, couldn't afford to go, they used to listen to the cheering from outside the ground. Ebeneezer and Lil, she was the one who used to sit me on her knee and sing 'glory glory hallelujah!' Ebeneezer he said he remembered a massive celebration in the streets, streets were full, that must have been when he was a kid, when they won the Cup in 1901."

Tottenham won with style, it won in glorious circumstances, it established traditions that endure and it made the world sit up and take notice. Of such stuff is legend made and, in 1901, the supporters of Tottenham Hotspur had perhaps just an inkling of what had been started.

The Tottenham public remained steadfastly loyal in the first decade of the new century. Home gates were usually between 7,000 and 10,000 for Southern League games and, demonstrating the appetite for Spurs' football, several thousand for the matches in the lesser leagues like the Western League where a full first team did not necessarily turn out.

The phrase 'taken the club as far as I could' is a modern euphemism for a departing manager's behind-the-scenes frustrations but when the triumphant manager John Cameron resigned in 1907 citing 'differences with the directorate', he had had enough of the board's lack of support for his team-building strategy. Instead their attention and resources were channelled towards ground improvements. Typical Spurs indeed.

The lure of the cup enticed significantly more through the turnstiles. In February 1904 the second round FA Cup tie against Aston Villa, one of the most famous clubs in the land at the time, had to be abandoned after 20 minutes after the gates were locked half-an-hour before kick-off with a ground record 32,000 spectators inside.

Expecting a big crowd and always on the look-out for extra income, the club added extra seats between the stands and the touchline. Accounts of what followed differ. One suggests that at half-time those occupying the seats walked onto the pitch – there was no fence to stop them – followed by many others from the terraces. An alternative view is that the overcrowding was obvious before kick-off. After one interruption with 15 minutes gone and Villa one up, the game was stopped again a few minutes later and the FA secretary decided it was no longer a cup tie. Quite how this would have helped the crush in the stands or the prospects of the match being safely completed isn't abundantly clear. However, the crowd did not hear of this until half-time, whereupon they took their anger onto the pitch.

The players and referee were rapidly escorted through the throngs to the dressing rooms and the game was postponed amidst pandemonium with the beleaguered police unable to clear the hundreds of spectators from the field of play. It was the closest White Hart Lane has ever come to a riot. Some fans tried to blame members of the press who had to be smuggled out of the ground by the groundsman and spirited away to Northumberland Park station.

Spurs were fined £350 and ordered to erect an iron fence around the pitch, inside which only authorised personnel were permitted. This incident provided extra reason for the already ambitious board to push ahead with the planned substantial ground improvements. They also resolved to remain in Tottenham because of their responsibility to the local economy. The centrepiece of the rebuilding was the West Stand, designed by renowned stadium architect Archibald Leitch (who would also design the East Stand 30 years later) and opened in September 1909. With 5,300 seats and room for 6,000 standing in the Enclosure, all under cover, it was the largest in the country at the time and the wooden gabled frontage remains familiar to many supporters because it was essentially unchanged until demolition in 1980.

As a final flourish, former Spurs amateur WJ Scott crafted from copper a large fighting cockerel atop a ball, which was placed upon the roof to overlook the pitch.

Also included were enlarged banks at both ends and concrete terracing, comparatively unusual at a time when most grounds had unterraced standing banks. By 1912, Tottenham could proudly boast a capacity of 50,000 with 40,000 under cover. These were the season ticket prices that year from the Handbook, price 1d:

Shareholders: £1
non-shareholders: £1 5s
shareholders: reserved seat £1 11s 6d
non-shareholders: £2 2s
Soldiers and sailors must in future pay.
Reserve games 4d adults, boys 2d

In 1908 Spurs joined the Football League, where standards were demonstrably higher and there was an appetite in the south for the rewards of fixtures against the big clubs from the north and Midlands. Spurs were also casting worried glances across the capital at the swift rise of Chelsea, formed in 1905 and heavily bankrolled, and Fulham. They did not want the Flower of the South to wilt.

As late as January 1908 Charles Roberts, still chairman, proposed reform of the Southern League rather than rejection. Only when this was turned down flat did he announce that Tottenham Hotspur intended to become leaguers. It nearly went wrong when Spurs' initial application was rejected, then the Southern League forced them into Division Two. At the last moment however, Stoke resigned from the Football League and this time Tottenham's swift re-application was narrowly successful.

The *Yorkshire Post* described Spurs as 'one of the most popular clubs in the country.' "The Tottenham Hotspur Club has always stood for everything that is good, alike in a playing sense and in that of good sportsmanship… the Directors like good sportsmen, laid their cards on the table… League football has been materially strengthened by the Spurs' election… Tottenham have always played good football, and they will be an attraction wherever they play."

However, that's not the whole story. At the time it was suggested that the sudden withdrawal from the League of a founding member was extremely convenient and that Spurs and Stoke may have come to 'an arrangement'. More accurate is the charge of big city bias. Spurs with their big crowds and national profile were good business.

Football crowds of the time were rowdy but peaceable. Predominantly made up of men from the skilled working classes, the middle classes were a presence at matches, as evidenced at Spurs with the privileges accorded to shareholders and the demand for seats. The club had expectations for the behaviour of supporters as set out in the Handbook at the beginning of the century:

"Learn the rules well before criticising [and they are included in the Handbook].

Respect the rulings of the referee and refrain from unseemingly [sic] demonstrations so common on many football fields when decisions are unpalatable; the best referees make mistakes.

Applaud good football impartially.

Don't let defeat discourage you. It is at this time that encouragement is most wanted by the players.

Don't express your disapproval of a player so that everyone can hear, it only upsets him, and he loses confidence.

This season's team should doubtless accomplish some fine performances. Don't in your enthusiasm, forget that there is such a thing as mistaken kindness where athletes in training are concerned.

Don't stop at home when the team goes away; they want your support more than ever when on opponent's ground.

Let visitors go away with the impression that the Tottenham crowd are good sportsmen.

Whether at home or away don't forget the 'Tottenham whisper'."

We can deduce from this that in fact the crowd most certainly got at opposing teams, referees and Spurs players who were not playing well. Then and now the terraces made up their own opinions and rules of behaviour regardless of solemn pronouncements in official publications. Impartiality would make a football crowd an infinitely worse place to be. It also shows that Spurs have a sizeable away following, enough to get them noticed at away grounds.

The "Tottenham Whisper" remains a mystery. In 2007 the question came up on the BBC 606 phone-in website. One suggestion is that it is another in the lengthy list of calls for moderation in the crowd. It's when you don't express your disapproval of a player so that everyone can hear because he will then lose confidence. Another correspondent says you whisper when telling other people that you are a Spurs fan as you don't want anyone else to know you support them.

One of the authors raised this in November 2011 during an appearance on the Fighting Cock podcast, after which Simon B e-mailed in: "This memory is hazy as it's from something my late granddad once told me. Apparently back in the day there was some kind of dig made at us Spurs fans for the manner of our support during the games. We apparently out-shouted, sung and cheered the opposition's fans so extensively that they actually criticised us for being too raucous (ungentlemanly behaviour old boys and all that). Apparently someone from our club responded by saying something along the lines of, 'Suck it up numptys, we were only whispering' (or whatever the 19th century equivalent would have been)."

So even when they whispered, Spurs fans drowned out the opposition.

Most supporters lived within easy travelling distance of the ground and local businesses identified with the club brand. Local business was alive to the marketing opportunities and the business generated by large crowds coming to the area.

Souvenirs and colours featured. 'ET Coombes hats caps scarves hosiery in Hotspur colours. Opposite the ground'. Jones 'the Spurs button man' at 708 High Road sold Spurs Comic Pictorial post cards 1d each, 1s (5p) series of 16 "very funny".

Sports goods featured prominently. Myall's Football Boots manufactured the special Hotspur boot 8/11 (45p) per pair, appropriately top of their range, which went down to 3/11 1/2. Their shop was opposite the ground. HR Brookes of 778 Seven Sisters Road, 'the cheapest house in town' and maker of the Spurs jerseys.

On matchdays stalls sold souvenirs and food but some enterprise was not welcomed. The programme regularly warned: "The public is cautioned against buying 'pirate' programmes. They are in no sense official. Our boys outside the Ground will in future wear caps labelled 'Tottenham Hotspur Programme'."

The pubs did good business. The Whitehall Tavern, nearly facing the football ground, boasted that 'results of all principal matches shown'. Pubs often provided this results service for their customers, with some employing people to call in with regular score updates as well as the full-times. Alternatively, connoisseurs of the electric piano could head for the Eagle in Chesnut Road (behind Tottenham police station) and luxuriate in the 'finest saloon bar in north London'. The Eagle was handy for the music hall at the Tottenham Palace, twice nightly 3/6 (18p) down to a shilling (5p) or if you were at the other end of the High Road the Empire Edmonton presented 'always a star twice nightly'.

Spurs were promoted in their first season in the League but found life harder in Division One. Despite finishing regularly in the bottom half, crowds improved compared with the Southern League days.

In September 1914 Tottenham prepared as normal for the coming season. Infamously the public were told that the war would be over by Christmas and life carried on. The first game of the 1914/15 season was a public trial against 'our friends the Gunners' in aid of the Prince of Wales's National War Relief Fund. In the same programme there's also playful mention of 'the annual cricket match against the Pensioners', i.e. Chelsea. In September, Cocky the cartoon cockerel (possibly latter-day mascot Chirpy's grandfather) who appeared on the cover of every programme, was able to joke about the war. After forward Bert Bliss scored twice to defeat Chelsea: 'Private Bliss, who scored two goals, receiving the DSO, Chelsea brigade completely wiped out'.

In contrast, in winter 1938 national foreboding of the inevitability of war against Germany is clear from the programme editorial and civil defence preparations almost a year before war was declared.

Football was under severe attack from a powerful lobby that saw professional football as unpatriotic. Papers refused to print the fixtures. The game pointed to the continuation of racing and the music halls, which stayed open as an example of the benefits of leisure during wartime and of how football was being singled out.

The local recruiting office had an advert in the programme and the band included patriotic marches in their pre-match repertoire. Lord Baden-Powell opened the specially constructed rifle range at the ground and the public were encouraged to come and practice their shooting. The players undertook military training when football training had finished. Meanwhile, Velanche's Football Dogs were on twice nightly at the Palace.

The tone turned sombre as the impact of war seeped home from the trenches. 'The boys in khaki' enjoyed their brief respite on the terraces as did "the wounded heroes from the Tottenham Hospital." Losses at the front became a regular item for the rest of the season and "soldier footballers" a roll of honour. On Christmas Day 1914 it was announced that former amateur Spurs reserve WHD Lloyd had been killed.

The 1914/15 season was completed in full. Perhaps Spurs wished football had been halted after all: they finished bottom, their team weakened as their young men joined up. Their fans were nevertheless grateful for their contribution to the home front. Crowds held up well: 18,000, 11,000 and 7,500 for their final three Division One home matches. White Hart Lane became a gas mask factory for the duration.

3

Tottenham Hotspur have done more for the shilling man than any other club in England

O N the evening of Monday 1 September 1919 Tottenham Hotspur beat Leicester City 4-0 at White Hart Lane, the first home league match after the First World War ended. Despite the 6.30 kick-off – no floodlights in those days – and that Spurs were playing in Division Two, a crowd of 21,060 turned up. Ten thousand were added to the gate the following Saturday as Spurs scored four more against Coventry.

This was more than just the relief of getting back to normal after the Great War, understandable though that may be. This marked the beginning of 20 years of high attendances, including the record gate for any match at the Lane, that proved beyond doubt that Spurs were an established force in London football and could draw crowds whatever the circumstances and regardless of league position.

During this period, three pillars of the identity of Spurs supporters became immovably established, although each had their origins much earlier in the club's history.

Arthur Rowe is the name most associated with the pass and move style of attractive football usually known as push and run. Under Rowe, Spurs swept to the league title in 1951 and then ten years later Bill Nicholson's Double side refined the style to as close to perfection as we are ever likely to see. This is the Spurs Way, attacking football played with style and swagger by skilful, intelligent players. Yet Rowe himself freely acknowledged his debt to Peter McWilliam, the Spurs manager in the early 1920s, who has links with the club dating back to before the First World War.

Second, the magic of the FA Cup. Spurs won again in 1921 and each year since then this is the most eagerly anticipated competition of them all, bringing record crowds to the Lane and inspiring performances that typically transcend the team's league position.

Finally, our rivalry with Arsenal, which after the war took on a darker hue after the most sinister episode in the club's history.

The fixture versus the Arsenal that is now known as the north London derby or to many just 'the derby' dates back to the 1880s when Tottenham had not yet become Hotspur and Arsenal was a mere suffix because they represented Woolwich in south London. Even then they were up to their tricks, fielding 12 men in an early fixture and getting away with it until they were rumbled well into the first half.

This was territorial, north v south London, until 1913 when it became intensely personal. Arsenal joined the Football League before the turn of the century but by 1910 were a club in decline. In particular, attendances fell after a large section of the Woolwich Arsenal itself was closed.

Henry Norris was a prosperous and ambitious businessman from west London who was to have a lasting effect on the supporters of Tottenham Hotspur. With a keen eye for an opportunity to increase his prestige and influence through football, he became the majority shareholder at Arsenal despite being on the board at Fulham. He decided to move to the populous north of the city after his plan to amalgamate the two clubs to form a London superclub fell through.

Considerably assisted by his connections with the Church, he bought a plot of land in Gillespie Road owned by the Church Commissioners. The contract was signed by the bishop himself. Local residents secured a council vote against the club using the land to build a stadium. Spurs and Leyton Orient both protested furiously but failed to gather enough votes to force the League to hold an emergency general meeting, which probably indicated that for whatever reason many clubs welcomed the move.

Supporters have long memories. In 2006 the following petition attracted over 4,000 signatures: "In 1932 a little piece of Islington's heritage was trashed when Gillespie Road tube station on the Piccadilly Line had its name summarily changed to 'Arsenal'. There is no place in the locality called Arsenal. There was, of course, a football club, but that is moving away in 2006, rendering the adopted name ridiculous. We are urging TfL to take the popular step of reverting to the historic original name in place of its soon-to-be nonsensical 'Arsenal'."

The club may have moved but the plea fell on deaf ears, perhaps because of the lingering suspicion that the signatories were not a balanced cross-section of local people and train-spotters. To this day Spurs fans call the Gunners the Woolwich Wanderers and chants encourage them to return from whence they came, in a hurry.

Arsenal's first match at an unfinished Highbury took place on 6 September 1913. Twenty thousand people turned up, perhaps the first ever north London gloryhunters. Norris was single-minded and ruthless but he knew his public. There was a huge demand for professional football in north London and he was not finished yet.

When league football resumed in 1919 the Football League increased the size of the top division from 20 to 22, a structure that remained in place until 1995 when the now Premier League reverted to 20 teams under pressure from UEFA. Spurs finished bottom of Division One in the 1914/15 season, the last before hostilities began. Above them in second bottom place were Chelsea, while Burnley and Wolves had been promoted and took their places in the newly expanded top flight. Arsenal had been members of the league for longer than Spurs, since 1893, but had been relegated in 1913, a full ten points from safety, and had finished sixth in Division Two in 1915.

The final two top spots were to be decided by ballot. This method was not unusual. The final places of the Football League were decided by election until 1986 when the top conference side automatically went up as the base of the league pyramid was widened. However, the result was that Arsenal and Chelsea were elected, Spurs condemned to a season in Division Two. A bitter rivalry thus began that lasts to this day, one that because of its origins runs much deeper than a mere dispute between neighbours.

We will never know exactly what happened behind the scenes. What is abundantly clear is that the president of the League Management Committee was less than impartial in his role as chair of the meeting. He advocated strongly on behalf of his preferred candidates. On his recommendation, Chelsea were nodded through without a vote. Arsenal were portrayed as the senior club in contention, when in fact both Birmingham and Wolves had greater claims to that honour.

Most histories of the club express bewilderment at this snub but are at pains to add that subsequent relations between the neighbours were entirely cordial. Partly this feels like any problems have been minimised, a relic of a stiff upper lip gentlemanly attitude to the business at hand. It's hard to imagine that Spurs' officials, however professional, could not have been angry at this incursion on their territory and source of income. This could only have simmered long into the 1930s when Arsenal became the most successful side in the land under ex-Spur Herbert Chapman.

However, this version of history takes no account of the feelings of supporters. Then as now their emotions, attitudes, and allegiances are taken for granted without any acknowledgement of their feelings or preferences. They turned up in droves and that was enough. The history of the ordinary fan remains unrecorded and unacknowledged for almost the entire history of British football.

At a distance of almost a century, it's almost impossible to redress this imbalance. However, there are clues. Undoubtedly Tottenham's core support followed the side around the country as well as turning the creaking, ratchetty turnstiles at White Hart Lane. For instance, in 1928 nearly 37,000 spectators braved miserable weather to see Spurs defeat Oldham 3-0, enticed by the magic of the cup even though Arsenal were also at home on the same day.

The principle that Spurs and Arsenal home fixtures should not clash had been established since the league resumed after the war. Interestingly, it appears to have been made primarily on the grounds of safety rather than because of its effect on attendances. The police had advised that the transport system was not geared to the influx of supporters into one corner of north London all at once.

In 1937 Spurs enjoyed yet another rollicking cup run that enthralled the supporters. A fifth round replay against Everton drew 46,972 on a Monday afternoon. They were not disappointed. In a match full of good football and incident, the tension was heightened by some debatable refereeing decisions hotly disputed by the crowd and the players, lest we fall for the stereotype of a 'play up and play the game' attitude from hardened professionals. One match reporter was clearly caught up in the atmosphere and "the electrical emotionalism of the great crowd that varied hearty cheers with a silence that could almost be felt". Trailing 3-1 at one point, Spurs pulled one back with four minutes to go, whereupon "there was by this time a continuous roar round the ground... Spurs levelled amid volcanic cheering" then scored the winner with seconds left to "cheering that was delirious in its intensity".

The lure of the cup drew an astonishing 71,913 to the home tie versus Preston, only to see Spurs lose 3-1. However, Preston returned to north London for the semi-final in dubious circumstances. The FA decreed that Preston and their opponents West Bromwich Albion should travel south to Highbury for the game. Then as now the convenience and safety of supporters was secondary to other considerations. Several grounds in the Midlands and north were available, plus Spurs were due to play a league match at home on the same day. The Tottenham board were concerned about the impact of other games on their gate receipts. A glance at attendance figures that season when Spurs were a mid-table Second Division side displayed a pattern. While league gates against the better known teams and local rivals held up well around the 30,000 mark, as the season went on against less august opponents numbers averaged in the low 20,000, with only 18,515 for the visit of Coventry that was moved because of the semi-final. In contrast, the cup drew 42,430 that year for our only other home tie in round four versus fellow Second Division team Plymouth Argyle.

Also, in those days many London football fans chose the best game in town. Travel by underground was straightforward and admission was cheap. This idea of the itinerant fan or choosing to see a game if your side was away seems odd in these days of entrenched tribalism and the rival attraction of football on television, but the main deterrent is of course cost. The idea of supporting a team but going to see another side in London was killed stone dead by high ticket prices and the disappearance of the informality and low costs afforded by standing terraces. However, it has disappeared only in the last 20 years or so. Many Spurs fans were regulars at the Orient, for example. It also seems certain that substantial numbers of fans went to Spurs one week and Arsenal the next. However improbable this may sound in the contemporary context of the tribal identity of supporters, this persisted well into the 1980s and 1990s, with fans having season tickets for both clubs until that became prohibitively expensive.

What is most striking is the number of spectators drawn to both clubs in such close proximity, one with established ties to the area, the other newcomers who could not have relied on substantial numbers of south Londoners travelling north every other week. Even allowing for the between the wars popularity of football, the numbers are admirable. The first match since the move in 1913 drew 39,221 to White Hart Lane in mid-January 1921 to see Spurs win 3-1. In those days teams often played the same opponents home and away in successive weeks. Arsenal won the return 3-2 but the crowd exceeded 60,000 even though both clubs were mid-table. Arsenal certainly had the impetus. They were new, shiny, exciting, making the headlines in a purpose-built stadium and their progressive planning off the pitch saw that later in this period they wisely invested considerable resources to ensure success on the field to match their supporters' expectations. Galling though this may be, they successfully attracted supporters from the growing north London suburbs and beyond.

Spurs put the indignities of relegation by ballot behind them, romping away with the 1919/20 Second Division by six points, a hefty margin in an era with two points for a win. Over 47,000 welcomed them to the top division when they were visited by Blackburn, losing 2-1.

Spurs achieved a creditable sixth place in the final table but found glory in the FA Cup in a year ending in one. After straightforward home wins against Bristol Rovers and Bradford City, a record crowd of almost 52,000 crammed into White Hart Lane to celebrate a narrow 1-0 victory versus Aston Villa, still one of the biggest names in the English game at the time, in the quarter-finals. Gate receipts of £6,992 were a record for any club game in England at the time other than a cup final.

The FA Cup Final against Wolves was played at Stamford Bridge, Chelsea's ground. The gates opened early at 10.30am because of the pressure of the queues that had already built up, fans cheerfully putting up with a soaking on the open terraces as the rain poured down for most of the day. To keep their spirits up, if not to keep dry, they sang popular songs, shook their rattles and sounded trumpets and motor horns. The days of chants were still a long way off. As the London side, Spurs fans were in the majority, having blue and white flags and wearing ribbons and rosettes in navy blue and white. Photos of the fans show that rosettes and ribbons were the order of the day, not scarves, and rest assured that the tradition of silly hats at cup finals stretches back to 1921 and beyond.

Some 72,805 were admitted before the gates were closed at 2.20pm – no all-ticket matches in those days – and as a concession to the elements the game kicked off hfive minutes early at 2.55pm. The heavy conditions underfoot hampered Spurs' passing game but in an undistinguished match Jimmy Dimmock's low shot across the keeper was enough to bring the cup to the Lane.

After the match the players jumped into an open-topped charabanc with the cup and drove through the West End and up the Seven Sisters Road to White Hart Lane where the crowds were waiting. Mounted police struggled to clear a path through the tumultuous crowds as the procession was led by the Tottenham Town Band.

The directors decided on a grand celebration dinner in the plush Holborn Restaurant. Undoubtedly terrace supporters would have not received an invitation but amidst the toasts and upright celebrations, significantly manager Peter McWilliam, associated with the club for so long now, acknowledged the relationship between the team and the supporters: "It is very easy for supporters to be enthusiastic and cheerful when we are winning the cup and doing well in the league, but much more we need their enthusiasm, their cheerfulness, and even their sympathy, when we are losing. I promise you that we will always do our best."

Tottenham Hotspur supporters were used to seeing attractive football with the game played the right way. Contemporary accounts make it clear this perception was not confined just to Spurs fans. Tottenham Hotspur stood for something. Our football had values, scruples even. The right way was the only way and supporters understood this. Then as now, they had high expectations not so much of success but more of achieving results by playing open, passing football. It was a style Spurs fans still refer to as the Spurs Way, and though it was the sides of first Arthur Rowe in the early 1950s and then Bill Nicholson which eventually took it to the ultimate level, it is also a style that has been adopted by some of the most successful sides in the world. Think space and shape, angle and incision, flexibility and interchangeability, keeping the ball on the ground and making it do the work.

Spurs and the Spurs Way was acknowledged and admired in the football world. It had meaning and significance in the contemporary world rather than being a construct imposed on the time by historians.

The perception of Arsenal however, contrasted with that of Tottenham Hotspur in that it was far more negative. Supporters of northern clubs in particular resented Arsenal who despite their dominance in the 1930s, or perhaps because of it, won few friends away from Highbury. Their sometimes physical approach was disliked and their ability to score late goals was the origin of the 'lucky Arsenal' tag. And they were resented for allegedly buying success though an aggressive transfer policy and dragging moneybags through the marble halls. Perhaps their worst sin was being successful and southern.

So behind the attendance statistics, who were these supporters, these flat-capped acquiescent masses patiently waiting for hours in the open for kick-off, the only distraction being an occasional passing photographer taking a picture for posterity or when a small boy was passed down to the front? We know they came in numbers, were loyal, were regulars, but there is precious little known about who they were or where they came from. Even the local paper made no effort to record their views or perspectives. There were no fanzines. There's nothing to record their impact on the club's fortunes even though Spurs could not do without them. They provided the backdrop to the big matches, extras in the background as the drama was played out. Consultation or feedback was unthinkable. Any comments from supporters in the paper were invariably from middle-class dignitaries or indignant letter-writers.

However, it is possible to draw some tentative conclusions based on historical research into football crowds in general. Working-class men were in the grip of a game that loosened only with the changing leisure patterns of a more affluent society in the late 1960s and finally were set free as the Premier League gorged on the wealth generated by national and global marketing opportunities, thus putting spectating beyond the reach of many.

Football soon became the people's game. Between the wars it cemented its place in the nation's heart yet the core support at matches was from the skilled working class who because of their higher income and relatively stable employment opportunities were able to afford the minimum admission set by the Football League, 6d before the war rising to 9d in 1917 and 1s (5p) from 1919 onwards. Thus for unskilled men and indeed many skilled workers with other demands on their wages, football was out of reach, especially when the costs of transport to and from the game were added. The margin between black and red on the family balance sheet was often small. Illness and even a short period of unemployment could suddenly create significant hardship.

This was particularly the case during the Depression where unemployment reached unprecedented levels and working families suffered through lack of work and income. However, the Depression did not affect the country in a uniform manner. London mitigated the worst extremes and Tottenham remained relatively prosperous during the 1920s and 1930s. Average crowds certainly rose between the wars. It is unlikely that the Depression had any significant effect on crowds at Spurs even though league rules did not allow a reduction in admission price for the unemployed. Reserve matches were much cheaper, however, and around the country these games drew crowds several thousand strong. In Liverpool, the streets around the ground on matchdays were lined with unemployed men watching the crowds going to and from the game but there is no record of anything like this happening in Tottenham.

Historians suggest the period between the wars saw the beginning of significant middle-class interest in the game although it is inaccurate to say they had been excluded until now. A cartoon in the Handbook depicts a packed carriage on the '2.38 From Liverpool Street to White Hart Lane' with men and boys of different ages and class, judging by their headgear. At Spurs there was clearly a demand for seats, which obviously were more expensive. The covered accommodation of the West Stand was augmented by 5,100 seats in the top tier of the East Stand, designed by the famous stadium architect Archibald Leitch and opened in 1934. This implies that Spurs were able to attract a proportion of middle-class supporters.

Also, the standing enclosure ran the length of the West Stand which for an extra sum offered a covered vantage point for those who wished to avoid the hurly-burly and discomfort of the open terraces. The enclosure remained in place until the West Stand was demolished and rebuilt in 1980. Access was via the West Stand and for a long time it was possible to pay for ground admission and then transfer when inside the stadium. For a period in the seventies and early eighties, the club introduced standing season tickets. Initially these were for the enclosure only, although many took advantage of the price savings only to slip round to the Shelf or Park Lane.

Women were a distinct minority although they were a presence. Certainly it is rare to see a woman in the crowd photos at White Hart Lane at this time. However, the club was aware of their needs, at least some of them. The 1932 Handbook reminded supporters not to barrack as it "is neither sporting nor gentlemanly" and bad language is "always objectionable and more so in view of the large number of lady patrons."

In November of the following year the programme printed this appeal: "A strong lady supporter of the Spurs writes a note that contains an appeal. I commend it to the sterner sex. She points out that she is on the short side, and her view of the game is often obscured by the bowler and trilby hats of the men. She asks me to request the men to be chivalrous enough to come to the matches in caps so as to enable those who happen to be behind them to get more than an occasional glimpse of the incidents on the pitch."

The vast majority of supporters lived within easy reach of the ground. At the beginning of this period, most probably walked – if nothing else it saved on fares. As the years passed, public transport became more affordable. The good transport links meant that Spurs was easy to reach by bus, train and tram. Support was strong in Enfield and further north in Hertfordshire and parts of Essex. These areas remain Spurs heartlands.

A picture of the ground taken in the early 1930s shows an advert for the Underground using Manor House station on the Piccadilly Line, the nearest at the time. This indicates that Spurs fans came from further afield. Advance tickets were available not only from the ticket office but also Alfred Hays in Cornhill and Bond Street. Also, the itinerant fan who chose the best game in London on any given weekend could easily put White Hart Lane on his list. From the early 1920s supporters were encouraged in the programme to: "Travel home by Metro after the match – electric trains to all parts of London, WHL to Liv St."

But the lack of a local Tube was identified as a problem for the club and fans, as shown by this note from the programme in 1938: "All hoping the time will arrive when this congested centre of population will have the advantage of a Tube. This is long overdue, especially in view of the fact that Tubes have been constructed in other districts where the demands for transport are much less than in this neighbourhood".

Supporters were advised to take the train to ease congestion at Stamford Hill but sadly not everyone made it home safely. This brief note appeared in the programme for 8 August 1933: "George Osborne 24 of 146 Walworth Road SE17 was run over by a bus on the way home from match on May 6th. Appeals for witnesses from his father."

Trams ran every minute from Finsbury Park and Liverpool Street in the late 1930s, when fan Harry Slater first went to games. "Sometimes I went by train when I was at Stoke Newington. That was a quicker way," he says. "Trying to get on a bus was impossible, particularly late in the day, if you got out early it was OK.

"I used to walk there or sometimes go by bike, an uncle of mine who had a cobblers shop two or three minutes', perhaps five minutes' walk from the ground, he used to take bikes in and charge a penny or tuppence, something like that, to park your bike. Of course I got mine free, but he didn't repair my shoes though!

"Those days there were a lot of cyclists going, of course there weren't many cars. My father never had a car."

Cycling was a popular form of transport. At many grounds, local residents hired space in their gardens to look after the bikes during the game for a few pence. One fan recalls cycling to and from Chelmsford for every home game in the late 1930s.

Season tickets for numbered and reserved seats were £3 10s (£3.50) at the beginning of the 1930s. Centre seats in the East Stand were 3s (15p), sides 2s with most available on the day but some you could book in advance by applying by post to the ticket office, from Arthur Hays or Keith Prowse travel agents in central London or by phone on Tottenham 0018. Supporters were warned not to buy from touts outside the ground and to beware of pirate programme sellers. The official variety had a peaked cap. From 1932 the left luggage office, tried as an experiment the previous season, became a permanent service by popular demand.

There were restaurants and buffets in all parts of the ground, with caterers Mecca granted a licence to sell alcohol, now available on all matchdays. Chocolates and cigarettes were also on sale. A hot restaurant meal cost 1/6. For the average supporter this was positively opulent, yet within the development was a conscious effort on the club's part to look out for the interests of the ordinary terrace fan. The directors stated it was their policy "to cater for those who in the past have been loyal supporters of the Club. This is why prices have been fixed, and that is also why the whole of the standing accommodation on that side of the ground, whether in the open or under cover, is the minimum admission charge of 1s".

This was by no means the norm. Shortly after the stand opened, the programme quotes from a letter sent to the club: "I have been on grounds where the convenience of the stand people is studied but the man who pays his bob can't get a cup of tea."

Charles Buchan, former centre-forward turned journalist and famous for his long-running *Football Monthly* magazine, knew the game and was an entirely approving independent voice. Writing in 1938 he praised the club for its attitude towards the ordinary supporter.

"Tottenham Hotspur have done more for the shilling man than any other club in England. It is a club supported through bad times and good by fathers. Mothers. Sisters and brothers. The Spurs have the most loyal and critical supporters in England. Why? They were the first club in London to place a cover over the shilling man, and the first to devote three sides of the ground to the shilling man. They were the first to install refreshment buffets for the shilling man, and the first to have an office where the shilling man can store anything while he watches. And they were the first to have a special safe section for the spectator-children of the shilling man.

"A conspiracy of silence hangs over the club. They never use ballyhoo. Quite right for a club that keeps advertisements off its ground and out of the programme. Price 1d that programme, by the way. The Spurs can find room for 60,000 people who pay one shilling. No other club can do that."

Perhaps this is a reason why the supporters remained loyal through the ups and downs of the 1920s and 1930s with promotions followed by relegations and no silverware to follow the cup triumph of 1921. It's a lesson that still applies in contemporary football that the club would do well to remember.

The crowd sang songs to keep themselves amused before and during the match, bearing in mind that to guarantee admission for big games let alone gain a decent vantage point supporters had to arrive hours before kick-off. Songs were linked to certain teams although there's no mention of Spurs having a song at that time. Equally, the popular songs of the day were shared among different crowds. Repeated football chants, however, came much later, popular from the early 1960s.

Football Favourite magazine printed the words to dozens of songs over several issues in 1927 for the benefit of supporters all over the country. This included *The Wearing of the Green* and *My Old Kentucky Home*. Popular songs could be changed to fit the game. Thus *Chick Chick Chick Chick Chicken* became *Kick Kick Kick Kick It* and *Keep the Home Fires Burning* turned into *Keep the Forwards Scoring*. It remains unclear as to whether these were accurate reflections of terrace culture or the creations of individuals, the equivalent of chants that appear from individuals on Twitter or messageboards today and make it no further.

It's impossible to pinpoint when the wearing of club colours to signify support actually began. The familiar injunction from street hawkers around the ground to "wear your colours" applied to supporters between the wars. Football scarves date from the first decade of the century, as do rattles, and fans for the big matches were decked out in ribbons and silly cup final hats. However, little of this is evident in the dour crowd photos of White Hart Lane, enlivened only by the slightly self-conscious grins of people unaccustomed to being photographed.

Harry Slater made sure he arrived in good time: "You had to get there very, very early. Idea was you get there early so you would get a good view. I mean, I was a giant compared with some, 5 foot 8 and a half [chuckles]. When I was a boy it was hopeless, they used to pass you overhead. Sometimes you ended up virtually on the touchline, they let you sit on that track. They used to have an enclosure for children, it was half price, go to this section. If you went with your parents, I never went with them but sometimes with my brother, you always have to go in with him because you know what it's like coming out of there. It was right in the far corner. Get there about 1 o'clock."

Mind you, Harry didn't always pay. The official figure for the highest ever gate at White Hart Lane, the fifth round FA Cup tie versus Sunderland in 1938, is out by at least one because Harry slipped under the turnstiles, and not for the only time: "Oh yeah, they [other fans] used to encourage you, say go on then, he [turnstile operator] can't see what's going on. Not saying I did it very often, two or three times. Also, they used to open the gates 15, 20 minutes before the game ended, get down there late and see something. Wait for the gates to open and go in."

A flavour of what these big games at White Hart Lane felt like is provided by the record of the fourth round cup replay the following year against Cardiff City in 1922. A midweek game and therefore with an afternoon kick-off on a work day saw nearly 54,000 inside and almost as many locked out. The High Road was completely blocked and the police overwhelmed by the chaos. A photo shows the then undeveloped single tier east terrace jam-packed with spectators precariously perched high on the large advertising hoardings at the back of the open stand.

Not everyone took a favourable view of proceedings. A correspondent to the *Herald* entirely disapproved: "At a time when the spectre of starvation, unemployment and misery stalks through every city, town and hamlet in the land it is unseemly that half the nation should go mad over a game of football."

The fans had clearly invested a lot in this one match, a benchmark tie against one of the big teams in the game at the time. The frustrations of previous indignities and snubs were let loose. Wagstaffe-Simmons described the scene after Banks scored Spurs' winner: "It was Bedlam (sic) let loose. It was what the followers of the Spurs had been waiting for during the past twelve months. Many hats must have been lost that were tossed high in the air, and surely the familiar rattles never rattled more loudly than on Saturday. Words cannot describe the outburst of cheers that hailed this gratifying achievement. It was really most impressive, and yet it all arose from a team scoring a goal at football. What strange people we English are."

Echoes of the stands and terraces can still be heard in the voice of the author of the programme notes. Despite editorial caution, the anonymous author, who occasionally signs off as 'Spurite', is not afraid to offer an opinion based on his view from the West Stand rather than the club's official line. His refreshingly indiscreet opinions are the closest we can come to hearing the authentic sound of the crowd during the inter-war years.

It is likely Spurite is a reliable source. He was a long-term supporter, at one point referring to his notes for 1912, and the style is consistent up to 1939. He went to matches home and away, plus the reserves who in those days drew crowds numbered in the thousands and played at a very high standard. He's also aware and honest. For example, in September 1926 he ruefully refers back to negative comments about Arthur Grimsdell written over a decade earlier, then reminding us of Grimsdell's subsequently brilliant career.

Our man begins the 1926/27 season in optimistic mood, hoping for success in league or cup but above all "we may expect to see clean and scientific football, for which the Club is renowned. The Spurs tradition will be maintained."

His notes are peppered with homilies, usually in bold: "Be chivalrous in victory and sportsmen in defeat", "Good play by the Visiting Team is worthy of our appreciation". Certainly in the earlier years of this period the programme displays an awareness of and non-critical interest in the wider game, such as how players of other clubs were progressing and who was playing good football.

However, football crowds have always been nonconformist. There were no chants or songs directed at the opposition or the referee for that matter but supporters were not afraid to vent their feelings. In early October Spurite admonishes the booing of Fred Reed, the West Bromwich Albion captain, after a tackle that injured a Spurs player. "Barracking is a most unnecessary and reprehensible practice. A section of the New Cross [Millwall] audience did their best to spoil the game with their jeering. After Saturday's match Mr W.I. Bassett, the famous international of bygone days told me that in his opinion London football crowds still need educating." Not just Tottenham then.

Testament to our away support is that our man was happy to be among the thousands of Spurs supporters who travelled to Villa Park in November to see a 3-2 victory. He makes a point of saying, albeit politely, that both Villa goals should have been disallowed, the first for an off-the-ball foul on the keeper, the second for an incorrect handball decision.

Then as now, refereeing decisions remain unfathomable. In autumn 1927 Spurs' thrilling late comeback ensured a win versus Middlesbrough but although he is "most reluctant to criticise a referee, because I realise how difficult his job is", he then proceeds to complain vigorously about a disallowed goal, then, enigmatically: "When is a goal not a goal? When the ball in transit hits a player's head and the referee mistakes the cranium for hands."

The following October, Spurs have six points from eight games, two off the bottom of Division One but only four off the top and unbeaten at home. Nevertheless our supporter is not happy. "There is too much individualism… it is stupid to try and beat several opponents while two or three other forwards are waiting unmarked for a pass that does not come along… selfish retention of the ball… more first time attempts to find the net… not be so much finessing inside the penalty area… now boys we want some goals."

He's not alone. He ends the programme notes thus: "Thanks to the correspondents for the letters suggesting it is necessary for certain steps to be taken. The Directors are fully alive to the need for action in the direction indicated."

The mood of the supporters does not improve as the month goes on. Manager Billy Minter makes several changes in response to the lack of goals but the experimental side loses 3-1 at home to

Everton. Spurite acknowledges the uncomplimentary reaction of the crowd towards the Spurs players. He is at pains to assure readers that both players and manager are upset and are working hard to lift their game. A couple of months on, he is forced to reveal that an unnamed player performs better away from home because of the crowd's negative reaction towards him.

Anyway, bad refereeing has played a part. After minutely dissecting two decisions and agreeing with the booing that ensued, he complains bitterly about the number of 'perfectly legitimate goals knocked off'. He's still at it the following week, imploring referees to not be swayed by the home crowd.

By the end of the month, Spurs have dropped to third from bottom and Spurite acknowledges that the fans want Tottenham to spend money on new players but articulates two very modern dilemmas. The club has to be certain that new players are better than those we already have and many of the suggested targets are not available: "The players Tottenham would like to secure are anchored to clubs that will not part from them, and the players who are obtainable are not up to Tottenham's requirements." Our man does use the programme notes however to deny a series of transfer rumours over the next few months.

In passing, Spurite notes another modern problem. After a heavy defeat to Fulham in the London Cup, he sympathises with the lack of enthusiasm of first teamers towards this less significant competition and advocates a change of competition rules rather than a change of attitude.

As the season goes on, Spurite is cheerful for the most part, praising the team's efforts and encouraging supporters to travel to away games to support them. However, there is tension in the air throughout an exceptionally tight season where with two games to go 15 or 16 clubs, including Spurs, remained in danger of relegation. At times he is flagrantly critical of the forwards for their wayward shooting and the defenders for not demonstrating any understanding between them.

Tension in the crowd from frustration and unrealised expectations. New signings not delivering. Early season impatience. Holding on to the ball for too long. Complaints about the board. Complaints about referees and injustice. Demands for money to be spent in the transfer market. Prioritising competitions because of too many games. The character of the Tottenham crowd has changed little over the years, loyal, wanting good football but not hiding their feelings when the side is not up to scratch. The contemporary supporter would feel right at home.

Barracking was an accepted part of the crowd's day out. The earliest Spurs supporters were censured for their raucous behaviour on the marshes. One writer on a day out at a game excitedly noted some of the daring phrases of encouragement and abuse: "Down him!" "Sit on his chest!" "Knock their ribs in!" Another recorded that "doubtful tactics by the home team are applauded to the echo, while the same actions by the opponents are met with hooting and groans". As we said, the modern fan would feel right at home.

Then as now matchday was important for the local economy. Food was available from stalls and souvenir-making was a cottage industry. Advertising in the ground and the programme was not allowed by the board but the proliferation of pre-war advertising from local business shows how important the club was to the local economy. Everything from hats to football boots and cigars had some link, however obscure, to the Hotspur. The pubs, cinemas and music halls encouraged supporters to make an afternoon and evening of it.

Some took it more seriously than others. In December 1938 after Spurs beat Millwall 4-0, the programme printed the following:

"At Tottenham Police Court on Tuesday a man charged with drunkeness said: 'I came to Tottenham to see Millwall play the Spurs.'

Magistrate: (Mr Whitworth): Did you expect Millwall to win?

The Man: Yes sir, and my friends gave me a whisky for each goal scored by the Spurs to console me."

He was fined 2s 6d.

Equally, the authorities saw the club as a way of appealing to the solidarity of supporters to be displayed in a different manner. In the autumn and winter of 1938, the country prepared for war and Spurs fans were encouraged to contribute. In October this appeal went out for volunteers to the Auxiliary Fire Service: "These are critical times. For months we have been on the verge of a volcanic outbreak. The immediate danger of war has passed away but peace cannot be guaranteed by any people or nation. We all hope for freedom from the arbitrament of arms, so that the nations of the earth may tread the road of well-ordered progress. But we must be prepared for all eventualities, and for that reason I earnestly appeal to Tottenham Hotspur supporters to do their bit towards making adequate preparations."

Spurs have a long tradition of going away. This was indubitably a time for celebration as well as watching a football match. Coaches were hired and special trains organised, the first football specials. The transport was decorated as well as the fans themselves and loaded up with crates of beer for a day out. Train companies responded to the demand from Spurs fans for away travel by running excursions that became more regular and not just for the big games. In 1927 Thomas Cook offered a trip to Portsmouth for 5s 9d (approximately 28p). The following year Cook's offered the same deal for the game in nearby Southampton even though Spurs were then in the Second Division, a clear sign away support held up regardless of league position.

In February 1928 tickets for the away FA Cup tie at Leicester were limited but available from the Spurs box office. The fare was 5/9 or 3/6 return on the train, depending on whether you went second or third class, while the London Midland ran a service from South Tottenham picking up at Haringey, Holloway Road and

Crouch Hill, fare 5s meal available there and back, 2/6. In 1933 you could travel by train to the Christmas Day fixture at Huddersfield.

Older supporters will remember the coaches run by the Henry Company. They had been active in this period, running trips to every away game by 1938. For example, Luton was 3s (15p), Birmingham 7s 6d (approx. 38p), from the ground and pick-up at Broad Lane.

Historian Matthew Taylor incorporates the match into the culture of support: "Drinking and gambling were part and parcel of supporting culture at this time, although we can only speculate whether this had yet formed part of a broader weekend cultural routine involving perhaps the public house, the bookmaker's shop, the sporting newspaper and the music hall as well as the match itself."

This may have been a golden age in terms of attendances but conditions at most grounds remained primitive throughout this period. White Hart Lane was relatively well appointed, especially after the new East Stand was built, which meant supporters could find cover on all four sides of the ground. The Lane had concrete terracing but many other big grounds did not: fans were packed in with no set safety limit and toilet facilities were nowhere near enough for the size of the crowd.

One aspect of contemporary crowd behaviour, football-related violence, was largely missing in England. Incidents of disruption have always been associated with the game. In the 1930s, Queens Park Rangers, Carlisle and Millwall faced ground closures as punishment for crowd disturbances. However, personal safety was not a major concern of Spurs supporters on their way to and from the Lane. Dave Russell in his book *Football and the English* describes this period as relatively peaceful. Indeed, the fact that innocuous terrace barracking was frequently reported in the press suggests minor indiscretions stood out.

Russell notes that the first major episode of concern over crowd behaviour between 1919 and 1922 was less about the actual extent of the problem and more about a supposed decline in public discipline following a wave of industrial militancy after the First World War. Authorities had real fears that an uneven transition back to ordinary life for millions of soldiers, tough, battle-hardened and expecting to have fought for something worthwhile to come home to, would create militancy and a potential threat to public order.

The football authorities and club owners paid no attention to the needs of fans, who were expected to turn up regardless of conditions, discomfort or safety. In that sense it is testament to the forbearance of supporters that their passion for the game and for their team was expressed in peaceable restraint.

This image of the peaceable, accommodating crowd, a coming together of strangers who co-existed in harmony, became important in the early 1920s and cemented in the public consciousness after the 1923 FA Cup Final. A non-ticket crowd at Wembley surpassed all expectations and spilled onto the pitch as kick-off time neared. However, it took the arrival of the King and a single policeman on a white horse to dampen the prospects of any disorder and to clear the pitch. The match went ahead without a hint of trouble, the supporters self-regulating and disciplined despite crowding the touchlines for the entire match.

This myth has passed into history – the horse was in fact quite dark, the nature of photographic processes at the time making it appear much lighter in photos and on film. It suited the times. Rather than being a threat, the masses became transformed into a reassuring image of the virtues of a nation. This threat was real because of the potential of conflict in industry as unemployment rose in the Depression.

Football has a meaning for its supporters that goes far deeper than the game as sport or a leisure pursuit. It provides friendship, camaraderie, a sense of belonging in an unsettled, confusing world. Results are never certain but loyalty to the club is the one thing that can be relied upon. For some it is a means of expressing attachment, emotion and passion that finds no outlet elsewhere in people's lives.

There's no doubt that many sought escape and excitement on the packed terraces at White Hart Lane. Living standards broadly rose between the wars and leisure time increased but it remained a precious refuge after a hard week's drudgery at work. They could let off steam, feel part of something and today's fan is no different in that respect. Post-First World War, the game gave an added sense of normality as the community struggled to re-adjust, creating new bonds and reinforcing existing ones.

The club remained important to the local community. As before the war, it gave a rapidly changing community a focus and identity. The players were different from the supporters only in their supreme talents. Predominantly from working-class backgrounds, the maximum wage meant they earned more than the average working man but not so much that it gave them a separate social status. Many augmented their reduced or non-existent summer wages by going out to work. Players and fans were neighbours.

This period became the first when it became easier to follow the fortunes of Spurs without necessarily going to the match. The spread of the game in society's leisure culture undoubtedly broadened its appeal as it took a firm hold on the consciousness of the nation.

The *Tottenham Herald* of course kept a close eye on the club, producing special souvenir editions to mark successes. National papers, particularly the popular press, devoted more and more column inches to football as they fought out a circulation war, using the popularity of the game to sell more copies and shaping perceptions of the game by gradually moving away from factual, blow-by-blow dry reporting to more dramatic, critical and personality-driven reports. This made national stars of several players in the 1930s, complete with advertising contracts and personal appearances if not quite the celebrity status of the Premier League superstar. Sadly no Spurs players moved into this exalted bracket.

Two London evening papers, the *News* and the *Standard*, published 'Late Final' Saturday editions, eagerly snapped up because this was the fan's chance to find out the scores on the way home from a game.

Football was first covered on the radio in January 1927, sadly with the questionable choice of an Arsenal match against Sheffield United. The Football League banned commentary of league matches in 1931 for fear of affecting attendances but the cup final and internationals were extremely popular. Despite the handicap of beginning with another Arsenal match, this time versus Arsenal reserves believe it or not, television broadcasts began in 1937 and quickly established themselves. Again league matches were banned but the annual ritual of watching the cup final, first covered the following year, signified football as one of the occasions when the BBC fulfilled an element of its charter and brought the nation together.

Football could be seen in weekly newsreels, shown as part of every cinema programme. Cinema-going was phenomenally popular in the late 1920s and 1930s. Tottenham had four cinemas between the wars, including the Corner Picture Theatre on the corner of the High Road and Seven Sisters Road, and the Electric Theatre in the High Road, later to become the Tottenham Royal dance hall.

Football betting was illegal but this was the age when the football pools really took a grip, allowed because the stake was collected after the results were known. Each week coupons were distributed with a list of all the league matches. You were invited to invest in whether a set number finished in a home win, away win or draw, although prediction of exact scores was not required. The ceremonial completion of the coupon, with smudgy ball-point ink in tiny graph-paper squares, was a feature of Thursday teatime in many households through to the seventies. Draws were the holy grail – perm any eight from 11 selections and you were on for a fortune. By the mid-1930s, between five and seven million people a week did the pools, staking £30m a year.

However, it's likely that by the end of this period, those bonds between fans and community had begun to loosen just as the bonds of support remained strong. The sound of the suburbs was absorbed into the dense urban conurbation of London. The better-off could move north and north-east to Hertfordshire and Essex. Also, the 1921 cup victory gave Spurs a higher profile in the south in a league largely dominated by northern and midland clubs until the rise of Arsenal in the thirties. Therefore Spurs undoubtedly attracted support from other parts of London from that point onwards.

However your support began, that sense of place remained, as it does to this day. The Hotspur played where they had always played, and you always came back to the same place, walked the same streets as the founding schoolboys, albeit you no longer had to get your boots dirty on marsh mud.

Whether the game generated wider loyalties across class is more debatable. The game itself was run by middle-class business people – supporters had no say in the running of the club even when the supporters' club was formed. Such involvement is extremely limited even now but then it was unheard of. Yet this went largely unchallenged, at least not in the form of concerted protest. There is evidence of supporters grumbling about the lack of football knowledge or transfer acumen of the board whenever Spurs were not doing well but there was never any concerted protest as far as we can tell.

The only instance of any political activity was around the infamous international match between England and Germany played at White Hart Lane in 1935, when groups opposed to the anti-Semitism of Nazi Germany organised protests inside and outside the ground.

Historians and sociologists have sought to explain the apparently docile attitude of crowds of working-class men in terms of class analysis. Here was a regular gathering of largely working-class men, treated poorly by the middle-class owners and directors, set in a social and economic context of large numbers of ex-soldiers returning home with experience of conflict, then the industrial unrest and mass unemployment of the Depression.

Some scholars suggest that the ruling class controlled football for its own interests. The safety valve it provided allowed working people to let off steam, maybe cause a bit of a ruckus but essentially never challenge those who ran the game and ran the country.

While there is some truth in this, crucially it denies working people the capacity for independent thought and action. Football grounds between the wars became places where working-class culture was given free rein. It became theirs. They reflected working-class character – bawdy, predominantly friendly and peaceable, hedonistically vulgar, fun. For a few hours the ground was theirs. Behaviour wasn't controlled, it was self-controlled. Within self-imposed limits fans could act as they wished and find a sense of identity.

This aspect of football culture remained a key feature of supporter identity. Patterns of support changed after the war as we shall see. Supporters took over an end, sometimes fought for it, but it represented something important about ownership and belonging. It's possible that the apathy and alienation of many contemporary Spurs fans relates in large part to the brutal awareness that we can no longer take possession of the ground and make it our own. For the first time since the very early days of the club, we can't go where we like, we can't spontaneously meet friends and watch the game together, we are stewarded closely, told to sit down, scrutinised by closed-circuit cameras. It feels like being allowed in to our grandmother's front room on Sunday but only if we take our shoes off, don't talk and keep our drink on the doilies.

Alan Russell quotes soccer historian Tony Mason, talking about how football helped individuals within social groups and that playing and watching football "had become one of those things which working men did".

Football was one of the social settings that fashioned a sense of class but one in which no link was made with any political message or activity. Russell concludes that football "perhaps generated a consciousness of class rather than class consciousness".

What is true is that on the raucous, boisterous terraces of White Hart Lane, you quickly understood that being a Spurs fan was part of your identity. You learned what being a Spurs fan meant, about the importance of good football, of loyalty even when your team dropped into the Second Division, of getting behind your team, of just being there and being part of a wider community of people who felt exactly the same as you did.

The majority of Spurs supporters between the wars were local to the area. Many others lived locally until relatively recently or their families did and the tradition was handed down. Yet as time passed the ties were less with Tottenham and more with Hotspur. There are many examples of how the club reflected back civic pride in this rapidly expanding suburb. The great and the good toasted the club's exploits on the pitch as a symbol of the borough's prosperity and of course their own social and economic status.

Tottenham fans and residents were Londoners too. And Londoners could choose from different teams. When one was away, another was at home. The loyalties and emotional pull of supporters in one- or two-club towns and cities are very different. Tottenham Hotspur wasn't inextricably linked to the economic well-being of N17 or London for that matter, as was the case in other one-club towns where broadly speaking the long-term fortunes of the football team and local economy ebbed and flowed in unison. Football in Liverpool was an intrinsic part of the city's culture. On big matchdays, some towns outside London would empty and decamp to watch their team play away. Slowly at first, then over many years, the link between the community and the fans began to unravel.

This is not to demean the passion and loyalty through the generations of Tottenham Hotspur supporters. But making this observation helps to explain why the ground itself has become so significant. This powerful attachment to place took hold between the wars. The club began there and stayed there. Supporters need identity and continuity: for Spurs fans, the Lane provides it. This was and is where we are drawn, a peculiar profound attachment to a now run-down piece of north London. Supporting a club needs a focus. Supporters need a place to be, a place that is theirs, somewhere around which the bonds of attachment coalesce. Tottenham supporters needed White Hart Lane to offer that reassuring, welcoming consistency, which is why the ground and sense of place is so important to a people's history of Tottenham Hotspur.

And it is at this point that the telling of that history takes on a different trajectory. From formation in 1882 to the end of the Second World War in 1945, it has been possible to follow the development of the club's support along that timeline. After 1945, as the crowds continued to grow and what we now recognise as the modern game began to take shape and extend its influence through media that was ever more easily accessible to the mass of people, the story of support develops along many different avenues. In the second part of this book we travel down some of those avenues, aided by research and first-hand memory, as our focus moves to reflecting the variety of experiences that together constitute a people's history of Tottenham Hotspur.

4

They played a different type of football

TURNING points. Examine the history of any institution or movement and you'll find them. Understanding why those moments matter, what caused the path to change, is vital in understanding the DNA of the force that experienced that change. In 1945, Tottenham Hotspur was at one of those turning points.

By the time football restarted after the Second World War, Tottenham Hotspur was a club of the past. The one-time Flower of the South had wilted. The club had lost its way due to lacklustre performances on the pitch and lack of vision off it. And yet, as we've seen, the crowds still came, through the days of football and economic depression, to see the Spurs. By 1945, the hunger for watching live football had not subsided. In fact, the dour circumstances of Britain in the immediate post-war years meant that the desire to spend an afternoon at the game was greater than ever.

Rationing was still in place, clothing utilitarian at best, consumer durables unheard of and, to add to the general greyness of a nation shattered by years of war, coal smoke pervaded the streets. Add to that the trauma of the loss of loved ones, or the trauma of those who had survived but, after what they had seen, wished they hadn't, and it's not hard to understand that there was a need for escapism. For years, football had been the escape for crowds of ordinary people. And in 1945 the people were eager for some regular football.

During the war football had been played in a restricted format, with regional leagues and guest players rendering club identity almost redundant. Add to that the initial restriction of crowds to just 8,000 and the fact that entry was by ticket only and you can understand that the football on offer during the war was not what one of the game's modern sponsors would call the real thing. Plus, of course, war tends to make most things – even football – comparatively irrelevant.

The fact that Spurs once again fell foul of the football authorities may also have kept loyalties alive. In 1941, the club was among the 12 expelled from the Football League for refusing to travel long distances for games. The refusal was based upon the fact that the clubs could not get their players released from war duties for long journeys but the football authorities, demonstrating as ever their acute awareness of the game's place in the grander scheme of things, did not consider a trifling affair such as a world war good enough reason to opt out of travelling. So the dirty dozen were expelled, and promptly formed their own competition.

Spurs fan Harry Slater tells a tale of what life was like for those left at home during the war. "I used to play for a team, firm called John Dickenson – they had a fantastic ground, the only one of a few pitches in London that was available in wartime. I ran a league, about six teams, a couple came from south London. It was towards the end of the war, we went to play on this particular ground. I got a phone call on Saturday morning from the groundsman. He wouldn't let me play because the ground was icy. So I said, 'Look, I've got these people coming from south London.' And I talked him into it.

"The following week, the same thing happens. I went over there and this time he wouldn't have it, so we got on the bus and went to

Tottenham. During the course of the match there was an explosion in the distance.

"I got in the office on Monday morning and this chap said to me, 'Do you feel lucky?' I said 'Why, what are you talking about?' He said, 'That V2 fell on the penalty spot of our ground. Wrecked the dressing room, groundsman's in hospital. There would have been 22 players on that pitch."

Slater remembers the football authorities "used to run a shambles of a league" during the war, and refers to the sharing of White Hart Lane by Arsenal and Spurs. "One time Arsenal played at Tottenham, and during the war they used to swap players. Hooper used to play in goal for Tottenham. They were short of a keeper so they played Hooper. He let in three of the simplest goals ever! We all enjoyed it! It was every other week, Spurs and Arsenal at Tottenham. We enjoyed it because Arsenal got beat."

That ground-share between Tottenham and Arsenal is interesting. The rivalry between the clubs was already well-established, in part due to the Gunners' move from Woolwich onto Tottenham's north London patch, and in part because of the controversial circumstances around Arsenal gaining a First Division place at Tottenham's expense. But those events were nearly 20 years past by the time war broke out, and the 1930s had seen Arsenal established as one of the country's top teams while Spurs languished. It's possible the two clubs were not seen as rivals, the modern day equivalent perhaps being the relationship between Leyton Orient and West Ham, where mutual dislike runs deep but where the gulf in playing level renders rivalry relatively minor. Certainly Tottenham fan Peter Jack, one of four generations of Spurs fans from a family who have lived in the area since the turn of the last century, doesn't remember any great issue when the lilywhites and the reds shared the green space at White Hart Lane during wartime.

"I used to go and see both," he says. "I used to go each week. I don't know if the people who went were Spurs or Arsenal fans, or people just going to see football. People weren't quite so ardent about their teams, they were quite nice about it. I can remember a few guest players playing, Stan Mortensen played for Arsenal, and I can remember Ted Drake. Strangely enough, I can remember a few guest players more than I can the Spurs players."

But Harry Slater remembers there was animosity between Tottenham and Arsenal at this stage. Fans "hated" Arsenal playing at Tottenham's ground, he says. "I used to go occasionally to the Arsenal stadium and do you know, they've got the worst clutch of supporters... If a player is having a bad game, what's the point of shouting and harassing the bloke? They should be trying to encourage him." Other people have been known to say much the same about Spurs fans.

It seems that the nature of the rivalry, and the reaction to the ground-share, was often very much in the eye of the beholder – a lesson perhaps for those who are quick to ascribe a single set of attitudes to a crowd. But it's also clear that, at this stage, the levels of antipathy that would be displayed in years to come were not present. Of course, the backdrop of something genuinely serious in the shape of a world war may have served to keep a mere football rivalry in perspective.

The hunger for 'proper' football in 1945 is perhaps best demonstrated by the huge crowds that descended on four British stadiums to see Moscow Dynamo in November 1945 – although the fact that the Soviets were still considered our valued wartime allies also had its effect. At Stamford Bridge, 85,000 got in and many thousands more were locked outside amid scenes of pandemonium. At Ninian Park in Cardiff, 40,000 turned out, with 90,000 packing into Glasgow's Ibrox Park for the final game of the tour. Between the trips to Cardiff and Ibrox, the Dynamos came to White Hart Lane, drawing 54,600 people to a game in which the Soviet side faced Arsenal, of all teams. Justice was done with the Gunners going down four goals to three.

It was against this background of hunger for the resumption of football proper that Arthur Rowe began to build one of the greatest

Spurs sides ever, and in so doing ensure the club's fame and establish a character that would have enduring appeal to future generations of fans.

There were signs, even at this stage in a shattered country with a war-weary population, that people were starting to take their leisure seriously. The Spurs Supporters's Club was formed in 1949 after leafleting home matches and holding a public meeting, and from 1950 published its own magazine, *The Lilywhite*. Facilities for away travel was one of their main concerns. However, from the beginning this was very much a social club as their constitution loftily notes: "The Club shall provide for the benefit and recreation of its members and the furtherance of the ideals of Sport".

Members looked beyond the football for their leisure in an age of self-reliance before rising living standards in the 1960s broadened the leisure opportunities available. Soon the club had a flourishing social side with matches against other supporters' clubs' teams in football, cricket, table tennis and netball. Snooker and darts had both a women's and men's side, while the appeal for recruits for a dance band, dramatic society and harmonica band resulted in a concert party that was still going well into the 1960s. The club was active all year with a full programme of sport, outings and concerts, plus a long weekend at various holiday camps. In 1962 they bumped into Jimmy Greaves in Minehead, also on holiday in the same camp.

There is evidence of some fans travelling to games as competition restarted. Albert Lee, a member of the Supporters' Club committee in the 1940s, tells of driving to away games with his wife, Kathy. "The relationship between supporters and players was very good in those days," he says. "The players always attended dances or social evenings that were arranged by the Supporters' Club. We had our own sales section with scarves, photos and other memorabilia and the players would always sign batches of photos at no charge."

But supporters' concerns do not change over the decades – tickets and getting to the game. Here are the suggestions from the 1950 AGM that officers were instructed to take to the football club:

- arrangements for away matches in journal;
- approaching Spurs for enclosure tickets;
- tickets for away matches for members compelled to travel by train owing to working on night duty;
- subsidised cheap travel for children;
- trains from Chingford to White Hart Lane arriving an hour before kick-off.

The Supporters' Club was proud of its good relations with "the parent club" as they repeatedly refer to it. It seems they worked hard on this. Goalkeeper Ted Ditchburn was the liaison officer between the club and the SSC, encouraging players to join in social activities with the supporters and arranging for tours of the dressing rooms and treatment rooms – the lure of 'going backstage' was strong even then.

This harmony was not always the case. Ditchburn reports that he first became involved so his coach business could gain the contract for away travel, then he hints at nefarious goings-on that caused him to tell his team-mates not to have anything to do with the SSC. The new board had a more positive attitude, however. Supporters' clubs at the time were viewed with deep suspicion at many football clubs so this cordial relationship was unusual. Certainly the football club board did not see them as a threat while the SSC itself had a deferential attitude towards the club, forever anxious not to rock the boat. They were confident however that they were closer to the club than their Arsenal counterparts.

The SSC carried on the tradition of loyal and large away support. *The Lilywhite* determined to carry the "Tottenham Roar" everywhere the team played and proclaimed: "The most luxurious coaches in London have been placed at the disposal of the Spurs Supporters' Club for travel to away matches. Each one of these coaches is fitted with a heater for the long, mid-winter journeys, and a radio for your enjoyment."

Prices were: Wolves 12/6, Aston Villa 11s, Chelsea 3/6 and Huddersfield 18/6, coaches leaving from the ground. Nearly 30 coaches travelled to big games, add those who went under their own steam by rail and Spurs were taking a sizeable away support across the country. By 1950 it was the largest supporters' club in the country with nearly 4,000 members, with ambitions to double that in the following 12 months.

Photos of the happy wanderers show them decked out in scarves, rosettes, silly hats and rattles. A couple of 'characters' pop up in most photos, obvious Spurs exhibitionist stalwarts, a man in a navy and white striped suit, bow tie and bowler plus Mr EHG Harris, alias Miss Spurs, who describes himself as "an 'old dame' in the club colours on away matches, plus large rosette and carrying a very large and noisy bell with streamers. This leads to many a good laugh, good natured comments, and clean wholesome fun amongst our own and rival supporters."

Notably women are prominent in the organisation. Daphne Edwards was one of the founders, there are women's sports teams and every photo of travelling fans over a decade and more has between a third and half of women. Two older members were well-known too, Ms Patten and Ms Fuller known respectively as Gert and Daisy after two popular comedy characters of the day. They were in their early thirties when they saw their first match, the 1921 FA Cup Final. Since then they had been to most home and away matches, covering 50,000 miles in support of the Spurs. Their biographer in *The Lilywhite* is in awe: "None will deny them their courage and fortitude, as in many cases when present at away games and surrounded by numerous men they are never found wanting in their cry of 'play up the Spurs' in all kinds of weather."

Not all the trips were happy occasions. In 1951 one of the coaches returning from Huddersfield suffered an accident in which many were injured and two young Spurs fans died. The club set up a fund for their dependants – Tottenham Hotspur donated 50 guineas and Fulham supporters' club raised funds too. The SSC helped ex-players down on their luck. A fund for Willie Hall, who lost his legs, raised £75 6s 1d including 10 guineas from Arsenal SC. Club funds were boosted by sales of 'distinctive club tea trays' 25s, Spurs School Caps with badge 7/6 or girls' berets 7/6. Or how about a club tie, only 8/3?

The Football League resumed properly for the 1946/47 season. It was a tough period for football. Many of the experienced players had lost their lives or were unable to play because of the injuries they suffered while fighting, while younger players had missed out on coaching. Spurs, however, had an advantage, having established a nursery club at Northfleet, an idea that had been the brainchild of the enlightened Scottish coach Peter McWilliam in the early 1920s. McWilliam had agreed to farm out young players to the club on the understanding that they learnt to play the game the way McWilliam thought it should be played – the quick, passing game identified in Jonathan Wilson's peerless history of football tactics *Inverting the Pyramid* as "the Scottish style".

What that meant was that, as football restarted and a hungry public came to watch, Spurs could call upon a core of young players who knew each other and who played in an identifiable, attractive way. The emphasis was on skill, teamwork and entertainment and this, it is not fanciful to suggest, meant that Tottenham Hotspur meant something to people.

It had taken a run of eight defeats in ten games in the transitional 1945/46 season to convince the club's board of directors that they should employ a full-time manager, and in January 1946 they chose Joe Hulme. As a player, Hulme had been a key part of Herbert Chapman's all-conquering Arsenal side, and since 1944 he had worked at Spurs. He helped lay the foundations for what was to come, taking Spurs to the fringes of the promotion spots in the old Second Division and, in 1948, steering the side through an epic FA Cup run in which Blackburn Rovers, West Bromwich Albion, Leicester City and Southampton were all beaten to take Spurs to a Villa Park semi-final with Blackpool. This was the Blackpool of Matthews and Mortensen and the tie may just have rekindled memories of that historic north v south, new challenger v established giant final in 1901 that so captured the public imagination.

Spurs came within four minutes of pulling off a shock win and reaching Wembley for the first time, losing to Blackpool's superior strength and experience in extra time. Here, perhaps, were laid the roots of the modern romance with the FA Cup. Spurs were making their mark, but to build on what they had achieved in difficult times, they needed to be in the top flight. So Hulme was sacked, and Arthur Rowe, a product of Northfleet and a disciple of the McWilliam passing game, appointed. He went on to become arguably one of the most influential managers in football history.

Rowe's team became known as the push and run team but, says Harry Slater, fans didn't talk of it in those terms, certainly not at first. "We didn't call it that," he says. "It was just terrific football to watch. Medley, Ramsey… it was a good team collectively. They played a different type of football. What they did, they changed the game of football and it took a couple of seasons for the other teams to catch up and know how to play against them."

This developing style attracted a new type of supporter. "More people went who were not technically supporters because Tottenham were a good team to watch, Slater says. "Spurs were known as a team that played good football? They always had that. People wouldn't go to watch a team that wasn't playing good football. Couldn't afford to."

In the 1949/50 season, over a million-and-a-half people paid to watch Spurs storm to the Second Division title playing Rowe's exciting brand of football. The average attendance at White Hart Lane was 54,405.

Slater remembers the atmosphere being very different in those days too. And that's atmosphere in the most literal sense. "You didn't notice the extent of smoking until you had the evening games," he says. "You'd be there and see all the smoke rising, and you say my god. I never smoked. And in those days you had the smogs.

"I don't remember feeling uncomfortable in those days, there were pub fights maybe but I never went to pubs before the game. There was never any segregation. I think there is less trouble when you don't segregate because it collects people together. When I was in the army up at Catterick, I went to Newcastle's ground when Spurs were playing, I was shouting, taking the mike out of Newcastle fans… that was all fun and games and they were joining in. In those days you could do that, you could say what you think."

Interestingly, while he remembers Rowe's push and run side as being great to watch, his take on the passing game valued today is not what you might expect. "Football was much better in those days without a doubt, now there's too much technology and planning, tactics. Passing the ball, that's the thing that's ruined football. Bloke gets the ball, straightaway he thinks I've got to pass this, not take people on. That was the excitement of football, running with the ball, one, two, three players and score, these days they don't seem to do that any more. Except Bale on occasion. When you are taking people on, you are drawing people towards you and opening the game up. But now, backwards and forwards, back to the goalkeeper, back in block formation, forward in a block, you cannot get the same sort of excitement as you used to. To me, football's more boring. You don't get as much movement, movement forward. There's too much tactics and not enough football."

But Slater, like many others, got the bug in that period. The Tottenham crowd as we know it was beginning to take shape. "We weren't exactly rich, but we were ardent fans," he says. "Once you get that, irrespective of how you do, you carry on."

It's worth considering Rowe's back story as well as the influence of his coaching style, because both influenced the way the club's support was to grow. Rowe was a Tottenham lad, born in the area in 1906. He had played for the club as a youth and as a senior player. We argue in this book that a club represents, and draws its strength and identity from, place, from community. When an individual becomes the manifestation of those ideas of place and identity it is a powerful thing. Rowe is a giant in the club's history not just because of what his teams achieved on the pitch, but because he was 'one of our own'. Any football fan will tell you there is always a warm glow of satisfaction when a home-grown talent makes it. That's not to suggest any small-mindedness, simply to state the fact that there is particular pleasure in home-grown success.

So with Rowe's appointment, the ingredients for that turning point we mentioned at the opening of this chapter were in place. A local lad and former star of the team who had studied the game in distant lands had returned, and proceeded to revolutionise the game. As journalist Brian Scovell says: "His chosen style of play was a clear change from most of the rather stolid, predictable norm of British football up to this point." And Rowe chose Spurs not simply because of old allegiances, but because of the roots that had been set down by former managers John Cameron and Peter McWilliam, under whom he learnt the game. What strikes other fans as the irritating habit of harping on about style of play, or is condemned by the sages of the modern sports press as an unreasonably demanding attitude, is actually something that goes much deeper – an appreciation of and a yearning for an approach deep in the club's DNA, and applied to devastating effect by Rowe's team.

Tottenham Hotspur's Second Division title in 1949/50 made the football world – already enlarged by the development of a mass media that recognised the potential in the post-war hunger for football – sit up and take notice. The following season they not only won the club's first league title, they did so by sweeping away the old order completely.

The turning point was arguably the 7-0 demolition of Newcastle United on 18 November 1950. At the time, Newcastle were the epitomy of the English style. That Spurs victory silenced the last of the doubters who questioned whether Rowe's new, suspiciously continentally-influenced game of passing and moving would cut it against the very best. It did. The *Telegraph* described that style as "all worked out in triangles and squares and when the mechanism of it clicks at speed, as it did on Saturday, with every pass played to the last refined inch on a drenched surface there is simply no defence against it." In the local *Tottenham Weekly Herald*, correspondent Concord said: "Spurs have proved beyond all doubt the vast superiority of their new-style soccer... Successful application of this style will, I predict, create a revolution in British soccer. Just as clubs found it necessary to discover an answer to the third back game, so they will have to remould their ideas to counter Spurs' system."

At the beginning of that season, Rowe had told the club's shareholders that he would not change the team's playing style to meet the challenge of top flight opposition. And not only did he pledge to continue, he posited the Tottenham way as something that stood in direct opposition to the Arsenal way. Along with Newcastle United, Arsenal were the big English team of the time – largely due, it can be argued, to the team's successful application of the new offside law. That, said Rowe, had introduced football "of a negative type". And he went on, "Our method is better." And so it proved in the heady days of the 1950/51 season.

Spurs fans had not only seen their team win its first title, they had seen it done in a way which had swept away the old and embraced the new. With the end of rationing still three years away, pleasures were to be appreciated and the sense that something new and exciting was happening also chimed with the prevailing optimism of the times. Spurs were the new, the exciting, the forward-thinking. Stunning success had been achieved under the leadership of one of our own, and in the process the methods of our closest geographical rivals had been exposed as outdated.

Rowe's side never achieved those heights again, something which exacted a terrible price on the great manager's mental health. But the modern idea of what Spurs were had been seared into the consciousness of its fans. And Rowe was also, in one of his final acts for the club, to secure the services of Danny Blanchflower, a craftsman and a romantic who, more than any other player in the club's history, epitomises its character. Blanchflower, along with Bill Nicholson, was to take the club on not just to more success, but to immortality. And in doing so he would infect the club's fans with all the appreciation, the yearning, and the agony of the glory for years to come. The modern Spurs were here. And crucially, at a time when horizons were widening in Britain. A country that had for so long felt itself at the centre of the world now began to realise its place in the world. Insularity began, slowly, to give way to an understanding and appreciation of what was beyond these islands. It was a painful process, but there was a confidence about the age that manifested itself in ambition, in seeking to cross new frontiers and achieve new heights.

As man began to conquer the planet's highest peaks and explore previously unreachable corners of the globe, the idea of landing on the moon began to exercise its grip on the popular imagination. Science and discovery and invention were embraced by a population eager to be modern and to break with the restrictions of the past. In sport, the urge to run faster and further, to record greater achievements, to touch greater competitive heights was at large.

The confidence of the age was also fuelled by a newfound mass affluence. The privations of post-war Britain were finally being shaken off, the benefits of the Welfare State were beginning to be felt, and incomes were on the rise so that something called 'disposable income' was available to many people. That meant people had money to spend on things that were not necessities, and so the consumer culture was born.

Here lie the roots of English football as a global consumer phenomenon. A game that already had a strong grip on a mass audience was perfectly placed to benefit from the new age of consumer affluence. And into this mix of heightened ambition and opportunity come Tottenham Hotspur.

Once the team of the suburbs, the proud flagbearers of local ambition with a distinctive style and identity, the club was now poised to capture imaginations further afield at the start of an age of global mass entertainment, an age when the lines between football and showbusiness began to blur.

As the great team of Arthur Rowe began to break up in the mid-1950s attendances dipped, and some of the reports from the time indicate the demanding nature of a crowd that had tasted glory and expected to continue doing so. When Bill Nicholson took over, his first match was watched by 38,000 – a relatively small crowd for the day. Those present were lucky enough to witness an extraordinary 10-4 victory over Everton – prompting Tottenham's Tommy Harmer to remark to Nicholson as he left the pitch: "It's all downhill from here." Of course, it wasn't, and Nicholson's side began to draw the crowds again, average attendance pushing up over the 40,000 mark in his first full season in charge.

Chris Kaufman was a young fan from Hackney who used to go to games as the crowds grew. "It cost about a penny happeny to go down to Spurs on the 149 bus," he remembers. "The first time I used to pay to get in it was nine old pence as a junior, then I remember getting chips when we came out, fourpence for a normal bag or sixpence for a big bag from Young Sams, it was, on that corner where the Red Lion is, near Bruce Grove.

"We'd turn up at least an hour before to get a decent view. As you came in you'd be confronted by a complete wall of bodies and it'd look as if it was impossible to get through. But being old hands we knew we could. I'd wait until there was a little chink of light somewhere and we'd just shove an arm in, and that'd make a bit of a breach in the wall, and we'd begin to get through."

Often it's those early experiences that shape the way we define support, and it's certainly the case for Chris, who told one of the authors when being interviewed for the 2004 book *We Are Tottenham* that he'd never really got used to the idea of not standing up in a crowd to watch his football. "I still haven't got used to the idea of sitting down," he said. "I feel it's like being at the theatre. You've really got to be standing up to watch a football match. Obviously you are participating if you're sitting down, but you don't feel like you are."

That's interesting, the idea of 'participating'. Because, by definition, a spectator is one who does not participate. But the notion of the 12th man is very strong in English football, the idea that by actually being there you are playing your part. Even so, Kaufman does not remember much in the way of organised singing when he began to go in the mid-to-late 1950s – that came, he says, during the Double season, and possibly not until the great nights of European competition at White Hart Lane.

Nor does he remember much expectation among supporters at the start of the 1960/61 Double season. "There wasn't all this pre-season hype for a start," he says, "I don't think anybody thought too much about that." But, he concedes, as the season went on and Spurs racked up victory after victory, "you began to realise something extraordinary was going on".

But in some football circles, for sure, there was expectation that this team could do what no team in modern football had yet done – win the league and the FA Cup in the same season. In keeping with the spirit of the times it was an achievement keenly pursued, with West Bromwich Albion, Manchester United and Wolverhampton Wanderers all coming close in the 1950s. Spurs had already caught the eye, with Nicholson's adaptation of Rowe's push and run style marking them out as a modern force distinct from the yeoman English approach. *The Guardian*'s David Lacey remembers: "The pre-Double Spurs side stick in the mind because of the impact they had on an era dominated by the breathless, long-passing style of Stan Cullis's Wolves. The subtler, more-thoughtful football of Bill Nicholson's Spurs gave the English game a new learning."

Club captain Danny Blanchflower famously told chairman Fred Bearman: "We'll win the Double for you this season", and the football press were pretty convinced from day one of the season that Bill Nicholson's Spurs would win the league. "If anyone should be rash enough to lay you a shade of odds against Spurs winning the First Division championship, jump in quickly," said the *News of the World*'s Harry Ditton, opening his report on Spurs' opening day

2-0 victory over Everton. In the same paper, the great Tom Finney called the performance "English soccer at its most superb".

Every fan will tell you their team is special, but the luckiest fans can identify a moment when their team was the kind of special that truly marked them out, which cemented a devotion. The Double-winning Spurs side certainly did that, bringing not only the 'new learning' David Lacey referred to, but a new appreciation. The team captured imaginations, including those of young girls in London's home county sprawl such as Julie Welch. Welch was inspired by that pioneering team to break new ground herself, eventually becoming the first woman to report on top-class football for the national press.

Winning the Double made Spurs arguably the first superteam of the mass entertainment age. Spurs were now not just the team of Tottenham, of the suburbs, of the south of England. Spurs were England's pride and, as the game finally began to shake off the shackles of insularity – in the face of determined opposition from those who ran the game – attention turned to how they would fare against Europe's finest.

The European nights at White Hart Lane occupy a special place in the psyche of the club and its supporters. These were the moments when the legend of the glory and the Spurs Way was firmly established. Chris Kaufman thinks this may have been the time when organised singing really took off. "I first became aware of singing at Spurs during those European nights, maybe during the year they won the Double," he says. "I know that whole *Glory Glory Hallelujah* business came around that time. I was at that game when Spurs beat Gornik 8-1. In the first tie we'd gone four goals down, and we'd managed to nick a couple of goals back. I remember such a wall of sound from the Spurs fans when they came out that the Polish players were physically diminished, they were white. I can't imagine what it must've been like for them. I'd never known such an intensity of noise."

Many who were there that night tell similar tales. And wily old Bill Nicholson knew how to use the atmosphere, the 12th man, to his advantage. Spurs fan and author Adam Powley's father worked on the gate in those days. He remembers his dad telling him: "Bill lined up the club staff before the game, picked out the biggest among them, and told them to line up either side of the tunnel when Gornik ran out onto the pitch." This was high theatre, and it is easy to see how it would have made its mark on those who experienced it. The noise, the passion, pouring from the darkness of the stands onto the floodlit pitch as teams from far away came to take on the Spurs, teams drawn in by the bewitching success of the greatest team of the century, crowds hooked on the strange, fascinating newness of it all, the atmosphere flooding into the newspapers and radio reports, even occasionally to the televisions that now began to take centre stage in every living room. Who could not be intoxicated by it all? What fan could not be hooked for life in these days when joy it was to be a Spur.

While Kaufman does not recall organised singing and chanting, there's evidence that the crowd had been making its presence felt from references in press reports and the letters pages of the local *Weekly Herald* newspaper to the Tottenham Roar. For some sections of the press, this wasn't quite the done thing, and there was criticism of the aggressive and intimidating noise the crowd could sometimes generate. Some fans wrote in to the local paper defending their right to cheer their team on as they saw fit, and after the Gornik game the club itself, via the official programme, had this to say: "It was thrilling to hear the old-time 'Tottenham Roar' at full blast, but though our supporters were obviously out to do their best to help the team… their vocal enthusiasm seems to have worried some members of the press. But what's the use of supporters if they do not support, the more so in such an important game? We, at any rate, were proud of our supporters, and of our players who made it such a memorable evening." The 12th man was now recognised by the club.

But supporters' concerns of the time will still seem familiar. In 1962 a group of fans protested at the low allocation to clubs of cup final tickets. This was in sharp contrast to very different attitudes espoused by the SSC in the early 1950s. At the time finalists got 24,000 between them, county associations 43,000, league clubs 23,600, with the rest going to the FA and Wembley. This topic has infuriated fans for over a century – the supporters make the occasion yet are denied tickets. However, the Supporters' Club backed a move that would decrease the number of tickets for finalists to 20,000 while increasing the allocation to the National Federation for Supporters' Clubs to 20,000. On the face of it, it was an odd move and certainly one not representing the interests of Tottenham fans should they reach the final. It seems being part of the 'football family' was more valued than expressing self-interest.

Also, then as now the 'prawn sandwich brigade', in those days called 'the fur coat brigade', using football to socialise at the expense of true fans drew bitter comment. One fan is quoted as saying: "Our lasting memory of Wembley 1962 will be of hundreds of 'socialites' who were streaming out of the ground 15 minutes before the end of the game. Many true supporters would have given their right arm just to see that last quarter of an hour with the sight of Spurs jubilantly carrying the Cup round the pitch."

Europe not only allowed Spurs to test the best of British against continental opposition, it gave the fans the opportunity to widen their horizons by following their team into Europe. This was before the era of mass travel to Europe on holiday, but the involvement of Tottenham Hotspur in European competition provides a foundation stone for that development. Spurs fan Aubrey Morris started organising trips for fans after successfully flying a small group of 47 to Sunderland's Roker Park for an FA Cup tie in 1960. Morris was from a family of Jewish bakers in Bethnal Green, a veteran of Cable Street and the D-Day landings and a London cabbie – as well as a member of the Communist Party. His company, Riviera Holidays, established itself flying Spurs fans across Europe in the early 1960s, and Morris went on – via the establishment of the England Travel Club on which he worked with Bobby Moore – to become recognised as the man who invented the concept of the modern package holiday.

What's interesting about those early travellers is that they weren't just the well-off supporters. As Morris said of the queues that formed outside Riviera's offices in Liverpool Street to buy tickets for a historic trip to Rotterdam for the 1963 European Cup Winners' Cup Final, "We had a real mix of people. We had kids queuing up, youngsters with the money, eight pounds ten shillings. They were just ordinary people."

The trip saw the largest movement of football supporters ever seen in Europe at the time. Riviera took 2,500 on a fleet of 33 aircraft. At least 1,500 more took trains, ferries and private transport. An extra ship was arranged because the usual two night ferries were overwhelmed with requests to travel. The Spurs Supporters' Club took 65 coaches. The *Weekly Herald* said: "The Berlin airlift had nothing on this. Never before has an English team had so much fantastic support on the Continent."

One of the fans who travelled was Roger Dean, who interrupted preparations for his engineering exams at East Herts College to follow Spurs to Rotterdam. He told the *Tottenham Hotspur Opus* about his experiences. "By the time we were 5-1 up we were singing any English songs that came to mind – *Land of Hope and Glory, Knees Up Mother Brown, Nellie Dean*… The Spurs fans were very festive but I saw no evidence of the poor behaviour that later became so common with excursions of this type. I was very proud of Spurs that night but of my fellow supporters too. I was dropped off at White Hart Lane about 4am, from where I walked home to Oakwood, carrying my friend's heavy rattle and two huge red Dutch cheeses for Mum, almost in time to get ready for work."

Morris too commented on how well behaved fans were, perhaps because they were so taken with the new experiences, as Morris clearly was when he talks about travelling to Lisbon in 1961 for the Benfica game, experiencing warm weather at 10pm and ordering live fish from a tank in the middle of a restaurant. The whole experience was new, and Morris and his colleagues often had to sort out basic tasks such as passports and currency exchange for fans who had no idea of what was needed on these trips – effectively sorting out the whole package and laying the foundations of the package holiday revolution. But even so, what a time it must have been.

There were, said Morris, about 100 who travelled to pretty much every game, and these were obviously the more well-heeled fans, otherwise they would not have had the money or the opportunity to travel quite so frequently. The travelling contingent had been noticed by the team, often staying in the same hotels on these trips, and Bill Nicholson took the time to thank the travellers for their support. But, in the very early days, the club and the official supporters' club kept their distance from the trips – ironic when you consider that, two decades on, it was the club's decision to move fully into the business of providing travel that really finished the Spurs Supporters' Club.

Interviewed before he died in 2008, Morris said: "It was a particular thing at a particular time in history – it was a good time."

As the reputation of the team grew, so too did the profile of the supporters. In fact, arguably for the first time, the crowd was being readily acknowledged as part of what constituted Tottenham Hotspur. And the crowd were not only being heard, but seen too – seen as part of the spectacle. In the first leg of the Gornik tie, the Polish press took exception to what it saw as an overly-physical approach by Spurs, and labelled the team 'No angels'. Spurs fans responded with characteristic wit, one group dressing as angels and parading around the edge of the pitch holding aloft placards with slogans such as 'Lift up thy voices as never before' and 'And it came to pass, Jones to White to Smudger – GOAL!'

It seems extraordinary now, in the heavily-controlled world of modern football where the struggle against sanitised and officially-approved displays of 'support' often seems to be in vain, that the club allowed these very DIY displays to carry on around the pitch itself for the best part of a decade. Before the UEFA Cup Final in 1972, a fan was photographed dressed as an 'Aspurnaut' in full space man garb, carrying a placard announcing 'Countdown to European orbit No.6'.

The Tottenham Angels – Dave Casey, Mike Curly and Peter Kirkby – became an established part of the matchday experience around Spurs on those early glory glory nights, but their activities during the celebrations that greeted the victorious team after the Cup Winners' Cup victory in Rotterdam led them into trouble. Their placards 'Hallowed be their names' and 'Praise them for they are glorious' offended the vicar of the local church, who sent a telegram to the Home Secretary, no less, urging prosecution of the club under the blasphemy laws. "This idolisation of a football team by taking quotations from the Bible is wrong and offends Christians," he wrote.

The fans defused the situation by apologising for any offence unintentionally caused, with Casey saying: "We have apologised to the people who felt offended. Against the few who object, there are thousands who have enjoyed our little performances without taking them in a way they were never intended." And the trio turned their attention to another issue – helping to organise a midnight march through London to protest about the allocation of tickets at the FA Cup Final.

It was at around this time too that the Spurs crowd began to be tagged 'difficult' or even 'fickle'. This seemed at odds with the large support home and away in those days but the slow hand-clap would sometimes spread around the ground, furtively at first then louder sometimes. This would be met with a chorus of admonition and was often shouted down. One fan, D Blakey of Stratford, wrote to *The Lilywhite*: "The weak slow handclap… is a continental habit which does not suit British sportsmen and is distinctly foreign and alien in its insulting vulgarity."

There is a pattern throughout the history of Spurs support of those who barrack the team being met with a volley of criticism saying the true fan always gets behind their team precisely when they are playing badly. While understandable, this latter view is incongruous, given that since 1882 spectators have gone to football as an antidote to the restrictions of working and family life and consequently want to let off steam. Abuse always has been and always will be part of the sound of the crowd. When Sol Campbell played his first match at White Hart Lane after his infamous transfer to Arsenal, there was a concerted campaign to meet him with organised indifference on the Spanish model, either waving a white handkerchief or the entire crowd turning their backs on him. In fact, his every touch provoked a tornado of booing and abuse for the entire 90 minutes. It's what British football crowds do.

David John is part of a family of four generations of Spurs support: "When I started going in 1968, I remember the whole atmosphere, even as a kid the moaning surprised me. 'It will never be as good as that team' [the Double side]. Blanchflower and that lot had all finished and they were hanging on to that glory of the Double being the greatest team and they were all disappointed. People couldn't get used to the fact that we were average.

"I remember there being not anger but just disappointment. The support would always be there but it's that feeling, like Liverpool have felt recently, Man Utd now, of end of empire. The fans were clinging on to the fact that we were the greatest team but it's over and someone else had taken over. We'd won the first cup in Europe, first Double, it's all that first time stuff, it was never going to come back."

While the grass roots organised, other fans were emerging as figures almost as famous as the players – none more so than Morris Keston. Since he began supporting Tottenham Hotspur in the mid-1940s, Morris has watched them nearly 3,000 times. He curses his triple by-pass operation because it broke his run of watching every home game since the early 1950s, but he missed just the one game. Such was his devotion, he 'converted' from Judaism to Christianity so he could enter Egypt to follow Spurs on tour.

Not only that, during this period he's known most of the Spurs and England World Cup winning team players and counts everyone from Moore, Greaves and Hurst through to Jennings, Venables and Crooks as personal friends. You name them, he name-drops. Don't forget Ali and Sinatra. The title of his autobiography is no publisher's hyperbole – *Superfan* he certainly is.

Keston is a successful businessman who started from nothing. Brought up in the Jewish East End, he was evacuated during the war but suffered from malnutrition because the care he received was so poor. His mother figured he would be safer in the comfort of his family, despite the rigours of the Blitz, so he spent the rest of the war in London, earning a scholarship and beginning a lifelong obsession with football. Leaving school at 14, he was sacked from his first job in a barber's after he refused to work on Saturday afternoons. Eventually he got into the *schmutter* business, *schelpping* around the country for a fortnight at a time, taking in third division reserve games and any football that he could, and co-ordinating his return to London with the Tottenham home fixture list.

It is tempting to dismiss Keston as a wealthy businessman with the time and money to buy his way into the club but that is misleading. His explanation of what Tottenham means to him in Hunter Davies' *The Glory Game* strikes a chord with many supporters: "I don't understand it myself. I've had ups and downs in business, lots of them, but I just seem to accept them. But Spurs worry me all the time. I don't actually enjoy watching them. I'm too worried. I must be a masochist. There's a magnetism that draws me to them, I've got to go. I can't keep away. These days I often leave about 15 minutes before the end because I can't stand it any more. Even if they are winning 1-0, there's no point in suffering any longer. I can't stand the agony of watching them lose their lead."

His access was astounding. Moore, Hurst, Greaves and others regularly popped in for a cup of tea during the 1966 tournament. When he was ill recently, a who's who of Tottenham players of the last 40 years queued up to wish him well. He clearly basked in the attention and was a serial entertainer but the players liked and trusted him because they knew he had their interests at heart, something which many ex-pros would say is a rare and precious attribute in football.

Yes, there were the parties but the players came round for a cuppa and a slice of his long-suffering wife's apple crumble. He entertained in his home, with home-made cooking. He ran charity events and testimonials, and made sure the players actually got all the money that was coming to them. He emerges not as a glory hunter but as a homespun, friendly and generous bloke, often a little star-struck, who is deeply in love with football and Tottenham in particular. It is hard to see such a relationship between player and fan ever being repeated. This is from another age, not so long ago, when the players enjoyed their fame and wealth but understood that they and the fans are one and the same, not a different class.

Keston stayed in the same hotels and travelled on the same planes when Spurs and England went abroad, and could get a seat in the directors' box for most games, the only exception being at the Lane where the Wale family who ran the club in the 60s and 70s regarded him with suspicion. Bridges were burned after the players left the official 1967 FA Cup Final celebration dinner, piled into a fleet of taxis and danced the rest of the night away at Keston's do at the Hilton. Davies asked the players – it was their choice, they just preferred Morris's parties.

This has more to do with the board's relationship with supporters than anything Keston had said or done. The supporters are fine but they should know their place. It is a view that prevailed for decades and persists to some extent today. To fans, the club, the team and the supporters are one and the same. The Wales, and Alan Sugar for that matter, upheld a Victorian attitude of keeping them firmly separate.

Keston again: "Fans never get any credit, not of any sort. I feel sorry for those kids who travel up and down screaming their heads off for Spurs. Their hardships are never recognised. But if gates were to fall, you'd soon hear the club complaining."

The huge crowds that watched football in Britain for years were now players in the drama, with distinct characteristics and identifiable characters. Mass media and the increased importance attached to leisure amplified the contribution made by supporters. And by now the love of the game and of clubs had been handed down through generations, traditions established and codes of honour and practice forged.

Being a Spurs fan meant something distinct.

5

Can I look after your car, mister?

SUPPORTING a club is about more than simply watching a sporting event. It feeds into a sense of identity and can provide points of reference by which we measure our lives. Brian Dennis and Bernie Kingsley are two fans who began following Spurs in the 1950s and 1960s, and their stories offer some insight into the part football clubs play in the lives of a fan, and to why football has such a hold on the national psyche.

Brian Dennis was born in West Green Road, Tottenham, in 1947, Kingsley in Hertfordshire in 1956. Family played a strong part in how both came to follow Spurs. "In 1950/51, I was taken into care," says Dennis, "and for the next eight years we actually went to live in Woodford, away from Tottenham. So I came back to Tottenham and my mother got us moved into a house in Northumberland Park, just round the corner from the ground and that's where we lived for another four to five years. I guess it's those years when we really came to support Spurs, when we came back to live in Northumberland Park. Being round the corner that became my playground – the actual stadium. As kids, we would play around

111

the stadium." For Dennis, the return to Tottenham helped him feel a part of something after some difficult times, giving him the chance to put down some roots. Being in care can be a rootless childhood filled with temporary, disrupted relationships. Supporting Spurs and living next to White Hart Lane gave him a sense of belonging, a history. It was more of a home than the house he lived in. "I was three years old when I was taken into care," he explains. "Me and my youngest brother and my next eldest brother. Because we were very young we were put into child care. My other brothers stayed with my father and eventually they went to boarding school. So there was a period of eight years where we didn't know the rest of our family. My father never came to visit us but my mother did so she was our connection with the family.

"So, when we came back to Tottenham, my mother brought the three of us together to Northumberland Park and we got rehoused there. And it wasn't until I was 15 when I met my brothers again. They came looking for us and we got back together through that. And my sister, she knew both sides of the family and she was the oldest so she got us all back in touch. But by then, of course, the damage had been done. They were Arsenal supporters and we were Tottenham supporters!"

The stadium and the club were central to Dennis's childhood. "I earned my pocket money at Spurs. I played around the Spurs ground. Our lives centred around the ground and the people coming and going. The footballers were all local. Most of them lived in the area. As soon as I realised I was moving back near the club, it was an inspiration to me, because all of my mates lived around the ground. In fact I took my first driving lesson, illegally, when I was 15, in Paxton Road. I crashed a Ford Prefect into one of the factories along there! We just about did everything around the ground."

Looking after the cars of the fans who turned up provided a lucrative stream of income. "You would pick your road," Dennis remembers, "you had your patch and there were probably about six or eight of us in our little gang and we always picked around

Northumberland Park, Worcester Avenue, that area. People would come from miles around. Easy to park, no restrictions and every road was full up with cars, bumper to bumper. And as soon as they pulled up on your patch, you'd run up to them and say 'Can I look after your car, mister?' Most of them would tell you to clear off but, percentage wise, you always got a few. Then it was your duty to be there when they came out. Now, it depended on two things. What they didn't know of course was the gateman on the Park Lane gates used to let all the kids in at half-time for nothing. He'd open the gates up and all the kids would run in, there were hundreds of us, and we'd watch the game and then five minutes before the end you had to disappear to get back to your pitch. So you never looked after their cars.

"If Spurs won, they were so happy they'd give you something – a penny, threepence, sixpence, a shilling depending on how happy they were. And, of course, you'd butter them up a bit by asking 'Did we win?' when we knew they'd won! It was a good little scam because my mum was pretty poor. She was on her own with three kids and she couldn't work because she was ill. To get half a crown out of a night's work or a day's work for a match, it paid for the fish and chips and a bottle of drink. We all went home happy but broke. That was how you earned your pocket money because I never got any from my mum. It was a lovely little scam and I've got great memories of it.

"Underneath the Spurs ground there used to be factories. For years and years, you could see Thermos flasks being made under the ground – that was in one factory. There was another factory that made Kitekat, which is cat food. I think there was one other but I can't remember who they were and then, if you come up into the middle tier of the ground, almost at eye level, there was underground car parking. We kids used to be able to bunk in and play all our football underneath the pitch but above the factories. We used to play all of our five-a-side football underneath the ground itself."

Dennis's memories of the first game he went to give a vivid insight into what it was like to be a spectator in the late 1950s. "I was 11, it was against Nottingham Forest. My brother and I were crushed almost to death because the crowd used to sway from the back, the Park Lane end especially. They were dangerous, football grounds. Very dangerous. It was absolutely terrifying because you've got probably a thousand, two thousand people behind you all pushing, surging forward for instance when they score a goal or there's a near miss and they're trying to look up and over the top, because the steps weren't that high and you'd be up against a crush barrier. And my brother and I virtually stopped breathing once and we thought that was our lot. We really did. There was over 70,000 in the ground that day. Too many.

"The nice thing they used to do, and I remember this from my very first game going with an adult (I got taken in with an adult), if you were halfway back, they would pass you down. Every kid got passed down to the front. You would get passed right the way along the crowd and you'd get right down to the front and eventually you'd look through that and that was the only way you could see the game.

"When you got passed down, you stayed there and waited until the stadium started emptying and then, whoever was with you, they would make sure you got out. There was no control over the crowds, you were that tightly packed in, you could virtually get out of the ground without walking. You were so tight together that the kids used to get carried! It was frightening and there was a hint of danger in the whole thing but it was kids, wasn't it? It was fun. As soon as you get in the ground, the fact that you grew up and lived there, that's your manor, your inheritance."

Getting into the ground presented a challenge the local kids were more than happy to take up. "There were ways of getting in, in corners of the ground," says Dennis. "When there were adults going through, you'd drop down underneath and go through at the same time. You just hung around. The ground wasn't filled in in those days and the corners were still open, so you could actually get over a fence or over a wall and nip in that way. Because there was no crowd segregation, you could get in one corner and walk round to wherever you wanted to be. So we literally climbed over walls. If you could climb a tree, you could climb a wall. It was great fun, trying to bunk in for nothing. You did the same at cinemas. You could bunk in through the toilet windows.

"Outside the ground it was chaos. There were huge crowds. Most of my time was spent looking after my cars and my pitch so it wasn't that often I actually went to watch a whole match – that would've had to be a special occasion as I was more interested in earning my pocket money and then getting in at half-time! But I remember hordes of people just getting into the ground and going where they wanted. They were like ants. Now it's much more orderly and controlled. You know which gate you're going into and so on.

"You always had your hot dog sellers and your rosette stall and your scarves. They've always been at football grounds for as long as I can remember. The tickets were just tickets. Or you paid on the day – cash. By the time the sixties came they started segregating and the fences went up. Once the segregation came in, that's when you started to see shirts appear and scarves and everybody started getting bolder. I think the away fans got more bold and showed themselves more. And there were police escorts for the away fans coming in."

Once inside, the nature of the crowd revealed itself. "Most of what I looked at were men in cloth caps and cheese cutters and things like that. All in their macs. Everything was very dour. Black and white. I don't ever remember seeing women in a crowd then, there must have been but I can't ever remember seeing one. There weren't the songs that there are now. I can't remember an awful lot of singing, apart from 'Glory Glory Tottenham Hotspur', which Man United stole. That's the only song that I can ever remember being sung. And it would be sung, of course, when we scored. There would be singing but nothing like it is today. It was all about making noise – with the rattles and things like that – rather than with the voice and hooters, we all used to have hooters and you made noise like that rather than with a singing voice.

"I never remember seeing any violence and nobody misbehaving as such. Maybe the odd swear word but nothing like you hear now when you're walking down the street and people are swearing their heads off, which I personally don't like. I certainly would have remembered it as a kid if there was bad language around. So I think they were pretty well behaved crowds.

"I never noticed the away fans in a sense that 'oh there they are, there' because the ground was open and non-segregated so the crowds just mixed in and you didn't often see an away supporter's shirt. Of course, that came in from the mid-sixties onwards. Nobody really had a replica shirt. You had a scarf, always had a scarf, and maybe a hat of some kind, a Tottenham hat, so there wasn't a lot of colour in the ground either. The only way to describe it was black and white. Everything was very dour.

Growing up when he did meant the attraction of Spurs wasn't only the fact that the team was local. "Billy Nicholson was an absolute legend to everybody," he remembers. "We were developing into – in the late fifties – we were beginning to take over again from Arsenal. They'd had their run. Man United, Liverpool, they weren't anywhere. As kid I was very, very lucky growing up in an area where eventually '60, '61, '62 and all the rest followed on. We had a big ten-year period where we were the top of the tree, the best club in the land."

With success came celebration, and Dennis remembers the big parade down Tottenham High Street after Spurs won the Double in 1961. "It was phenomenal. They started at Edmonton Town Hall and four to six hours later got to Tottenham Town Hall. It felt like there were millions of people. There wasn't a single spare space of road all down either side. It was like the Jubilee. It was monstrous. We walked down to Edmonton Fore Street and got behind the bus and tried to follow it but you got separated and pushed all over the place. But yeah. And I've never seen crowds like it. The whole of Tottenham was proud of the players and wherever you looked it was blue and white. All the shops were decorated, the houses were decorated. I can still see all the bunting up, the blue and white and the rosettes and the crimplene paper, like paper chains, all that would be out and all the shops would decorate their windows with Tottenham stuff in there, replica cups and the like."

Bernie Kingsley was drawn to Tottenham Hotspur by a mixture of family, fame and reputation. "I actually can't really remember when I started supporting Spurs," he says. "They won the Double when I was four. By the time I was six or seven, I was conscious that my Dad used to go. He'd been one of those people who went to Arsenal and Tottenham but certainly by the early 1960s he was a Tottenham supporter.

"Jimmy Greaves was the first player who really caught my imagination and I had pictures of him plastered all over the place and, by the mid-sixties, I was very into it. I liked football generally and I remember having pictures of West Ham and even Arsenal, but I certainly felt like a Tottenham supporter and then I became conscious that my Dad would go to matches and he'd bring the programme home.

"My Dad was one of those people that, if there were team changes, he'd write them on the programme, and the time that the goals were scored, and I kept wanting to go. And then finally, when I was ten, he took me to the last game of the season. It was against Sheffield United, about a week before the cup final against Chelsea in 1967, and he took me and my cousin."

The Kingsley family were not from the ranks of the suburbanites who had embraced the Spurs as their team. They lived in Hertfordshire, 30 miles north of London, from where increasing numbers of supporters travelled as London continued to sprawl across the south-east. And, like an increasing number of supporters, they travelled to the game via private transport. The car was arguably the foremost symbol of newfound consumer affluence and independence. Between 1951 and 1961 car ownership in the UK grew by 250% and in the London area alone there were 1.5 million cars registered by the mid-sixties.

"Dad always drove," remembers Kingsley. "He usually went with friends and he parked in White Hart Lane alongside the cemetery that day because that's where they usually parked. Within a year or two, it was difficult to park there and we parked in different places. A lot of people drove.

"It used to take about an hour to drive from home up to Tottenham. We'd come up through Cockfosters and Southgate. I remember that because I subsequently went to live in Southgate and I remember, when I was a kid, driving down this road with all these nice houses and thinking 'Ah, it would be really nice to live around here.'"

Kingsley remembers his first glimpse of the ground vividly. "From where we parked, you could see the floodlight pylons and that was the first vision I ever had of White Hart Lane. We walked to the ground and we sat in the back row of the upper part of the East Stand, level with the halfway line. Spurs won 2-0. Jimmy Greaves scored. I missed his goal because I was taking down the half-time scores. They used to put them on the boards around the perimeter in those days."

Bernie went with his dad a few more times the following season, including once to a game on a Friday night – very unusual. "From that point I was totally hooked," he says. "I wanted to go every week. Mum wasn't too keen on me going every week but Dad, well, we started going increasingly to games.

"My Dad and his mates and I would go. Dad always used to stand in the old enclosure – inside the front of the West Stand – where you paid an extra sixpence (two and a half pence in today's money) to get in there. There were no crush barriers and not that many steps but it was much safer because it was a lot more controlled and there was less crushing in there. We'd always get there early.

"The gates would open at one o clock and we'd be there for the time the gates opened so you'd be standing inside the ground for two hours before the kick-off. Dad made me a box to stand on, which he painted in navy blue and white. Later on, he made me another one, which was a bit more sophisticated – the legs folded up and it had a little handle! We used to get there early so we could get right down the front. I could stand on the box, leaning on the railings, about level with the penalty area at the Paxton Road end, and that was our spot for years."

As the crowds flocked to White Hart Lane, so a little matchday micro-economy began to develop. Kingsley remembers, "People with boards where there'd be scarves hanging, and rosettes. They used to sell rosettes in those days and they'd have a tray. There was one shop, which I don't think belonged to the club and that was in what's now Bill Nicholson Way, along the side of what was then the White Hart, which became Rudolphs. It was literally a hole in the wall with a kind of shutter that opened up to become a temporary roof for customers and then just a counter – that was the souvenir shop at Tottenham.

"And outside the old Supporters' Club at Warmington House there was Jack and Kay's programme hut. That was my great interest because I used to go and buy all the programmes from the home games, but I'd buy a programme from every single away game because that's what they used to sell.

"You did feel like the football club was in the middle of much more of a town. It feels a bit separated now. It's a lot more run-down than it was. It was never an affluent area, but along the High Road you had things like Star Furnishings and there were houses on all four corners of the ground and that made it feel more closed in. The old stands were still there so when you walked up Bill Nicholson Way it felt more closed in. As you walked along, on the right-hand side was the old ticket office and some club offices along there and then you came to the gates. And then, past the gates was a big corrugated iron fence that had some big gates in it but you couldn't see through them and that was the players' car park in there, so you felt like you were almost walking up a bit of a tunnel. And then you had this big stand open in front of you with 'Tottenham Hotspur Football Club' and steps that went up to the West Stand upper tier. If you were going into the terrace, you'd go underneath the staircase to where the turnstiles were and there was a real sense of wonder. You'd go behind the High Road and there'd be this big football ground.

"It was very friendly when I first started going. You could walk all the way round the ground inside. There was a tunnel under the West Stand in which there was a big gate which they sometimes closed – it was behind the enclosure – but it was possible to walk round all four sides of the ground. When we first started going it was something like four or five shillings to get into the ground and sixpence to get into the enclosure. You used to pay on the turnstiles, and inside the West Stand you had another set of turnstiles where you'd pay the extra sixpence to go inside the enclosure.

"You weren't particularly conscious of it being a home end or an away end to begin with. Perhaps for games against Manchester United or Arsenal there would be – I can remember a game when they were all in the Paxton Road end but there was no segregation then. People just went and somehow the away supporters would gather together."

Going to the football needed less pre-arranging in the days before credit cards and membership systems made everything easier for us, and for most games it was just a matter of getting there early enough to get a good view. But some of the bigger games did take a bit more getting into.

"There were one or two games when we had to get tickets," Kingsley recalls. "I remember going to a match against Manchester United probably around 1969/70. The lad who was my best friend at the time was a Manchester United supporter so we took him. There was a massive queue coming out of the entrance of the West Stand, round into the High Road and into Park Lane. We just walked along this queue and thought "What are all these people standing here for?" and we got to the front about the time they opened the gates, so we just walked in. We basically queue-jumped the whole thing! And nobody said a word! You know, two lads."

He also remembers the turbulent scenes before what he calls "the infamous game in 1971 when Arsenal won the league on a Monday night as the first part of their Double. We went up – my Dad and his mate and a school friend who was a Spurs fan. In the mass of people outside, we lost Dad and his mate at some point.

"We were there by half past four, in the crowd. The gates were there then and the whole of what's now Bill Nicholson Way was absolutely jam packed. There were times you were moving forward with your feet off the ground. We got to where the gates were just as they decided they were going to close them. We just managed to get through and they shut behind us. So we got into the West Stand but the enclosure was already completely full so we had to work our way round and we spent the match hanging off the front of the Shelf. We discovered afterwards that Dad and his mate hadn't got in at all. They spent the match sat in their car listening on the radio and assuming because we hadn't come back that we'd got in."

By now the crowd itself was playing more of a part in the spectacle of matchday. "There was certainly organised chanting and singing which probably came mostly from the Park Lane end or the Shelf," remembers Kingsley. "The Shelf seemed to be older guys. They probably weren't that old but it felt like the young lads would go to the Park Lane end and the older guys would go to the Shelf and it would be two distinctive groups – but you could get atmosphere from all around the ground. The West Stand, that's where you got the barracking from. But then sometimes you got a barracking from the Shelf, as well. I saw Terry Venables play and he wasn't very popular with the crowd at all."

But the crowd's passion didn't always manifest itself in friendly way, and as the sixties turned to the seventies hooliganism became an increasingly common feature – changing the way crowds would be treated and organised for ever. "I think the turning point where it became noticeable was the game in September 1969 when we lost 5-0 at Derby and the Spurs fans wrecked the trains on the way back and got kicked out at Flitwick and Harlington. There was a lot of press coverage of that and that was when you started to see skinheads and lads wearing butchers' coats and bovver boots." The Spurs support started to gain a reputation, one that attracted more trouble and in turn fuelled the reputation. Kingsley says: "I don't think it was Spurs more than any other club although, obviously, I saw it more at Spurs because that's where I went but I'm sure that sort of thing happened at other places as well. That incident after the Derby game got national press exposure and the football hooligan thing was starting and they just did a big thing about it. Maybe we were just unlucky as a club that it was us that got that exposure. But that's when you felt the atmosphere start to change."

At White Hart Lane, he remembers, "they started putting fences in and sectioning bits off". And that led to the decision to block off what had become the popular terrace at the Park Lane end – which wouldn't be the first time the club destroyed an area of the ground supporters held dear. "I think it was because they'd put the fences up and the ones that wanted to fight, particularly the Spurs fans who wanted to have a go at the away fans, some of them started moving out of the Park Lane 'cause they knew they couldn't get at them so they went somewhere else where they could get at them," says Kingsley. "So, then they thought 'let's put all the away supporters in the Park Lane end and we'll control them there'. I can't remember exactly when they started putting the fences up but that would've been in the seventies. They originally only put them up at the Park Lane end for the away supporters."

Kingsley also started travelling to away games when he was a teenager, and his experience provides further illustration of how extended communities of fans grew and melded. Kingsley's dad was a manager at the Post Office and some of the postmen were Spurs fans who went regularly to away games. "Dad was never particularly interested in going to away matches so when I started saying I wanted to go to an away match, he let these other guys take me," says Kingsley. "I'd go with them and it'd be a car trip. There'd be four or five of us. One of my first away games was at Stamford Bridge. We drove and parked very close to the ground. God knows how, you couldn't do that these days! And we got there and the blokes I was with said 'oh we go in here' so we're walking up to these gates and I suddenly realised we were in the Shed End and there's all these Chelsea fans just staring at us! They knew we weren't Chelsea fans because we clearly didn't know where we were going. We ended up walking out and walking round to the other end.

"I went up to Leicester and I remember my first trip to Highbury. We left the car at Southgate and got on the Tube down to Arsenal. We were late, the game was just about to kick off, so we came out of Arsenal Tube station and one of my mates said 'we go in over there'. Of course, that's the North Bank so I watched my first Arsenal/Tottenham match at Highbury in the corner, but as part of the North Bank. Spurs won 2-0, which was great! The vast majority of the Spurs fans were down at the Clock End although there were a few others in the North Bank and, as the seventies wore on, more and more Spurs fans went into the North Bank to the point that, when we went to Highbury, half of that was our end. We'd just take it over. And it was kind of bravado really."

By now the terrace culture was growing, and informal organisation was becoming a regular feature of matchday. "I don't know how," says Kingsley, "but you just knew where people were going to go. By that stage, when I went to White Hart Lane, I was standing in the Park Lane end, so I was mixing with the lads who used to go to the away games."

There were also indications that the friendly environment Kingsley had noticed when he first started going to games just a few years before was slipping away. "We went to Maine Road, Manchester," he remembers. "We got there quite early and parked the car miles away. We're coming down this street leading down to the ground and there was a policeman on this corner. One of our group went up to him and almost whispered: 'Where's the best place for people not from Manchester?' and this copper just looked at us and said: 'You mean Spurs supporters? There is no safe place.' And he proceeded to send us on a route of all four sides of the ground before we got back to pretty much where we started from and the place we were supposed to go in, which was definitely not the safe place in the ground."

Kingsley also remembers the terrible events surrounding Spurs' defeat in the UEFA Cup Final in Rotterdam in 1974. It was the first time he'd travelled to Europe to watch the team.

"I was still at school, just about to do my A levels," he remembers. "The game took place during half-term. By that stage I was going to home games either on my own or with my Dad's mates and I was using the Supporters' Club in Warmington House. I found out that they were running a trip to Rotterdam for £14 and the match ticket was £1.25. You got the coach from King's Cross the night before, went over on the ferry, arrived in Rotterdam for the game. My parents were absolutely horrified when they found out I was going but they didn't actually try to stop me. We arrived around lunchtime, early afternoon, found a bar, had a couple of beers, went out, found some kids playing football in the park and had a massive game of football – all very friendly. We got to the ground at about six o'clock in the evening and started seeing all these Spurs fans who were covered in blood and bandaged up. We became aware there'd been lots of trouble in the town. We got in the ground as soon as it opened and got to our position, which was a terrace at the top – very steep – big iron railings fence one side of the section, chicken wire fence the other side. And Dutch fans in seats either side of us.

"Way before the game started, bottles started flying – you could get bottles of beer inside the ground. To this day, I don't know who threw the first bottle. Obviously, our bit was filling up more and more and then the trouble kicked off big time towards the end of the first half and then continued really badly into half-time.

"Spurs fans ripped the iron railings out of the concrete to start having bigger fights. The police came in from that side, the riot police. We were on the chicken wire side. When it became apparent the police were just going to come across and clear everybody, there's no way we could have got to the exits and if we could have got to the exits in our section, we wouldn't have got out because they were just absolutely rammed, so we scaled the chicken wire fence.

"Fortunately, the Dutch fans on the other side were much more sensible and they let us get over and then we tried to get out of the exit there. But you couldn't go down the stairs because the story was, and I believe it was true, that if you got down to the bottom of the staircase there were loads more Dutch fans down there with knives and chains. We heard the second half kick off but you couldn't see it because we were out on the staircase and we weren't that interested. All we wanted to do was get back to the coaches.

"Eventually people started venturing downstairs and I think the Dutch lot that were down at the bottom must have got fed up and disappeared, so we got out and sat on the coach and waited for everybody else to come back. It was another good hour or two before we left. We arrived back in London the following afternoon."

Only a game? The simple act of watching a sport ripples far beyond 90 minutes of action on a pitch. These two lives in football are not untypical. Fans remember their experiences vividly, measure their lives against them, use the act of going to the game to find identity as well as to escape and to enjoy. In every crowd there are thousands of stories and experiences. These two individual histories are unique but the themes they bring out are not uncommon. Weave these thousands of stories together and you begin to understand that football is more than just a business, and why it is the business it is.

Some of those stories were sent to long-established fan site Spurs Odyssey several years ago, when owner Paul Smith appealed for fans' memories of the famous Shelf terrace, itself to be the focus of tension between the fans and their club as we will discover in a later chapter. Their voices provide ample commentary.

"I always used to stand on the Shelf. In the late 1960s it cost 50p as a kid to get in. The kids' entrance was on the corner next to Paxton Road. The moment it opened I'd rush straight up onto the Shelf, best view in the house from the front."

"I used to stand in the Shelf, starting in 1981. I was a 13-year-old girl, often going on my own, and I couldn't have felt safer. I used to get in early and stand in front of a bar so I didn't get crushed. But on the odd occasion I fell, I was always picked up and dusted off with several people checking I was OK."

The Shelf especially was a kingdom within a kingdom, an anarchic, rumbustious area which was largely left to get on with itself, something that seems strange in the modern era of tightly-controlled grounds but that wasn't uncommon for many years. Surges on the terrace were a regular occurrence, prompted by choruses of the old music hall classic *Knees Up Mother Brown*. Anyone coming back onto the terrace with a tray of beer would lose their round as it was sent flying.

"I first started going in the Shelf when I was about 11. We used to get to the ground for noon to be the first in the queue, so you could sprint to the front fence, as this was the only way we could see anything. We slowly moved towards the back as we got older and did the *Knees Up Mother Brown*."

"Being 14 and very short it was always a struggle for me to see. And though occasionally fun, when people started singing *Knees Up Mother Brown* my feet would often not touch the ground for quite a while as I was transported around by the crowd."

"It was perfect for watching football. It was the also the best view of the game in any of the 80 or so grounds I have been to. To get the perfect place you had to be in there at about 2.15 for most games and 12.30 for Manchester United or Arsenal.

"The crowd up there were very loyalist, but not stupid. I never saw any trouble up there. However, it was so packed that there was no going out for a slash at half-time. You would never have got back in again!"

"There was a spot where there was a gap between crush barriers, and you always used to get the biggest surges when we scored. I remember just after the Holsten sponsorship the club had the fine idea of selling two-pint buckets of lager. I was too young to drink then, but if we scored in the first five minutes of the second half, you'd be guaranteed to get a soaking."

The Shelf had its own subculture and characters, and the men who used to wander through the crowd with large paper sacks of Percy Dalton's peanuts were a regular feature.

"There used to be some mad bastard who used to squeeze himself in and out of a jam packed Shelf, selling peanuts and shouting 'peanuts, fresh roasted'."

"The peanut seller looked like Alan Mullery. He would throw a bag to whoever wanted one, and the coins would be thrown back and he always caught it. Not once did he throw a bag with no money not coming the other way. How trusting is that."

It could also be a dangerous and threatening place, especially in the era when violent confrontations between rival groups of fans became commonplace.

"One Boxing Day, from the Shelf vantage point, I saw a West Ham crew gather below us on what is now the East Lower. It was really sinister. None had club colours, all older blokes, in their 30s, they just mingled with the crowd but exchanged looks and a few signals. I thought something was up, should have told a steward, then about 30 of them just piled in on some bloke, absolutely no reason, totally random, just for the sake of hurting a Spurs fan. Then they just melted into the crowd."

But even in the midst of this, fans were growing up and experiencing life. One fan who replied to the appeal for memories of the Shelf sent back a story that won't be to everyone's taste, but which evokes the times.

"One of my memories of the Shelf involved a game against Arsenal in the mid-1970s. Their mob was gathering further down towards the Paxton end but I was distracted by this rather brassy looking girl standing behind me. Being a lively 16-year-old virgin I reached back and put my hand on her leg, half expecting to get whacked. Well what do you know? She didn't flinch. For the next ten minutes I was massaging her thigh with my back to her and without even saying hello. Then the scumbags piled into the Shelf proper for the tear-up. Absolute carnage but I wasn't going to let that get in the way of a bit of old-style courting. I got behind her, tried to protect her and stop her from falling, all the while desperately trying to grab her tits. The romance just isn't there like it was in those days."

There was also a fair smattering of terrace wit, as these two writers recall.

"In Terry Venables' first game in charge, we were playing Liverpool and were getting a real football lesson, couldn't touch the ball. There's a break in the game due to an injury to Neil Ruddock after 60 minutes or so and as the players all hovered about the trainer as they do, some wag behind me shouts out, 'Don't just stand there Tottenham... PRACTICE!'

"In the 1965/66 season we were playing Blackpool who fielded a fireball called Alan Ball. He upended a couple of Spurs players, and while he was being booked the ground had a quite period. Some wag called out in a really educated voice which echoed all round the Shelf, 'We don't have that kind of behaviour here, Ball.' This bloke really meant it and the whole Shelf burst out laughing."

The terrace culture was loved because it was something fans created. But in modern times, the crowd itself has also begun to be marketed, treated almost as a product. There's a familiar narrative about loyal, dedicated supporters and the image of happy, cheering, supportive crowds is used as a key selling point by the game's marketeers. But support manifests itself in many ways, and there's a more anarchic, edgy side to support too – a side that is just as much a part of the story.

A large crowd wait patiently in the East Stand to watch Spurs play Sunderland in January 1912. A fair sprinkling of bowlers among the flat caps show the middle-classes watched football too.

An ambulanceman keeps the sweltering fans cool before a home game in September 1913, although no one has taken off their hat or tie.

OFFICIALS & PRESS.

Supporters waiting for the main gates to open before the cup replay against Cardiff City FC in March 1922, played on a Wednesday afternoon. This must be mid-morning – later the High Road was blocked by fans drawn by the magic of the Cup. Thousands were locked out. The White Hart, later Rudolph's, is in the background on the right.

20 February 1937: Fans up for the Cup as the football special departs from Euston, bound for Cheshire to play New Brighton FC in February 1937. Silly hats go way back. These and a version of the famous cockerel on a football are lovingly homemade.

The Double team parade their trophies along the High Road in front of hundreds of thousands of ecstatic fans.

The Spurs Angels encourage the Park Lane to 'Lift Up Thy Voices As Never Before' prior to the second leg of the European Cup semi-final on 5 April 1962.

Get there early: it's Sunday, 7am and already the orderly queue for tickets for the European Cup Winners' Cup-tie with Slovan Bratislava in March 1963 stretches along the East Stand. Most seem indifferent to the eager placard-carrying fan publicising another meeting in Trafalgar Square.

Fans on the pitch during the tense relegation derby versus Chelsea in April 1975, a game disrupted by violence on several occasions.

Another pitch invasion, this time a demonstration of loyalty when Spurs were relegated in 1977. The crowd stayed behind, peaceably invaded the directors' box and chanted their support for the team.

The Shelf bathed in sunlight as it fills up before the league game against Nottingham Forest in 1988.

A group of delighted young fans display their tickets for the 1981 Cup Replay. On sale the morning after the first drawn game, many queued all night or came straight from Wembley.

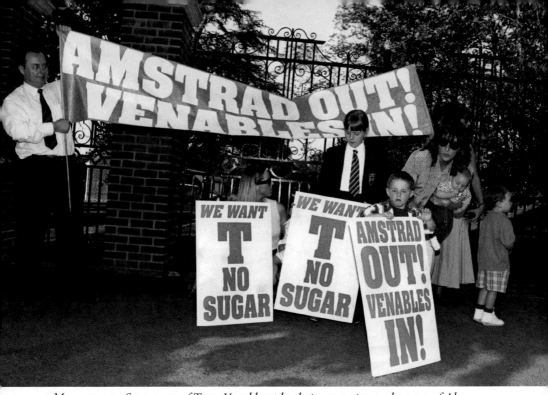

More protests. Supporters of Terry Venables take their campaign to the gates of Alan Sugar's Chigwell mansion in May 1993. A day out for all the family by the look of it.

The Bricklayers Arms in Tottenham High Road, the famous Brickies, visited by Spurs fans from all over the world, as evidenced by the flags and scarves hanging on every inch of wall.

6

I go for the football but I don't mind if the fighting's there

"PEOPLE seem to think that if you go to away games that you're football hooligans, and they say we're all illiterate, but you go down Tottenham and half the people are pretty well-educated." The quote is from a fan named only as Keith in Paul Wombell's 1978 college project *Tottenham Boys We Are Here*, a publication that has achieved cult status among some Spurs fans.

Produced between 1976 and 1978 with the aid of a grant from the Greater London Arts Association, it featured an extensive collection of photographs of Spurs fans during the season spent in the old Second Division, plus interviews with the fans themselves. Those first-hand interviews are interspersed with some commentary about media coverage of football fans and football violence.

The subject of Spurs fans who get involved in violence is a controversial one. For many, these are "not real fans". But that's not true. While individuals may attach themselves to football crowds in order to get their fix of violence, the vast majority of fans who have got themselves involved in what's been referred to under the catch-all term of 'trouble' are knowledgeable and passionate about the club they support. As authors Adam Powley and Martin Cloake pointed out in the 2004 book *We Are Tottenham*: "To ignore this aspect of Tottenham's support would be to ignore a crucial aspect of the club's modern character."

One of the fans they interviewed, who went unnamed for reasons that become obvious as the interview unfolds, had been actively involved in football violence and his inclusion prompted criticism from some fans.

Doubtless some readers will bridle at a chapter focusing on this section of support, but no people's history can be complete without including the stories of these fans. And, the fact is, the lines are blurred in any case. One observer's 'character' is another's 'hooligan' and the nature of football support is that the crowd is a fertile mixture of background, attitude and experience.

Hunter Davies recognised this when he included the chapter The Skinhead Special in his 1972 classic *The Glory Game*. He takes a train with a boisterous group of fans on the way to see Spurs at Coventry. One says to him: "The club call us hooligans, but who'd cheer them on if we didn't come? We support them everywhere, but we get no thanks." In conversation during the day, some of the views aired tap back into the feelings about identity and pride that we've traced throughout this book. There's resentment at the media's perceived obsession with northern clubs, anger at the way the fans are treated by the authorities, and more than a hint of the attitude summed up in the phrase "love the team, hate the club".

For a significant section of fans, identifying with the club means remaining fiercely independent of it. The dedication to and passion for Tottenham Hotspur is no less than that shown by other, straighter, sections of support but the presence of an outsider culture that does not seek official approval or permission for how it shows its support is a key element of the bigger picture.

Much has been written elsewhere about the growth of gang culture from the late 1950s onwards and what this means about those who take part in it. At Spurs, it's not until the late 1960s that we begin to hear of the emergence of a set of supporters distinct from a main mass, with their own set of values and often their own look. Older fans talk of a time when there was more respect but, as we've already seen, the stands at a football stadium were robust arenas long before the emergence of youth culture in the 1960s, and reports of violence at football can be traced back decades from the 1960s – as far back as the 1901/02 season, as we have seen from reports of scenes at the Aston Villa FA Cup tie.

That said, the 1967 FA Cup Final against Chelsea seemed to mark a turning point, with reports of clashes between gangs of Spurs and Chelsea fans. In 1972, in *Time Out* magazine – then still in touch with its counter-cultural roots – Chris Lightbown wrote an article on The Football Gangs of London that mentioned an early terrace face at White Hart Lane – Frankie Parish, "the popular 5' 6" dynamo who has led the Park Lane revival". As is the case with much writing on football gangs, there's a fair bit of knockabout and one-upmanship in the piece, but Lightbown's knowledge of the scene and figures such as Johnny Hoy at Arsenal and Micky Greenaway at Chelsea ties in with much of what has been handed down by word of mouth among the crowds over the years.

The article was written in the same year as Davies's book, and in that chapter on the Skinhead Special the journalist describes the look of the Spurs boys. "Most of them had blue and white scarves, in either wool or silk, which they had knotted around their middles. Some wore rosettes, but not on their chests. The season's fashion was to pin rosettes on their thighs." Photographs of fans at the time reveal a preponderance of heavy council donkey jackets, Oxford bags, v-necked sleeveless jumpers, sleeveless denim jackets and lost of scarves and pin badges.

Davies describes the Tottenham supporters arriving in Coventry and forming a large mob marching noisily to the ground, and recounts how through sheer force of numbers they infiltrate the home end and push Coventry's fans out. At first, there's little if any violence, but just before the teams come out punches and kicks are exchanged as Coventry make a determined attempt to retake territory. Lightbown's article makes reference to Spurs fans having gained a reputation for overrunning Midlands grounds and what Davies describes was a fairly typical afternoon at the football at the time. But two years later, Spurs supporters were involved in an incident that gave them notoriety across Europe.

Many thousands travelled to the second leg of the 1974 UEFA Cup Final against Feyenoord in Rotterdam on a night that saw some of the worst rioting by English fans in Europe and that left 200 people injured. Some fans say trouble started on the ferries, with heavy drinking fuelling the violence. Others say they witnessed nothing until just before the game, when they saw bloodied and bandaged fans and began to hear stories of trouble in the town centre. Journalist David Winner, however, while working on a documentary for Dutch TV in the run-up to the 30th anniversary of the riot, spoke to a retired Dutch policeman who alleged police chiefs had encouraged officers to crack some heads when the English fans arrived.

At the time, coming as it did just two years after fans of Glasgow Rangers had rioted in Barcelona before and during the Cup Winners' Cup Final in what was the first instance of mass football violence to be widely reported internationally, the Rotterdam riot cemented the idea of hooliganism as "the British disease". The club was banned from playing its next two European matches at White Hart Lane, but the notoriety gained by a section of the club's support attracted more of the same, and White Hart Lane developed a reputation as a fearsome place to go.

In 1977 the *Daily Mirror* ran two pictures of a named Spurs fan, Mark Scott, fighting with fans on the terraces at White Hart Lane in 1975 and 1977 on page three of the news section under the headline 'Caught in the act' and claiming "Mirror picture power puts a soccer thug behind bars". Scott is quoted in Wombell's book, saying he'd got separated and surrounded by Manchester United fans after "a load of us broke through the old bill, ran across no-man's land and jumped over the spiked fence to get at them."

Interestingly, while Wombell's book, and the terrace song from which it drew its title, talked of "Tottenham boys", there were quite a few Tottenham girls not only going to games but also involved on the edges of this section of support. Wombell interviewed two, named as Mandy and Tina, who told him: "We started going about six years ago. Me dad and his gang has always been Spurs supporters and we live in Tottenham as well. I go for the football but I don't mind if the fighting's there, as long as it don't spoil the game."

The club's spell in the Second Division took fans to grounds such as Millwall, Cardiff and Stoke City, known to have fierce reputations themselves. Tottenham fans followed the team in numbers throughout this season, gaining a reputation for loyalty and also, through incidents in and around grounds generally considered to be tough to visit, for being more prepared than most to fight. Wombell's photographs show some instances of general running around in the streets outside games, but also shows packed and raucous pubs and groups of fans singing and drinking outside pubs that are still packed on matchdays, such as The Bricklayers' Arms on the High Road just north of White Hart Lane.

There's still a fair bit of the biker gang and donkey jacket look, long hair and silk scarves tied to wrists and waists – a style described by Liverpool fan Peter Hooton as "Giant Haystacks with donkey jackets". But in a few pictures there's evidence of a new look, neater knitwear, crew-neck adidas t-shirts, polo shirts… As with so much else in football's counter-culture, claims about who adopted what look and why as the new 'casual' or 'dressers' scene developed need to be taken with a pinch of salt. But it's clear that around 1980 a section of Spurs' support began to shed the old look. In Ian Hough's book *Perry Boys*, about the casual gangs of Manchester and Salford, he agrees with an observation made by a Liverpudlian veteran of the scene that "Tottenham brought the first Cockney teams up in the early 1980s… Tottenham came to Old Trafford in green windjammers, Doc Martens and skinheads in late October 1981 in the League Cup and then we played them again in mid-April 1982 in the league and there they all were, in Ellesse and Tacchini trackies, black guys sporting gold and top training shoes."

There was a look, a set of values, a lifestyle developing around football, something created by the fans themselves which valued keeping ahead of media influence and being genuine and organic. At Spurs, this developed with its own characteristics. There were known faces, like Parrish, and like Keith Robins, who was known for organising the coaches that took vast numbers of Spurs fans all over the country. But unlike at other clubs that had more centralised, single gangs such as the ICF at West Ham or Chelsea's Headhunters, the Spurs 'firm' was harder to pin down.

As the fan interviewed in *We Are Tottenham* said: "What you've got is a collective of little firms… a lot of them are run by geezers and you know them by the fella's name – so-and-so's firm, so-and-so's mob…"

That loose collective and lack of names serves an obvious purpose, and telling the story of this side of the Spurs support has always proved difficult because of a rule that's always been stuck to – if you're involved, you don't talk about it. One fan who had been involved, Trevor Tanner, wrote a book in which he laid claim to being the main man at Spurs. It did not go down well and reportedly words were had.

For some years, The Bull pub on Tottenham High Road was a focal point for Tottenham's more hard core support. Richard Cracknell knew the pub as a teenager when his mum and stepdad took over the tenancy in 1985. "Me mum was Leyton Orient, so was me nan and me uncle," he says, "but me stepdad was Spurs and when him and me mum got married I was Spurs and that was it. He took me to my first game in about 1976 at home against Birmingham City and I remember being bowled over by the crowds.

"We were living in Collier Row in Romford, and money was tight, so I didn't go often, it was a special treat. When I was about 12 or 13 I started going with a few friends, I got adventurous with the buses. I used to stand on the Shelf, but only on the lower Shelf, I weren't allowed up in that middle bit. Up the top always looked a little bit too adult for me, I hadn't got me wings."

Already, Cracknell was picking up on the subtleties of how the crowd organised itself. In the early 1980s, football made you streetwise very quickly. And if the terraces were a school, The Bull was further education.

"It was Bob McNab's pub," Richard remembers. "He sold it to Terry Scales, the landlord. It got turned into a place called Kartels, because his missus was Karen. So Karen and Terry, Kartels. Typical 80s look with a naff awning out the front with Kartels splashed across it, painted funky colours inside, pinks and whites with pink lights running up steel bars. At the time it was state of the art. When we moved in I was 15, it was 1985. Me dad was the manager.

"Terry who ran the pub bought me a season ticket in the West Lower, it was £370 if I remember rightly, which was a lot of money then. I had to work Thursday nights in the pub collecting the glasses and that paid for the season ticket, and then I had to work Friday, Saturday and Sunday and I got a fiver for each night. So one night for me season ticket, three nights for a bit of spending money. My sister and I still went to school in Collier Row, because me mum wouldn't have us going to school in Tottenham. She'd taken a lot of convincing to move to Tottenham, that's for sure. It was tough round there. And the police had a really bad name. Those years were the biggest education of my life."

Perhaps surprisingly, in an area that would soon become synonymous with one of the worst urban riots in Britain when the nearby Broadwater Farm estate erupted, The Bull was "Taylor Walker's most successful pub in London" according to Richard. "It was rammed most nights. There was an odd mix of people who would come at weekends and then go off to the local nightclubs,

Websters, the Tottenham Royal… Sam Fox had a bar up the road, Sam's Bar. Some came just for the football, some for the evening out, others a bit of both. This was the time when you'd open lunchtime, close for the afternoon and open up again in the evening."

On non-matchdays, he says, it was still 'Spurs only" – not through any formal membership, but simply because "if you weren't Spurs you just wouldn't go in there. Everyone knew it was the Spurs pub". Matchday regulars who lived elsewhere would travel to have a drink even off matchdays – the pub was very close to Seven Sisters station, a location that was also key to it becoming the place from which the Spurs firms would 'welcome' visiting fans. But in those days plenty of the regular support still lived locally.

"When we moved in, it was a Sunday and on the Monday Dad opened up for lunchtime. We'd get the college brigade from over the road, looking for half a toasted cheese sandwich and half a pint with three straws, that type. After half an hour a bloke comes in with half a sawn-off shotgun under his coat and asks for some bloke by name. The old man never gets flustered by anything so he just says, 'Well, you can see who's in here.' So the bloke says: 'I'll wait.' Me dad says: 'You ain't waiting in here.' So off he went. We never saw him again."

Cracknell agrees that the reputation a section of the club's fans had got attracted a crowd who "wanted to go to the football and have a fight at the weekend" but he says, "Even then there were factions. You'd have one little group of five who used to drink in one bit, and another little group over there. Little gangs within the bigger gang, it was quite an odd dynamic. A real mix of ne'er do wells, people who had a bit of money, a real mix."

He remembers, too, younger fans mixing with an older crowd who had been involved over the past ten years. "There was a lot of Harrington jackets, sta-prest, Gabbicci and Sergio Tacchini tracksuits, adidas mamba, samba and bamba, all that," he laughs. "The older lot didn't dress so much but the younger ones had what I call that London look, the sportswear.

"It was almost like football was the internet then, because the only interaction you really had with other people around the country was on your awayday travels. So you'd see how people were dressing, all that."

Arrangements for meeting up were very informal, "They'd go on the trains but as people started being kept an eye on there would be more just going in little groups in cars," says Richard. Not everyone, though, who drank in The Bull was there to look for trouble. Because going to the match could be a risky business in those days, there was an element of safety about being somewhere and being with people who you knew wouldn't be messed with. "It was always busy, people loved the buzz of it, but at a time when pubs would get smashed up, I think people felt safe in there.

"People were into their football. I always found the hooligan element were quite knowledgeable about their football, they'd watch the games. I don't remember many who tagged along just for the trouble. Everyone who got involved was genuine Spurs." Cracknell, like many others, knew of Keith Robins and the coaches, but he says Robins wasn't really a regular and he doesn't remember coaches being run to matches from the pub. "The only ones I remember going were the ones to the race days."

Working in The Bull was certainly an experience. "I always remember midweek night games being so much more edgy," he says. "We always seemed to play teams we'd have trouble with midweek. Portsmouth stands out, around 85, 86. We'd played there in the cup and drew, and then at home and lost. A big load from The Bull went down to Portsmouth – I never went because the old man was having none of it. He knew too much. Everyone plotted up in a pub on a council estate down there – how everyone knew to go there I don't know. It must've just been a series of phone calls – no mobiles in those days – but this pub was packed apparently. Someone came in who no one knew and asked if they knew 'John the Spurs fan'. No one did, then someone clocked this fella was Portsmouth so they said, 'Now you know we're in here you can go and tell the others where we are.' About ten minutes later all the windows came in, their 6.57 crew. That really kicked off and I remember Trevor MacDonald on *News at Ten* that night talking about this disturbance at a pub in Portsmouth.

"The replay night I was working and I got told to make sure I got the bottles and glasses collected double quick. We opened up and it was pretty quiet, then about 15 blokes walked in we hadn't seen before and my old man says 'they must be Portsmouth'. Some of our lot are in there clocking them too and the next thing everyone's ordering light and lagers. None of them would drink that, it was all pints of lager, but they all wanted a pint glass and a bottle so they had two things they can chuck. Luckily the old man kept a bit of an eye on them and they left after one drink with nothing happening. But I remember it ended up being absolutely heaving in there that night. A big mob of Portsmouth got walked up the High Road but they had so many police around them that nothing could happen.

"The maddest day was a Saturday when Liverpool played Southampton in an FA Cup semi-final at White Hart Lane. The pub opened and a load of the Spurs boys came in – my Dad and Terry had said to them come down just in case so we've got a few bodies here. They'd decided it would be a Southampton pub because nobody wanted Scousers in the pub. So the door staff are checking people in and about one o'clock a great big load of Scousers turn up at the door and get told 'sorry lads, it's Southampton only'. So there's a bit of a row and a few of them got a bit lippy and there was a stand off on the forecourt. The door staff locked the doors – the place was like a fortress, it had grills over the windows, the lot – and the Scousers are lobbing a few bottles. The Spurs boys started to go outside, they asked the Southampton lot but they said 'no thanks', and as the door opens there was this big Scouser standing by these railings by the edge of the pavement. He draws this half sword out of his jacket, couple of foot long. And he makes the stupid mistake of whacking this sword on the railings. And it bent in half. It was plastic! Course, the Spurs boys see this and whack – he's sparko and the rest of them got chased up the High Road. Even in the fraught moments there were moments of comedy."

It's the characters and the stories that make cultures, shared experiences that bind people together, and Cracknell says that when he tells people about some of them people often find it hard to believe he's not spinning a tale. "They'll go 'no, that's Boycie from *Only Fools and Horses*, it's not real,'" he laughs. "There was Johnny Castles the car dealer – could only be a car salesman with a name like that, couldn't he? – and his dealership was on the one-way system behind the Robert E Lee pub. His office was a caravan on the site – that's Arthur Daley, isn't it? He wasn't into football but he used to drink in The Bull.

"He was always buying and selling stuff. He bought a great big batch of cowboy boots, proper they were, must've been worth a fortune, but at the time they just weren't the fashion. He tried to convince me Dad and Terry to have a country and western night at the pub so he could flog all these boots he'd bought unseen.

"There was one quite odd bunch of lads. Fella called Drunkard – no one really knew anyone's names – and his mate Boag and a few others. They were professional shoplifters. Drunkard was really bright, well-educated. Went to work in the City when he left school, quite a high up job, but he got fired after two days because he'd gone down his boss's bag and nicked her purse. Kleptomaniac. These days he'd get treatment for it as an illness, but then it was just 'he's a thieving scumbag'.

"They lived in the flat next to the pub. Boag had a pitbull called Sensimilla. It was a lunatic. They got drunk one day and went back next door. Boag had been holding the dog back and letting go, and Drunkard had a towel round his arm and they were letting the dog go for his arm like they do in the police training. Anyway, the dog's getting really wound up and he goes for Drunkard really hard. He dodges out the way and the dog misses him and goes through the glass window. I was outside on the forecourt and there was this almighty crash and showers of glass, and the dog landing in the bus lane – it cleared the forecourt and the pavement. It just got up, shook itself down, and run back up the stairs to have another go.

"They had a big bunch of keys on the table one day when I was collecting. I said; 'What's that?' So one of them goes, 'That's the show cabinet at Woolworths at Wood Green, that's the Comet in Enfield…' They had keys for showrooms and shops all over. They'd go on thieving holidays to Exeter for example, fill a van up with stuff they'd lifted and flog it in the pub.

"There was a big West Indian contingent, never any problems with race but there was a two-tier system there. The older ones really disliked the kids who they thought always wanted to cause trouble, but there was never anything from the white drinkers about black people. There was about 40 of 50 of these black fellas who'd come in regularly because there were girls in there and we had soul music on, and quite a big contingent went to the games and got involved. But they really hated these younger local black kids. At the time there was a police advert on the side of the buses in Tottenham that said '95% of the crime in Tottenham is committed by the same 65 people' and one of the younger lads saw this and said: 'That'll be all the lads off the estate'."

Perhaps surprisingly given the social tensions at the time and the robust environment around the club's support, there was never really the issue with racism at Spurs that there was at many other clubs. "Spurs, I don't know why, just seemed to be somewhere it wasn't an issue. Some of it might be down to regular fans being black, people like Norman Jay were known for travelling, and Sammy Skys was involved with the boys. They followed Spurs, faces if you like. Sammy was always in the forefront, there's a picture of him and a couple of other West Indian lads in the middle of the High Road fronting off a big load of West Ham – that's on the net. But I don't know why it worked out like that. Some of it would have been people coming along because they knew they wouldn't get any racial stick here.

"There was never really any of that amongst our own. But I remember it was bad with other fans – Everton were particularly bad. I remember one game sitting in the West Stand and Terry from the pub who had the seat next to me had given his ticket to a West Indian bloke who drank in there. This bloke in the Everton crowd, every time he caught the eye of the bloke next to me he was doing monkey actions and shouting over, and a few of the others were joining in. This fella was not a bloke to be messed with and at the end of the game he shot straight off around to the away end. He was looking for them, he really was not happy."

By the late 1980s, mainstream media was picking up on the football fan scene, and Richard remembers a documentary that was screened on a midweek night that featured some of the Spurs lads. "There was no iPlayer or anything so everyone came to watch it in The Bull. We were one of the first pubs in London to have a big screen so the place was packed. There was some footage of the Spurs mob coming out the station, away at West Ham I think it was, and one of the main boys – he was in there that night – the picture shows him slip off the kerb as he's walking out and he got dog's abuse that night. Someone videotaped it and it ended up getting watched quite a few times."

Another legend among away supporters was Tottenham Arthur, although Cracknell remembers him from later life, rather than as a regular at The Bull. He lived on the streets, sported a grizzly beard and a jacket covered in metal Spurs pin badges. He followed Spurs all over, and fans used to club together to get him a ticket or pass on spares. At one stage he used to get lifts on the team coach if he was spotted. Cracknell remembers seeing him at away games during the 1990s "with a bloke we used to call David Bowie. Because he looked like David Bowie. Arthur just used to turn up, didn't he? No one knew how he did it."

Early in 2016, it dawned on a few people that Arthur hadn't been seen, and the word went out in the pubs and on messageboards to find out if he was alright. The rumour that he had died began to circulate, but checking the wellbeing of a homeless man with no known relatives is next to impossible. What's for sure is that Tottenham Arthur has not been seen at an away fixture for some time. It's a poignant moment, not just for reasons of basic humanity but also because a little part of what football support was before everything became organised and corporatised may just have gone.

Despite the notoriety of The Bull, Cracknell never really remembers any heavy policing at the pub until quite late in their tenure. "I think there was a bit of an attitude of boys will be boys," he says. "Occasionally if some of the local shop windows got put in the local MP – it would've been Bernie Grant at the time – would have a moan and there'd be a few more police on but it was all up near the ground. Me Dad left the pub in around 1987 and a bloke called Tony took over. It still carried on like it was but the crackdown had started and I suppose our time there was a bit last days of the Roman Empire really."

From the vantage point of today, the late 1980s certainly were the last days of English football as it had been. Great change was around the corner, much of what was familiar would be lost, and for many the connection they once had with the game became more strained. That has led to an apparent nostalgia for the days of bad behaviour. A thriving literary sub-genre of hoolie-porn has provided vicarious thrills for a wider audience who would never have been involved themselves. And meanwhile much of the fan scene of the 1980s has been reduced to little more than trackies and trainers as the fashion industry commodifies it.

But those days retain their hold because of the sense of connection that ran through them. The modern game likes to portray what went before the commercial boom as simply the bad old days when football was plagued by hooligans. The rough edges, raucousness, blurred edges and even anarchy of the old days is anathema to the modern game, with its straight lines and slick organisation. The experience of being a fan feels more regulated than ever, and it feels at times as if we are being sold a culture that we created, that we owned in the first place.

And that's why it is important to hang on to those rough edges. The stories told in this chapter remind us of a perspective that cannot be missed out of any genuine people's history. That's not to romanticise much of what went on, simply to present a more well-rounded picture. And what would happen to the people who watched football into the final decade of the century was anything but romantic.

7

A tiny part of Tottenham Hotspur plc

I N 1981 a car-load of Spurs fans spent the journey home from Leeds whinging about another below-par performance and slating the board's lack of drive and ambition. Scarcely out of the ordinary. In fact, the sort of post-mortem conducted by generations of homeward-bound Tottenham fans before and since. What was different about this lot was the response: one of them decided to buy the club.

From the outside looking in, Spurs were perceived as a wealthy club, a 'moneybags' team who were part of the so-called 'big five' most influential sides at the time, Manchester United, Spurs, Arsenal, Liverpool and Everton. Supporters had a reputation to match, affluent rather than flash. The media often called the Spurs crowd 'fickle' because supposedly they quickly turned on their team as soon as things did not go well.

Irving Scholar was hardly a typical supporter. Based in Monaco to avoid tax, Scholar still managed to attend virtually every Spurs match home and away and was prepared to share his encyclopaedic knowledge of Tottenham minutiae with anyone prepared to listen and many who were not, to the point of aggravation. Travelling to and from games by plane and Bentley was a far cry from his teenage years spent on the Shelf, ironic given what happened during the East Stand redevelopment that he masterminded. To describe Spurs as the first fan-owned club stretches credibility to snapping point but there's no doubt Scholar and his associates were long-standing fans with a deep and lasting feeling for the Lilywhites.

Since the late 1930s, the Wale family and their close associates had run Spurs. Making money from the club was not their concern. Scholar, brash and ambitious, was in the vanguard of a fresh generation of Thatcherite free market entrepreneurs. In 1982 the Football League abolished the regulation restricting the dividend payable to shareholders to 7.5%. This rule had been in place for a century to prevent owners investing in clubs for the sole purpose of profit. Now, directors could run a football club and make money for themselves.

Changing times demanded radical solutions and in October 1983 Spurs became the first club to float on the Stock Market. To be more precise, the football club became a wholly owned subsidiary of Tottenham Hotspur plc. Within minutes, 3.8 million shares sold out. Echoing the rhetoric used by the Conservative government as they sold off nationalised industries, the launch of the share issue trumpeted that Spurs fans could be fully involved in the club's future.

Buy a bit of Spurs – as shareholders they owned the club, and 14,000 small shareholders invested, not for profit but to be a part of the club. Such a wide spread of ownership also fragmented any potential opposition to the board. That Christmas THplc shares solved those nagging 'what to buy a Spurs fan who has everything' problems in an instant. One of this book's authors had a framed share hanging forlornly in his toilet for many years.

Jill Lewis remembers the wave of optimism which, looking back, was misplaced: "I bought the minimum number of shares, my mum bought the minimum number of shares and I think dad bought double the minimum number of shares! It was exciting, there was a sense of being pioneers and I do remember that feeling. Obviously it was an amazing period for the club because of the games, there were some incredible matches, the UEFA Cup Final night at the Lane, but I can't come away from that with any positivity, it's led us to where we are now…"

Tottenham Hotspur and everything connected with it became a commodity, something that could be bought and sold. Football fans have always been consumers, paying for admission, buying food, drink and tokens of allegiance like rosettes, scarves and rattles. What changed was that the pursuit of revenue and wealth became the defining characteristic of the club.

Spurs became one of the first clubs to aim to maximise income from merchandise. The Holsten shirt sponsorship deal was signed whereas just a few years previously the ground and programme carried no advertising of any sort. The proud cockerel itself was usurped to become a copyrighted property of the club. Scholar bought a few clothing companies, including Hummel, to generate more income. Another first: the first television advertising campaign for a football club, featuring the 'team' emerging from the tunnel, a mix of self-conscious-looking players and fans, including West Stand loyalist satirist and comedian Peter Cook, and 'Mrs Ridlington', a beaming white-haired granny.

Gates had been falling, matching a national trend. Living standards had risen. People had more spare cash, more leisure time and therefore more choices. Also, the image of the game itself was being tarnished by the perceived extent of hooliganism. The Double year saw Spurs averaging gates of over 53,000. In 1970, this fell to 36,000, by 1980 it was 32,000 and in 1986 hit a low of just over 20,800.

Big matches were electric, other games, no problem in finding a good spot on the Shelf or the Park Lane at 2.50 and popping out during the match to get a beer, no queues, bring them back to drink on the terrace itself. You probably wouldn't have missed much anyway.

Supporters received these developments initially with incredulity – was this our Tottenham, showing football the way, being innovative? – and then welcomed them. This was a good time to be a Spurs fan. Basking in the glory of back to back cup wins in 1981 and 1982, Spurs gained a lot of favourable publicity. We had lost the Park Lane to away fans but the Shelf experienced a renaissance, not only loud but also a place where young and old fans mixed. This optimism was short-lived.

By the mid-1980s, the experience of being a football supporter was about to undergo profound change – and the catalyst for that change was the experiences of football supporters. It's possible to identify a particular turning point – May 1985, the bleakest of months for English football. At Bradford City's Valley Parade ground, 56 fans died when an old wooden stand caught fire during a match against Lincoln City. The stand went up in flames terrifyingly quickly. Many fans, including children, were burnt alive huddled against turnstiles and exits padlocked to stop non-payers getting in.

Just 18 days later Juventus and Liverpool fans in Belgium for the European Cup Final were grateful to find a bit of space on a neutral terrace at the Heysel Stadium, away from the main clusters of their respective support. There was a charge by a small number of English fans, Juve fans tried to get out of the way, a wall collapsed, and the crush was inescapable and tragic. The game went ahead to a backdrop of seething violence on the terrace and dead bodies draped with makeshift shrouds; 39 fans, almost all Italian, died, and 600 were injured.

Both events had a long-term impact on safety in sports stadia. But, as Ward and Williams point out in their book *Football Nation*, this wasn't a problem confined to football. The 1980s saw fatal deficiencies in public safety exposed by a litany of disasters including the King's Cross fire, the sinking of the *Marchioness* pleasure boat on the Thames, the capsize of the *Herald of Free Enterprise* ferry and a crash at Manchester Airport. Ward and Williams's damning analysis applies to football too: "Under neo-liberal governments that stressed private enterprise and profit over public good, the nation lacked adequate and well-maintained provision in public space, leisure and transport. This was an era of public inquiries rather than public safety. Analysis of these disasters revealed poor communications, poor situational awareness, a lack of leadership, poor decision-making, inadequately trained staff and dilapidated public facilities."

At the time, Bradford saw an outpouring of national grief, Heysel of condemnation. The latter received more attention. Blame was laid squarely on the shoulders of misbehaving football fans, the impact on English fans immediate. Elected on an unwavering law and order platform, Margaret Thatcher's Conservative government saw an opportunity to be seen to crack down on violence in general and football hooliganism in particular.

Fences were erected at grounds around the country. Banning orders came into force. White Hart Lane escaped the worst of the measures, perhaps because club chairman Irving Scholar, as a former terrace fan, understood the issues better than some of his peers. Wire fences went up behind both goals but not down the sides. This relative freedom was respected by supporters and not abused. Movement inside the ground became greatly restricted, with fences on the terraces themselves, and it was no longer possible to walk from one end of the ground to the other at half-time. More turnstiles and exits eased fears of a potential crush outside the ground.

To put this in perspective, the government pushed for a national Identity Scheme for football supporters, something that would have removed from football fans the freedoms afforded to every other British citizen. Football supporters alone would have to carry an ID card. Ken Bates, the Chelsea chairman, seriously advocated electrified fences, while Allan Clarke, the former Leeds and England player and now a manager, advocated public flogging of hooligans as punishment and deterrent.

The decade ended in tragedy. The failure to recognise that these disasters were matters of public safety more than the behaviour of a tiny minority of football fans contributed to the deaths of 96 Liverpool supporters in 1989 at Hillsborough. Fences meant to protect football did not protect supporters in the Leppings Lane end, and the mindset that football fans were a problem meant cries for help went unrecognised.

Tottenham supporters have to this day a special bond with Liverpool fans because in 1981 Spurs were nearly the victims. Tottenham were allocated the Leppings Lane end for the semi-final against Wolves. The crush built up before the match to the point where supporters were lifted off their feet. Some were injured, including broken limbs. One of this book's authors recounts the experience: "I took the football special and was marched by the police from the station to the ground. But that was normal for away games in those days. I got in early and chose to stand towards the right of the terrace away from what I anticipated to be the main crush behind the goal. Everybody around me was complaining that the terrace was too small and that we should have had the other, more spacious end.

"It was packed well before kick-off. I couldn't move but at least I felt safe. Behind the goal itself, people were shouting to stewards to stop more fans coming in or to help those who had been hurt. Loads of fans were pulled up by their mates into the seats above. It was so packed no police or stewards could get in even if they wanted to.

"Then they allowed some fans on to the pitch. The police opened a couple of gates in the fence. The fans sat on the cinder track, then later – play carried on while this was happening – they marched hundreds round the pitch to space in the Wolves end. I thought it was certain to have consequences.

"All the fans were properly behaved apart from a bit of arm-waving and chanting in the general direction of the Wolves fans but I remember thinking the papers were bound to say it was a pitch invasion.

"By the end of the game I had been pushed down to a few feet from the very front. The lowest steps of the terrace were a few feet below pitch level, so if there had been any more problems there was nowhere to go. It was the worst crush I have ever experienced in nearly 50 years of watching Spurs, but funnily enough, I felt safe. What stays with me is how thrilling it was, the game and being part of the experience."

We now know that the decision to open the gates probably saved the lives of many, many supporters, including that of the author quoted above. It was that close to disaster. The football authorities and the police did not heed the warnings. Hillsborough did not have a safety certificate for the 1981 semi-final. Liverpool fans were the ones who suffered.

The season after Hillsborough, pitchside fences disappeared from grounds for good. The Taylor Report led to all-seater stadiums two years later, a belated recognition that English football grounds were not safe for large crowds in the modern era. Terraces had gone for good. The experience of watching Spurs play would never be the same. At this stage, being a football supporter wasn't cool. In the mid-1980s, the game and its supporters were under sustained attack from all sides. Hooliganism was the folk devil of the times. Any violence related to football, however remote the relationship, was subsumed under the category. The problem, so the argument went, was not just the danger at games, it marked a deterioration in the moral fibre of the youth of the nation. This moral panic meant that 'something had to be done' even it meant that the interests of our national game suffered too.

Violence or more accurately the threat of it put off many supporters. White Hart Lane felt safe, as it always had. Fighting was rare in the ground, as much because of Spurs' reputation of being able to hold their end as the safety and segregation precautions. Opposition fans rarely tried to infiltrate the Shelf.

Bernie Kingsley was a steward at the time and gives a flavour of the lack of organised crowd control as well as the threats. "They gave you about ten minutes' training and a bib. Yeah, we did have a little bib – a bit like a hi-vis jacket, except it wasn't hi-vis.

"I had to go and open the gates at the end of the game, or just before the end of the game – but I also had to time that right to stop people coming in. The away end was sectioned so they'd open up one pen after another and I used to cop a lot of flak. I'd be standing in the empty one with the key to the padlock to open up to let them through and the police would be standing down on the pitch. I'd be saying 'we need to open this up' because it was absolutely packed at the back and the police would be saying 'there's room down the front'. Of course you couldn't get people to go down the front so when I finally did get allowed to open the gate, I'd nearly get killed in the rush.

"There was a pre-season game against Rangers in the mid-1980s where I've never seen so many drunk people in one place at the same time. They smashed through the turnstiles. I've no idea when the game started as I was just dealing with all sorts of mayhem underneath the stand. I think the game had been going for 20–30 minutes before I even realised it had kicked off."

Bearing all this in mind, it's tempting to wonder what made Bernie, and other fans like him, ask to work as stewards. "It was quite simple," he says. "In about 1980, we'd had an FA Cup replay against Liverpool and they'd made it all-ticket, so we had to go and queue up on the Sunday before the match – all the way round the ground.

"While I was queuing I found out that if you sold Spurs Lottery tickets, you got a ground pass, so you could get in for nothing for every game. So I signed up as a lottery agent. I did that for a couple of years and got my ground pass and went to all the games without having to pay to get in.

"After a couple of years I got fed up with having to sell these bloody lottery tickets and thought 'how else can I get in for nothing?' So I applied and went for a very brief interview with the then Head of Security.

"Pay? It probably started at about £5 a game and went up to £10. I got stationed on Block Z. It was one of the smaller blocks and they used it mainly for the youth team players and their families, even though it was in the away end. At the bottom of the staircase to Block Z there was a gate and that was the one they used to use to let people through, in and out, particularly the people who'd got complimentary seats in Block Z. That's why it was there. There was a game when the bloke who was supposed to man the gate didn't turn up so they gave me the key and said 'Do Block Z but also look after the gate'. And that was it. I became in charge of that and gradually got moved up because they worked out I had a bit of a brain.

"There was a game when quite a lot of the stewards didn't turn up, including some of the senior guys. Me and one or two of the others went into the West Stand, to the Security Manager's office, to complain about the fact that we'd been left short-handed and we bumped into Keith Burkinshaw in the lift. He told us off for being in there. Then he pacified us by saying he'd make me a supervisor and give me an extra quid a game or something like that. So then I became basically in charge of the corridor."

Bernie and his colleagues had entered what could be seen as a bit of a grey area between being a fan and being a club employee. "I felt a bit more part of the club and yes, you were compromising your experience as a fan because you weren't necessarily able to see all of the game," he agrees. "But we were treated like just the lowest of the low level staff. We did get quite a few perks though. The people who ran the bars would give us free beers. There were a couple of times when we'd probably had far too many beers than we should have done. The people who ran the Chanticleer Club would let you use your steward's pass to get in there through the back door so, after the UEFA Cup Final in 1984, we were in there until two, three o'clock in the morning, mixing with minor celebrities and one or two of the players. It was quite nice but after a while you thought you'd quite like to sit down and watch a match."

Eventually, Bernie and one of his stewarding colleagues opted to move on. "We decided that we'd get season tickets. It was the summer when they'd already got Gascoigne, and we signed Lineker. We got our season tickets and two weeks later, they sold Waddle. Typical Tottenham."

Away matches were a very different matter, where segregation exposed Spurs fans on their way to and from grounds and police protection from host cities was often less than half-hearted. Home or away, travelling to and from grounds exposed fans to the risk of unpredictable and often indiscriminate violence.

In October 1983 Tottenham Hotspur supporters took part in another first, the first league match to be televised live since early experiments with TV on the box began in 1960. A few years later, chairman Irving Scholar led the move to increase revenue from television rights. The resultant stand-off led to no agreement being signed and football's absence from television for the whole of the 1985/86 season.

This compounded the nation's growing dissatisfaction with the game. No *Match of the Day* or *The Big Match* on Sunday afternoon on ITV did not mean as the clubs had hoped that the public would crave football or that crowds would rise exponentially. No TV meant no football conversation. The diehards carried on regardless but public interest dwindled.

Football had a place in the nation's heart, it's just people did not pay to watch it so often. League attendances reached their post-war peak in 1948/49 when over 41 million spectators clanked through the turnstiles. Numbers fell away steadily from then on, apart from a slight resurgence after the 1966 World Cup win.

At the beginning of the 1980s, the figure had fallen to just under 22 million, bottoming out in 1985/86 when only 16,488,577 thought the game worthy of handing over their hard-earned cash.

Living standards had risen since the late 1950s and people chose to spend their increased leisure time on things other than football. Cars were much more affordable now so the growing range of alternatives were more accessible. English football did nothing in response.

Spurs' average attendance in the Double year was an astonishing 53,124 but could not escape the changing patterns of football spectating. Despite being a well-supported club during a period of relative success, the average gate fell from 35,100 in 1981/82 to a low of 20,859 in 1985/86. This compares with 33,417 in 1977/78 when Spurs were in Division Two. Supporters harking back to the atmosphere of this period would do well to remember that for every big game (usually a cup tie), many league games were played in front of sparsely populated concrete and the blank stare of upturned wooden seats. The greatest occasion of the decade, the UEFA Cup Final in 1984, attracted 46,258, below capacity. As Spurs get set to build a new 61,000 capacity stadium, talk is about whether it will be filled or not, yet for the past 130 years the ground was seldom full.

The official report into the causes of the Hillsborough tragedy, the Taylor Report, recommended that football grounds in the top two divisions became all-seater. A few lone voices suggested that terraces themselves did not create the conditions for the disaster and that they were safe provided they were properly maintained and the right number of spectators were admitted. Frankly there was little appetite for those views. Blame was resolutely placed upon the behaviour of unruly fans, although there was a recognition in the report that the management of big crowds had to be improved, especially policing and stewarding. Also, the notion of better facilities fitted the increased expectations of the standards expected of leisure pursuits in general.

It was the combination of the growing recognition of the need for better facilities, the strained relationship between football, its fans and wider society, and the economic and cultural changes of the 1980s that led to a watershed moment in the relationship between Tottenham Hotspur and its fans in 1988. It was the year in which the full implications of the club's decision to float on the Stock Exchange five years before really began to dawn on the majority of fans; a year when, in many ways, a template was set for the relationship between football clubs and their supporters that lasts to this day. It was the year in which they took the Shelf Side.

Fans had been concerned for some time about what the club was planning for the Shelf. A few had found out that in 1985 the club, without consulting the supporters, had applied for permission to completely demolish and rebuild the East Stand. Haringey Council rejected the application because the new structure would have encroached too far back onto Worcester Avenue. In January 1988, the club submitted another application to Haringey, this time for "refurbishment" of the East Stand including the building of 36 luxury boxes and the loss of 11,700 standing places. Among those listed as consulted were two local head teachers, the local police superintendent, the Borough Education Officer, 140 local residents and the Borough Engineer of Highways. No supporters on that list.

In March, Spurs fan Annelise Jespersen wrote to club secretary Peter Barnes, asking if the club had plans to redevelop the Shelf. He replied: "When the club has made a decision, rest assured we will inform our supporters accordingly, as we value your support." Supporters were to be informed, not consulted. The reply was written when the club knew full well that Haringey Council had taken the view that there was little reason to oppose the application. The date of 11 April was set for the key planning committee meeting, at which it looked as if the official thumbs-up would be given. The club then looked at the fixture list and rearranged home fixtures so that they would finish before 11 April. The game against Derby County, scheduled for 7 May, was rescheduled – with the permission of the league and Derby County – for 1 March. As Stuart Mutler, editor of *The Spur* fanzine at the time, observed: "Luton Town would slip in as the last fixture, allowing the bulldozers to slip nicely in on 12 April without the supporters hearing a word."

Unfortunately for the club though, word was out about what was being planned. The London *Evening Standard* ran a back-page piece on the plans in February, and Spurs fan Richard Littlejohn, then on that paper's staff, also wrote critically about the plans. Fans began to contact the club, but Barnes's response was to say that no decision had been taken, and that: "When there is some news we will make an announcement in the press." Spurs fan Steve Davies says: "I wrote to Irving Scholar to complain and he rang me at home. I had a long conversation with him. The reason he advanced to me in that call, which I had never heard before, was the police had complained to him that the supporters in that area were too rowdy! He then gave different reasons and was generally unconvincing."

Another fan, Steve Beauchampe, who edited a fanzine called *Off the Ball*, called Craig Brewin, the chair of the London Football Supporters' Association (FSA), to see if a campaign could be organised. Brewin, a local government worker, had contacts in Haringey's planning department and managed to get hold of a full copy of the plans. He read the contents out in early April at a meeting of the London FSA. Those present, including a number of Spurs fans, were stunned. One of those fans was Rick Mayston, who was the press secretary of the Spurs Supporters' Club. Mayston was also involved with the London FSA's work supporting the efforts of Charlton Athletic fans to get the club back to their ground the Valley, and he set about using his knowledge of supporter organisation and council politics to organise opposition to the plans.

On 11 April, 20 Spurs fans, including Mayston, Davies, Jespersen and Brewin, turned up at the council planning meeting to register their objections. Tottenham Hotspur was so confident the decision would be approved that it did not send a single representative, something that, wrote Mutler in *The Spur*, "etched, once again, a huge question mark over the club and its claims to be a professional organisation".

Haringey Council was under the impression there was no opposition to the scheme, and were very surprised at what the 20 fans had to say. The council agreed to defer a decision until 3 May. The fans, however, knew this was just the start of a long fight. Meeting in a small room at Haringey Civic Centre after the decision to defer had been taken, they set up a campaign group, with Mayston as coordinator and Davies, Jespersen and Brewin on the committee. "We called it Left on the Shelf," says Mayston, "because that's where we wanted to be – left on the terrace I had stood on since I was a boy. Scholar thought 'left' was political, but it wasn't." Davies says: "We were against it because it was a great standing area, the focus of support, as the Park Lane had been 15 years earlier and the plans would cut the atmosphere and the capacity very drastically, in favour largely of executive boxes."

LOTS set about organising a bigger lobby of the 3 May meeting, and informing Spurs fans of the very real threat to their terrace. Davies points out: "It is difficult to conceive now how challenging organising a campaign pre-internet was. You needed to get news into the press, which was not always possible." LOTS set about telephoning every contact they could think of and contacting newspapers, TV and radio stations. The FSA helped to print 10,000 leaflets that were given out on the away trip to Liverpool, asking fans to come to a public meeting to discuss the plans. Media attention and fan anger was growing and, to make matters worse for the Spurs board, Luton Town had inconveniently not been knocked out of the FA Cup, which meant they could not face Spurs until 4 May. Then the council put the 3 May meeting back to 10 May due to a clash with another meeting – giving LOTS just the opportunity to organise action at a home game that the club had tried to prevent.

Haringey Council also insisted the club call a meeting with fans to consult with them. The club did so… by calling a meeting for 9am on a Wednesday morning, 20 April, with very little advance publicity. The meeting was held in Warmington House, the building in front of the West Stand in which the Spurs Supporters' Club had its offices. "Irving Scholar and Peter Barnes arrived, and they brought Terry Venables with them – obviously hoping to deflect the questions on to football," remembers Mayston. For a while, the tactic looked to have succeeded, with fans asking the affable Venables about various team matters, but the focus soon turned to the plans for the Shelf. Scholar, who had also arrived with a policeman at his side, again tried to claim that "rowdiness" on the Shelf was the reason why it had to be redeveloped. Mayston immediately contradicted this claim, saying that, as the FSA member who met regularly with the police at New Scotland Yard, he knew there was no more trouble in that section of the ground than anywhere else. And yet in response to letters from supporters objecting to the scheme, Scholar had implied that the impetus for change was coming from the police.

Time and again Scholar was asked why the fans had not been consulted. Looking increasingly shaken, he replied that it was difficult to come up with a plan that would please everybody (which is why, Mutler mused in *The Spur*, he chose to tell no one at all). Speaker after speaker accused the club of "pandering to the rich", "trying to push the plans through quietly" and "showing disregard for the supporters". But in spite of all this, the club's officials continued to say that, however the fans felt, if planning permission was granted, the redevelopment would go ahead. Mayston reported that one member of LOTS had phoned the club posing as a potential buyer for one of the new boxes, stating they were worried about the action group's demonstrations and asking if it was certain the plans would go ahead. The club answered "yes". The conversation had been recorded, providing evidence of the club's sheer arrogance and disregard for its own supporters.

LOTS now focused on a demonstration at the final home game of the season, against Luton, and the lobby of the hearing on 10 May. The demonstration was held "because we wanted to make our statement", says Mayston. LOTS was clear it wanted a dignified, peaceful demonstration that would not give Scholar fuel to peddle his line that the terrace needed to be brought under control. On the day, remembers Mayston, "The Shelf was pretty full, we had over 5,000 people." A wreath bearing the words 'In Loving Memory The Shelf 1936-1988' was paraded around the ground. The heart of the demonstration converged on the corner of the tier nearest the Paxton Road stand and throughout the second half kept up a barrage of chants and songs.

When the game finished, they sat down on the terrace, staying put for 40 minutes, before moving off to the front of the West Stand and waiting for the directors to slink out. "It was the largest sit-in ever staged at an English football ground," says Mayston, "done with full police support and carried out entirely peacefully." Jespersen remembers being pleasantly surprised at the turnout. "I was amazed at how many stayed behind on the Shelf – I feared there would only be a few of us," she says.

Stuart Mutler in issue 2 of *The Spur*, remembering that last game watched from the much-loved terrace, after the sit-in, wrote: "As we filed peacefully out of the Shelf for the very last time, hung onto the wooden gate as we passed down the stairs was the wreath which earlier had been above our heads. I could almost sense that each and every one of us wanted to reach out and take it for ourselves, but in a strange way did not. It was like showing respect to a dead friend."

Attention now turned to the council meeting. Hundreds of fans turned up, packing the public gallery of the council chambers and spilling over into the streets of Wood Green. Scholar decided not to turn up and face the fans, opting instead to send the unfortunate Peter Barnes along with the architect, Bill Jenkins, who had drawn up the plans. Barnes's approach was to say to the council that since the fans had now been consulted – by means of the meeting at Warmington House and a drawing of the proposed new stand that was printed in the programme for the Luton game – would the council now grant permission? The councillors' response was to point out that consultation meant the club was actually supposed to listen to what the fans said. They also expressed anger at being put in the middle of a dispute between the club and its fans.

Barnes bungled his way through the meeting. When asked where the people who would be displaced by the siting of the new executive boxes would go, he said they would be able to stand on a new 'kop' in the North Stand – that was yet to be built and for which no plans had been submitted. At one point he described a contradiction as "Irish" – drawing shouts of "racist" and "tell that to Chris Hughton" from the gallery and singularly failing to impress a staunchly left-wing council. Jenkins then stepped in, announcing that when he had completed his survey the previous November, he had concluded that the Shelf was a death trap with the potential to make the Bradford fire look like a small flare-up. He was asked why, if that was the case, fans had been allowed to stand on the terrace in the intervening months. After some delay, he replied that a gas leak had only been discovered in the last two weeks.

The club's case was in ruins, and the council asked Barnes to agree to a compromise. He replied, feebly, that "I haven't got the power to make a decision", prompting disbelief and derisive laughter in the gallery. The council told the club to rethink its plans and voted to defer any decision for a further two weeks.

During those two weeks, the council had private discussions with the club – once again, no supporters were involved – about some possible compromises, with the idea of a Paxton Road kop hinted at again. On 24 May, the meeting reconvened. This time Spurs sent vice-chairman Douglas Alexiou, and from the off it was clear Spurs had decided to play hardball. Alexiou insisted the whole business must be approved by the end of the meeting, and rejected one of the suggested compromises that would have seen terracing retained in front of the executive boxes because the fans may upset the box holders by swearing! He also said the boxes had to go on the Shelf as this provided the best view – a fact that had not been lost on Spurs fans since 1936.

As the meeting went on, Alexiou's annoyance became evident. He said that if planning permission was refused, the club would seek costs from the council, withdraw a £45,000 donation to the local community, reduce standing capacity in the East Stand even further, or withdraw the plans for a Paxton Road kop. As Mutler reported in *The Spur*: "At that moment it seemed to the gallery that an air of blackmail had entered the room and placed a dark shroud over its occupants." Then came the discovery that sealed the fate of the Shelf.

Alexiou pointed out that, under the planning rules, only the external changes needed permission. Any internal changes could be made without permission and so the club could go ahead. The council suggested full permission could be granted on the understanding that the club would start building the kop within three years. Alexiou refused to sign any such agreement. The council voted that the club should resubmit its plans for the features that needed approval.

The campaigners left the meeting in a dispirited mood, although some believed the club would not start its work until the full plans had been rubber-stamped by the council. They were very wrong.

A few weeks after the LOTS campaigners had walked away from Haringey Civic Centre uncertain about what would happen next, Mutler received a letter from the club. He'd applied for one of the two-year standing season tickets the club had offered for the Shelf some time before, and the letter told him that "if I wanted to have a standing enclosure season ticket it'd be on the lower tier, because basically work had started". Mutler had been one of those who thought LOTS had managed to slow the plans enough to be able to organise more opposition to any redevelopment the following season. The letter brought home the stark reality that building work had started almost immediately after the fateful 24 May council meeting, and that the Shelf had been destroyed.

Our story now moves forward to 27 August 1988, the opening day of the new season with Spurs at home against Coventry City. At ten o'clock that morning, Mutler's phone rang. It was co-editor Matt Stone. "Have you heard the news?" he asked. Mutler wondered what signing had been announced, but what he heard surprised him more than the news that one of the transfer targets Spurs were linked with but never signed had actually put pen to paper. "They've called off the game."

"I was," wrote Mutler, "absolutely dumbfounded." In a press release, the club said the game had been called off by the police after a safety inspection of the building works revealed the ground was unsafe. Mutler and Stone went to the ground, milling around with hundreds of other fans who had begun their journeys to the ground before the postponement was announced. Some of those the pair spoke to had come from as far as Norway and the Netherlands. Mutler and Stone found Worcester Avenue blocked at both ends by huge boardings, suggesting that work on the stand was far from completion. They also noticed that club had decided to keep selling matchday programmes and keep the club shop open, despite the fact that no match would be played that afternoon. To be fair to the club, it did refund match tickets. But travel expenses were not subject to refund, and Mutler and Stone reported "an air of bewilderment, disbelief and anger" outside the ground.

It was a humiliating development for everyone associated with Spurs, and in the angry aftermath the blame game began in earnest. The media wanted an explanation from Irving Scholar, and he provided not one, but several. On TV's *Thames News* he said that "ultimately the chairman must carry the can". Although the reason the match had not gone ahead was the "contractors' fault". A few hours later on Radio 2 he said the postponement was due to Haringey Council and LOTS opposing the plans for redevelopment. By the Monday, his line was that essential safety works had not been completed. But as *The Spur* pointed out, "working on the safety aspects of the East Stand did not require approval from the Council. So this reason should not have been used as one of the club's reasons for the game's postponement". The line that the club had decided to call the game off also contradicted the line that the police had called the game off, given in the club's press statement and widely reported in the media. Scholar later went on to say that the club had wanted the game played and had suggested to the police that the East Stand be closed off to enable it to go ahead. As *The Spur* said: "This revealing comment now just about confirms that… he doesn't give, er, two hoots about us, the real supporters."

There was no satisfactory explanation, either, of why the game had been called off at such a late hour. Fans who had visited the ground during the summer contacted *The Spur* to say that the building work never looked like being completed in time for the new season. One, Steve McDonald, was a contractor for building firm Wimpey and he said that what he saw when going to collect his season ticket in July convinced him there was "no way in which they'd get it ready by August". National newspaper journalists who had visited the ground during the summer also expressed doubts about the chances of completion before the new season when they saw the scale of the work.

The whole affair was a turning point in relations between Tottenham Hotspur and its fans. Certainly in the context of the times, with the Thatcherite philosophy of worshipping the rich and blaming the poor for their own misfortune in the ascendancy, ripping out the popular terrace and replacing it with executive boxes looked like class war. And the club's utter contempt for its fans, shown in the failure to properly consult, the frequently changing and often scarcely believable explanations for its actions, and finally the attempt to blame the fans themselves for the whole mess, would not be forgotten. Perhaps most importantly, a new generation of fans who were organised and had expertise football clubs could not conceive of mere fans possessing had seen how their clubs would treat them given the chance.

So what of the campaign and those who had been involved? Rick Mayston of Left on the Shelf says: "We had a certain amount of success, a compromise success. We still had standing." He is referring to the eventual outcome of the redevelopment, in which a thin section of terracing, dubbed "the Ledge" by rueful fans, was retained in front of the executive boxes – at least until the authorities decided to make grounds all-seater in the aftermath of Hillsborough. Steve Davies of LOTS says: "The sit-in and the campaign itself got lots of publicity and support and forced the club to engage with its supporters, having ignored them, so it was a victory for democracy and it showed the fans at Spurs they could have a voice."

Annelise Jespersen, in one of two articles she wrote for *When Saturday Comes* at the time, said: "Spurs and their fans are becoming a tiny part of Tottenham Hotspur plc, a company which depends on the fans' loyalty to the team (I know of no supporters who have any feelings of warmth for the actual club), a company which knows that, no matter how much we protest, if we lose the Shelf we will still renew our season tickets."

While Davies is right in saying the LOTS campaign convinced many fans we could have a voice, subsequent events also showed much about how much the club wanted to hear that voice, and the complications that could arise when entering the political arena. Haringey Council had insisted the club sign an agreement to set up a Consultative Committee with the intention of improving relations between the club, the council, the local community and the supporters. LOTS staged a vote that saw Rick Mayston and another fan, Steve Harvey, elected to represent fans. At the first Consultative Committee meeting, no fans were present, as the head of the committee hadn't thought to invite them. At the second, the fan reps arrived to find some 30 other reps acting on behalf of various sectors of the community. Mayston reckons the council was interested in "planning gain – they were using us as a lever". Already a wedge was developing between Spurs fans and the local community.

The club announced, in the programme, that it would be staging elections for a Community *Liaison* Committee that would "keep interested parties *informed* about developments at White Hart Lane". The italics are the authors' emphasis. Note the disappearance of any reference to consultation. The club was also unwilling to recognise the LOTS vote, something the group accepted in as much as it agreed that the election should be open to the widest constituency of Spurs fans. The trouble was, the club seemed to be having trouble organising an election.

In the October 1989 edition of *Spurs News Monthly*, information on how to vote two supporters onto the Community Liaison Committee finally appeared. It gave fans 12 days to submit their vote, and the pen portraits of those standing were extremely vague. There was no mention of the fact that Mayston and Harvey had been elected to stand by members of LOTS. In addition, there was no mention of the vote in the matchday programme, which was much more widely read than *Spurs News Monthly*, and the monthly itself mysteriously seemed to be less available than usual.

The club had also pulled a sneaky stunt, putting forward the suggestion that the supporter reps should be one man and one woman. It seems a reasonable suggestion until you remember that LOTS happened to be a mainly male organisation – Annelise Jespersen had been the most prominent female member and she had gone to America for 18 months. Having seen the club at work, and noticed the make-up of its senior levels, many fans questioned this apparent conversion to the cause of equal opportunity, seeing it instead as a tactic to marginalise LOTS. As the whirl of committee politics gathered speed, the fans' group and the council committee began to drift apart. Fans became more convinced that the Liaison Committee was inadequate, while the committee seemed more and more susceptible to the club's implied criticism that LOTS wanted to take over the running of the club. Looking back, it may be a fair criticism to say that LOTS was not equipped for the Byzantine world of 1980s local government politics it found itself being drawn in to.

LOTS was, says Mayston, "just about one issue". Davies agrees, saying: "It wasn't an organisation or a structure, just a campaign." After the campaign, LOTS dissolved itself and agreed to donate any remaining money to the Back to the Valley campaign in which Charlton fans were campaigning to get their club back to its own ground (a campaign which would see the Back to the Valley Party win 15,000 votes in elections to Greenwich Council). Mayston carried on his involvement in the FSA, "There were other issues, things like the Thames Valley Royals (Robert Maxwell's plan to merge Oxford United and Reading)," he says. He wondered at the time whether in fact it was LOTS, rather than Scholar, who were out of touch, reflecting on why more fans didn't get involved in the campaign to retain the Shelf.

He also feels that the energy put into LOTS and, subsequently, the Tottenham Independent Supporters' Association, should have been put into reviving the existing Spurs Supporters' Club. But for many, the traditional SSC had no future. As far back as 1963, SSC president John Agran was complaining of "rowdyism" among the fans, saying "no member of the Spurs Supporters' Club or indeed any followers of the team were involved. We are very proud about that. One example of bad conduct was the practice of throwing toilet rolls from behind the goals. It was agreed that fortunately this now seemed to be on the decline but club members were asked to do all in their power to stop other people who might still be doing it."

There is a sense here of a separation between the SSC members and the new, younger and lower-class fans attracted to the game. They were disruptive, attention-seeking and unorganised, everything the SSC were not.

The Supporters' Club had moved into Warmington House in 1964, a building in front of the West Stand, and continued to run travel and put on social events. But interest gradually declined as fans made their own arrangements to get to and from games, including football special trains and coaches put on by British Rail and private coach companies. Supporting Spurs had changed. People didn't want to wear club ties any more or have a week away at a holiday camp. They lived too far away to join the social events. Support changed but the Supporters' Club did not.

Like many of the National Federation of Supporters' Clubs members, it was suspicious of the critical stance the new wave of fan movements took towards their clubs. And the club itself seemed to treat it with contempt, pushing the SSC out of Warmington House when the lease ended. In *The Spur*, Stuart Mutler wrote: "Now seems the time to copy the excellent efforts of the Chelsea Independent Supporters' Association and form our own independent supporters' club, away from Spurs' control."

That eventually happened in 1990, ironically when Robert Maxwell seemed set to take over the club as a result of the mess Scholar and his board had made. Davies says: "It turned out the club couldn't afford the East Stand redevelopment anyway – it was one of the main reasons for the financial crisis a couple of years later. Like many Scholar ideas, it showed little evidence of being thought through and the consequences were damaging. Ultimately Waddle and other players were sold and the team damaged." With Spurs in dire financial straits, Maxwell saw another opportunity. The idea horrified many fans. Davies says: "He had no evidence of any interest in football, his record was one of contempt for fans and tradition – shown by the plans for Thames Valley Royals – and he generally appeared entirely untrustworthy." Again with the help of Craig Brewin and the FSA, a campaign was set up, this time with an organisation called the Tottenham Independent Supporters' Association behind it. "It was unconnected with LOTS and Rick Mayston never got involved. I'm not sure why as he would have been welcome, but we went forward with those that did want to be involved," remembers Davies. "As coordinators that was me, Bernie Kingsley, Annelise Jespersen and James Loxley with a number of other people closely involved." [One of those people, we should say in the interests of full disclosure, is one of the authors of this book.]

TISA's campaign against Maxwell was an extraordinary success, with visible fan protests at televised matches and some forensic examination of club accounts at a much-postponed THFC plc AGM that saw Scholar and his board embarrassingly have to rely on their own majority shareholdings to defeat calls for their resignation. What eventually emerged was that Scholar had secretly negotiated a loan from Maxwell that was subject to a confidentiality clause Maxwell had insisted on. Scholar said this was why he could not tell the board about the loan, but the clause actually said that if he told the board, it too would be bound by confidentiality. Scholar rewrote that clause to fit his own explanation, and backdated it to cover the period of a subsequent investigation into the Maxwell loan. That investigation, the Ashurst Report, found this was "improper" as it had the effect of "misleading the board".

With even his own board unhappy with him, and with huge fan protests calling for 'Scholar Out', he eventually resigned in October 1990. "TISA was one of the first to take on a major issue, get national publicity and become a major influencer of the issues it sought to address, something we say a lot of clubs' fans emulate," says Davies. "So it is something I think we should be proud of." Jespersen agrees, saying: "I think TISA did incredibly well to mobilise so much support and to be so credible in the media, especially at a time when there were no real alternative outlets to the mainstream media."

But the chaos at the club continued, with TISA and many Spurs fans opting to back the consortium fronted by Terry Venables to save the club. Venables succeeded, but soon became embroiled in a battle with one-time partner Alan Sugar. That prompted more fan protest, with Venables seen as the football man being ousted by Sugar the businessman. In truth, the situation was far more complicated but when Sugar won, the chances of fan involvement in the club were set back years.

Not the most collegiate of operators in any case, Sugar also didn't see why he should talk to people who had opposed him. He told TISA's Steve Davies and Bernie Kingsley he didn't believe they represented anyone. So a vote was organised. Sugar told Davies he didn't trust him to count the votes fairly. So the Electoral Reform Society was brought in. Fans could vote for up to six reps – Davies got 99% of votes cast, Kingsley 96%. Sugar accepted the decision and there were regular meetings with TISA over the next two or three years, but the concept of supporters having a view of how the club he owned was run was not one he embraced.

The seed of organisation had, however, been planted, and was to make its mark at Tottenham Hotspur. Meanwhile, the final demise of the Shelf side standing came when seats replaced the terrace in both the East Stand and Park Lane. The Paxton became all-seater the following year. Building work continued, including redevelopment that saw the Paxton closed for a time to build another tier. By the end of the 1997/98 season, the work was complete and White Hart Lane was the ground we see today. The two screens at either end, rejoicing in the gloriously nineties name of 'the Jumbotron', were the first in the league to be purpose built and to show the match in real time.

Capacity was 36,240, small in comparison with other clubs in the top division and a far cry from the 56,000 of the grand days of the Shelf. Being part of a big game at White Hart Lane would never be the same again.

8

"We would sell a few thousand copies. We would publish pretty much anything!"

WHETHER you perceive the ideas Irving Scholar had as a brave new world or dystopian horror, his ideas undeniably transformed English football. High ticket prices, an overriding commercial sensibility, maximising income, astronomic television rights, clubs as public companies, investment from the City, all are part of the language of contemporary football, all are products of Scholar's vision.

If Spurs were among the first to benefit, they were also the first to be exposed to the risks. And while other clubs reaped the rewards, Scholar's vision fast turned into a nightmare. Inconceivable though it may appear, Tottenham Hotspur nearly went under. Scholar's legacy exposed a generation of supporters to a decade and more of underachievement, frustration and disappointment, and arguably continues to shape the relationship between fans and club to this

170

day. It's not an original observation to make that unease over the people's game becoming the money game is a significant factor today, but at Tottenham Hotspur that tension is arguably more pronounced. Because this is one of the game's biggest names, one which led the charge into the football business, the big-time charlies from flash Cockney bastard London, but which has consistently failed to benefit from the commercial boom it ushered in and indeed has been overtaken by once lesser rivals.

So when Spurs fans see their club described, often by itself, as a successful business, it strikes a nerve. Because wasn't being a successful club what Spurs were all about, wasn't that what gave these business types the chance to do business? It often seemed to Spurs fans that becoming a business and winning trophies were becoming mutually exclusive.

Yet supporters are resilient. From the faded glory emerged a distinct and vibrant identity inextricably intertwined with the club's history and origins. It values heritage, loyalty and a sense of who we are and what we want as supporters, which rises above the club's status in the league table or on the Stock Market.

None of this was immediately apparent. The new West Stand opened in February 1982, behind schedule but impressive none the less. The West Stand had always been, and still is, a touch more exclusive ever since the Lane was first built. The wagon as the only seating area gave way to a stand with the directors' box and expensive seats plus the standing enclosure in front. The new all-seater plus the executive boxes did not make much difference to most supporters. It was imposing without dominating the other three sides of the Lane while the design echoed the old structure with seats in the Lower West replacing the shallow terraces of the Enclosure. Players now entered the fray from a central tunnel flanked by the two benches rather than jogging up a few stairs into the fresh air in line with the Park Lane penalty box.

However, the double rows of executive boxes with their smoked glass windows impenetrable to the outsider's gaze came to symbolise the growing divisions between the terrace fan and a new class of football spectator. The occupants walked a few yards from their exclusive car-park to their dedicated entrance where they were greeted by a doorman. Clanking turnstiles became scrap. The new breed took the lift to the carpeted hospitality suites to be served pre-match food and drinks by their own waitress. They came to wine, dine and schmooze their guests. Business was done in tax-deductible cocoons where the game took second place and the raucous world of terrace culture could be kept at bay. Flick a switch and the crowd went silent. The unique atmosphere generated by a football crowd that had enticed and captivated generations became an optional extra.

To begin with, the boxes had no impact on the average Spurs fan. Fans on the Shelf had the same view for a fraction of the cost and when the light was right and you could see in, it was obvious that many had gone unsold. Income from non-footballing activities, like the premium on the boxes and corporate hospitality, would benefit everybody by providing more money for the team while the terrace fan was still being looked after. In hindsight, it marked the beginning of a decisive shift towards putting the needs of the new fan ahead of those of core diehards, the effects of which still reverberate today.

These changes, significant though they were, at the time provided a mere backdrop to success on the field. The 1980s had begun with the famous 1981 FA Cup Final victory, the first final ever to be replayed at Wembley. Tickets were easy to come by, going on general sale at the stadium itself as well as the Lane on the Sunday morning after the first match ended 1-1. Spurs fans made up about two-thirds of the crowd that saw Ricky's Villa's mesmerising winning goal, arguably the greatest ever scored in a cup final and undoubtedly the most vivid moment for two generations of supporters.

At first it seemed as if success was coming with a new approach. Another FA Cup win followed in a season in which the treble was briefly on. Then there was success in Europe. A cluster of stars who would become legends, such as Hoddle, Ardiles, Mabbutt and Perryman playing open, adventurous football with steel provided by Roberts and Miller lit up the ground. The UEFA Cup triumph on penalties against Anderlecht remains the most memorable atmosphere at the Lane since the Double.

Two years on, David Pleat rebuilt the side with a lone striker up front and a five-man midfield interchanging positions. Clive Allen scored an astounding 49 goals in competitive games. Tottenham were innovators but remained true to the Spurs Way. Expensive signings like Chris Waddle joined stalwarts like Gary Mabbutt to play fluent, attacking football. The blow of defeat in the 1987 FA Cup Final via a cruel deflection off Mabbutt's knee was softened by the promise of future success. This gifted side was bound to get better.

Pleat's tenure as manager came to an abrupt and undignified end when out of the blue, news came that he had been found guilty of kerb crawling. The board panicked and sacked him. Progress stalled momentarily but Scholar picked up the momentum later with what appeared to be the perfect managerial appointment. Terry Venables had a worldwide reputation as an innovative modern coach, popular with players and fans alike. Moreover, Scholar believed he could be trusted to embrace football's brave new world, at ease with the media and with investors as much as he was with his squad.

After a slow start, funds were made available to buy stars in the Tottenham mould, notably Gary Lineker from Barcelona and Paul Gascoigne from Newcastle. Mabbutt represented stability and continuity. They chose Tottenham ahead of other suitors because of what the club could offer. Or so it appeared.

In 1991 Venables went one better than Pleat by winning the FA Cup. The semi-final against Arsenal in that cup run is arguably the most memorable match of this period, more so than the final itself, because it was the first ever semi-final to be held at Wembley, hitherto sacrosanct for finals only. Both clubs received ticket allocations higher than for finals, which scandalously were at the time as low as 23,000 for each finalist, therefore it felt like a true occasion for fans. Spurs shook off their underdog tags to win 3-1 in an excellent team performance.

However, Spurs imploded on the threshold of progress. It was to become a feature of the club in modern times that supporters soon became wearily accustomed to. Looking back, cracks started to appear early on. The unassuming Keith Burkinshaw, who created the successful team of the early 1980s, left at the height of his prestige after a disagreement with the board. His parting shot, "There used to be a football club over there," was in fact penned by a journalist, but while little attention was paid to the comments at the time, they have since become a mantra for supporters disenchanted with the club's development.

Players may have been coming in but stars were being sold, notably Clive Allen in 1988, Chris Waddle the following season, then Gazza in 1991, all at the height of their powers and all who had a special place in supporters' hearts.

The full reasons were not obvious to fans at the time. Burkinshaw clearly felt that the club put business before the interests of the team. Behind the scenes, the club was a small step from total disaster. The value of investments can go down as well as up, but Irving Scholar had not read the small print. The expense of the West Stand rebuilding and financing other loans drained the club's finances. The businesses designed to support the balance were not profitable. Now the Hummel shirt worn by the players during these glory years is a collectors' item. Then, Hummel was the ultimate in naff.

The merchandise and services for supporters was of limited value too. Scarves, hats, badges and, less popular now, rosettes could still be bought from traders in the High Street with their pitches in front gardens or open space to avoid being moved on by police on the public highway. These were homespun entrepreneurs, displaying their wares from home-made wooden creations with a board and box crudely nailed together.

The club took an aggressive stance to limit the freedom of non-licensed products to be sold. They were replaced by all manner of new goods in the club shop – baseball caps, key rings, posters, Tottenham Hotspur aftershave. This was complemented by Spursline, a premium rate phoneline giving recorded information from the club. "You are through to Spurs, Spurs, Super Spurs, Oh! Super Spurs..." To listen to all 11 programmes a week would have cost £25, profits shared 50-50 between Spurs and the telephone company. While the service quickly degenerated in quality with blandishments replacing any real news, it was the only way to get information about the club other than through the back pages of the papers. Many fans of that era recall pressing a substantial pile of coins into the phone box as groups of pals huddled round the receiver.

Alan Sugar ended Scholar's misery by buying the controlling stake in the club in 1991 with Venables actively involved in the deal. We now know not only how close Spurs came to administration but also that Robert Maxwell was a phone call away from taking over. His business interests collapsed after his death in a sailing accident that November and Spurs could have gone down with him.

Alan Sugar's takeover saved the club, of that there is little doubt. The question remains, at what cost to the supporters? Sugar made sure the ground changes were completed but paid only lip-service to the interests of fans. Sugar claimed to be a Tottenham fan, but he was also a consummate businessman who saw a golden opportunity in the club. He understood that football clubs could generate a profit but, more significantly for his purposes as the major shareholder, could generate wealth too. This is part and parcel of 21st-century football finance. Twenty years ago, Alan Sugar was one of the first to recognise the possibilities and he used Tottenham Hotspur to put his vision into practice.

Sugar perceived non-football-related activities as a distraction. Substantial turnover came from matchday income, i.e. through the gates and in corporate hospitality. The real gamechanger however, was television rights. Tottenham had been one of the leading lights in the early negotiations to form the Premier League. Alan Sugar enthusiastically carried the torch for a television contract that represented the true worth of football. He pushed for the breakaway of the top division in English that led to the formation of the Premier League, which began in the 1992/93 season. That he was allowed to carry on as a prime mover for the contract for live football with Sky TV when his company Amstrad stood to make a fortune from the consequent sales of satellite dishes remains a serious question mark over the way the game is run. But never let it be said that Alan Sugar does not know a good deal when he sees one.

The development of the people's game was taking it further from the people, and at Spurs this meant the club of the suburbs, of the rising south, of Tottenham, was becoming a global commodity – albeit not as successfully as some of its rivals. Annelise Jespersen's comment about the fans becoming a small part of the plc was looking increasingly prescient. And it was this increasing sense of alienation that, in part, fuelled a new strand of support. Fans began to organise and develop their own voice on a wide scale for the first time, not just around travel but about all the things affecting them as fans. They wanted to challenge the view of fans as predominantly hooligans, and the efforts to marginalise traditional support. In doing so, they began to change a situation described by the author, academic and fan activist Rogan Taylor as "a period of football supporting without a history to its name". It's a great irony. The people who made the people's game did not really develop a voice until that game was being taken from them.

It's true that writing about the game was popular from the late 1930s onwards. Dedicated football magazines were enormously popular. Charles Buchan's *Football Monthly* was one of the best known. Started in 1951 by the eponymous England international turned journalist, it featured player-focussed articles accompanied by smiling Brylcreemed headshots of the stars on the training ground plus vivid action shots. At its peak in 1967 it sold 250,000 copies a month. Later, offerings like *Shoot!* were weeklies aimed at the same younger market in a format that was a hybrid of comic and tabloid.

The first publication that we would now call a fanzine was *Foul* magazine, that ran from 1972 to 1976, published by Cambridge graduates and featuring a mixture of humour and serious pieces about the state of football. But it was *When Saturday Comes* that changed the face of football writing in Britain. Its first issue in 1986 was forthright, funny and looked as if it had been put together with a typewriter and photocopier. Which was because it had. Author Mike Ticher only printed 100 copies because he had no idea how well it would be received. Following a positive review in *The Guardian*, the following month he printed 1,000 copies and the magazine is still going strong today. It inspired and empowered Spurs fans like Stuart Mutler, part of a generation of supporters frustrated that the game was covered in a way that distanced them from their experiences on the terraces.

"I remember reading in *Time Out* magazine, early 1987, about what would become the first well-known football fanzine, *When Saturday Comes*," he says. "I sent off for it, and straight away – from learning that people were setting up their own club-based zines – realised this was something I wanted to be a part of. The only literature that fans had was the club programme; two weeklies aimed at teenagers (*Match, Shoot!*); and the more-serious monthlies (*Football Monthly, Football Today, World Soccer*). If you have grown up only with the net, this may be hard for you to accept – but until *When Saturday Comes* there was absolutely nothing we fans had which reflected our issues, culture or humour. Nothing. It was seminal."

Mutler, by his own admission, came into football relatively late but often it is the converted who become true zealots. "While I was at primary school, pretty much all the boys had a team that they followed. This was the mid-to-late 1970s. So despite living in semi-rural Kent, the majority of my schoolmates supported Liverpool. I didn't have a team. I didn't like football. Dad's side of the family came from King's Cross and mostly followed Tottenham; my maternal grandparents had moved to Kingsbury from Gateshead, and were Newcastle supporters. Both sides of the family tried to get me to follow their respective clubs; plying me with a tracksuit, footballs and kickabouts down the local park. But neither Spurs nor Newcastle were successful back then. So I never really got it.

"Then in January 1981, my paternal grandfather said to me (perhaps realising we had the genesis of a decent team, and knowing that the year ended in a '1'): 'Watch Tottenham's cup run this year, I think they'll do something.' By the Saturday morning of the semi-final at Hillsborough, I was gripped. Of course after we won at Wembley in May following that now mythical replay, that was that: I was a Spurs supporter for life. I was 13."

Mutler became part of a fan culture whose vibrancy was never reflected in the media or in the negative image ascribed to football supporters at the time. It made him angry. "In the eyes of the government, police, the majority of the media and general public, football fans were nothing but hooligans. While violence was fairly commonplace in the mid-to-late-80s, it's unthinkable now – but death could happen in grounds too (think: Bradford, Heysel, Hillsborough). For this and more, all fans were to blame. We were vermin. Through the vast majority of people I was meeting, I knew this was not the case.

"I wanted to start a Tottenham fanzine to better reflect and give vent to this type of Spurs supporter, and to redress the balance. As I did not have the confidence to start one on my own, I wrote to *When Saturday Comes* and they published my appeal for a co-editor in late '87. I received a handful of letters. The person who I had the most in common with, and therefore thought it best to get the fanzine started with, was Matt Stone.

"While I was working in London, Matt was studying at Warwick. We wrote, phoned and met a few times. Back then there was no email or mobiles. The first issue appeared at the tail end of the 1987/88 season."

The Spur was published (pretty much) monthly during the season and was available either through subscription or on sale outside the ground, home and away. From the start, *The Spur* was professionally produced – it looked good and the content covered not only the team and the club but also terrace culture, both good and bad. Doug Cheeseman, who had worked on *When Saturday Comes* as a designer from its earliest days, worked alongside freelancer Ben Edgell to develop the ideas Mutler had for the look and feel of *The Spur*. Cheeseman continues to produce fine football publications as well as retain a hand in the production of WSC, which is still going strong. The beauty of it all was anyone could join in. Suddenly anything seemed possible – supporters had something to say and could do it themselves.

Matt Stone remembers the time well. "I had been going to Spurs since the turn of the 1980s and always felt that fans were badly served with information about the game. There was *The Big Match*, newspapers and the match programme, that was pretty much it after you gave up *Shoot!* Nothing interactive, the fans' views were patronised and ignored. In the mid-1980s I went to Division One games in the press box for a university newspaper. I was amazed how little the journalists knew about the players, how they had to ask who was that youngster, even who had just scored. In my experience all fans had a tactical understanding of their team and many had an encyclopaedic historical memory too.

"It became cheaper and easier to publish a fanzine or magazine and the fine example of *When Saturday Comes*, coupled with Sportspages bookshop in London, as an outlet meant an explosion in club fanzines. Spurs obviously had to have one and they had to have one with style. Stuart Mutler and I bonded over Chris Waddle and Smiths lyrics.

"We borrowed £400 off Rick Everitt of *Voice of the Valley*, the Charlton fanzine, and printed Issue No 1 with a mocked-up picture of Kenny Sansom on the cover. It sold out and we were on our way. Kind of. Issue No 2 was ready for the new 1988/89 season. Massive excitement at the Lane, we'd signed Gazza and Paul Stewart. But the first game was called off as the Shelf was declared too dangerous. We had a lot of unsold copies…

"The period 1988–91 was rocky for Spurs and football. Hillsborough changed football forever and Spurs nearly went out of business with £10m debts, loose change nowadays. But there was also the 1990 World Cup and a growing awareness that fans weren't animals. Hopefully fanzines helped push this sea change.

"Getting Gary Lineker to pose under a neon halo was amusing, we were responsible for the 'Gaz mask' phenomenon at the Lane and it was always a pleasure to see Spurs fans reading the magazine at half-time. Mostly though we met such great people who were only too happy to help, many I'm proud to be mates with. I like to think that Left on the Shelf and the Supporters' Trust grew out of the group of friends involved in the magazine. Good times."

The innovation, enthusiasm and spirit of enterprise amongst Spurs fans meant, as always, they had something to say and fanzine sellers around the ground became part of the pre-match atmosphere in the next 15 years. Jostling for attention alongside *The Spur* were *Off the Shelf*, *Follow the Tottenham*, *The Golden Cockerel* and *The Spurs Screws*, among others. Some were short-lived, others had more stamina. *CADD (Cock A Doodle Do)* was a glossy production during the mid-and-late 90s. *My Eyes Have Seen The Glory* (*MEHSTG*) began life as a printed fanzine in the early 90s. Run by a true Spurs enthusiast writing under the pseudonym Wyart Lane, it was the last print fanzine, struggling bravely on until its demise in 2007, finally forced under by the rising costs of print despite Wyart's resilience.

It remains very much alive online, espousing the spirit of the original fanzine ethos. Design and font endearingly untouched by contemporary design, it is a vast archive of Spurs fandom, still uploading a report for every match and still encouraging contributions from anyone who wants to write.

Fanzines were the *Private Eye* of football, a jokey front cover and inside an assortment of jokes, cartoons, history and comment about players and the team. The content of *MEHSTG* in November 2005 was characteristic: Supporting Spurs not slagging Arsenal, A Review of Hoddle's management style, John Duncan profile, Spurs songs, The Pleat/Hoddle Relationship, Ralph Coates, Spurs in Europe 1962, Shirt numbers through the years, Darren Anderton, young players misbehaving, What If …Arsenal Were Still Woolwich Arsenal and, not the most prescient of articles, Iain Duncan Smith – the Man to Lead Spurs Into a New Era. Player profiles and comment were always popular, there's a continuing obsession with our north London rivals and debate about how the club should be run. Nothing changes.

The fanzine spirit included football culture and politics as well as gags. "It was a step into the unknown," says Mutler. "Who knew where it could go? We would meet all sorts of people. We would sell a few thousand copies. We would publish pretty much anything! On the whole, though, the overwhelming majority of supporters ignored us.

"But it was invigorating (especially from a political point of view) covering the activities of Left on the Shelf, who had already formed, and, after that, TISA. I believed – still do – that the full potential of the supporters has never been realised. It was great to give space over to voices that, until then, had not been heard.

"Despite us knowing that most football fans were decent human beings, there was an element we did not agree with. So mostly through the early articles of Doug Cheeseman, we would publish pieces that were about racism and sexism, which we hoped would influence people for the better. It was especially exciting around the time of the World Cup in 1990 when there was a watershed moment for the nation. This was mostly down to the achievements of the England team, the more thoughtful style of coverage by the BBC, and the open display of emotion from Paul Gascoigne following his booking in the semi-final.

"Incredibly, overnight it seemed that football had turned a corner and become socially acceptable. For Spurs, for whom

Gascoigne and Lineker had shone, it looked like we may finally begin to achieve something. But like so many times before and since, it was a false dawn for the club and team. And it did not affect our sales for the better, either."

For many, particularly those in their twenties and thirties, fanzines became part of the experience of being a Spurs fan. Their critique articulated what these fans wanted from the game and from the club, and at the same time made them laugh. Supporter culture progressed beyond casual clothes and the occasional ruck. Nick Hornby's book *Fever Pitch* communicated what being a fan meant for him as he grew up, a ground-breaking expression of male emotions. Football enabled him to express himself, to feel a sense of belonging and a certainty of self. He articulated something meaningful that struck a chord with a generation. Talking about the feelings associated with football became legitimate. And despite his allegiances to the other side in north London, in the film his Arsenal-supporting dad is played by Neil Pearson, a season ticket holder on the Shelf.

Supporters had something to say, and said it in a way that was different from mainstream media. Fanzines reflected all elements of fan culture. They were funny and original, often rude and crude. Above all, they reflected a fan culture that was dynamic rather than passive and accepting, that supported their team with a passion but were not going to be told what to think. Behind the passion lies a restlessness and unease about how clubs treated supporters, some of which was to surface in later protests about the distance clubs and players have created between themselves and fans.

Sometimes fanzines had a real and lasting impact, as Stuart Mutler reflects, albeit at some personal cost: "The creative and social side were hugely enjoyable. But all the other crap (which was pretty much everything else) made it next-to-impossible. For six-plus years, I gave everything. In turn, it consumed everything. Within a very short period of time, that took its toll. It then became a question of how long I could fend things off before they finally caught up with me. Today, I describe the experience as 99% agony, 1% joy... a bit like following Tottenham.

"Personally, it meant a five-figure debt. Plus: for a few people, myself included, a handful of lifelong friends. While there is an awful lot I would do differently if I had that time again and if I had to do a fanzine again, for the friendships that were gained – and the experience – I don't regret it. Critically, I think it was a success. *FourFourTwo* said it was "king of the fanzines". Financially it was an unmitigated disaster.

"Amongst Spurs fans, I would like to believe it influenced some behaviour. I remember the very first match we sold at, away at Anfield, April 1988. There was a group of Tottenham fans that held up an inflatable gorilla and, thinking they were taunting the Liverpool fans, chanted John Barnes' name. Six years later when the magazine closed, and especially now, I don't think you would see that type of thing. I'd like to think we played a part in that."

Supporters now spoke for themselves. In 1995 *CADD* published an article by Ivan Cohen and Jacqui Cawley. Both were members of the Spurs List, a group that shared information, match reports and general Spurs chat via e-mail and a forerunner of social media sharing.

They also introduced readers to a new phenomenon. "For the uninitiated, the Internet remains a mystery, in much the same way as team selection by England managers... In addition to the [Spurs] List there is a graphic interface to the Internet known as the World Wide Web (www or web). The Spurs supporters' pages are run by Jacqui Cawley. Started in 1994, they are 'visited' several thousand times a month, not only by Spurs fans, and from all over the planet..."

Spurs' fan writing and debate migrated onto the net, starting in earnest in the early 1990s. Costs were low or non-existent and design was straightforward using pre-existing templates. All you needed was a computer and some ideas, you could reach Spurs supporters worldwide with a single click of a mouse.

Some sites were started in the mid-1990s by users of the Spurs List, most notably Bruce Lewis and Paul Smith, who founded the website *Spurs Odyssey* which is still going strong. *Spurs Odyssey* is an example of those early sites, a mixture of match reports, club information and a messageboard where fans could get together online, discuss all things Spurs, share a joke and abuse each other. Messageboards were the first online fan communities and remain popular despite the rise of Twitter and Facebook. Using modern technology, they replicate to a large extent the traditional patterns of support – feeling part of a fan community, chatting with fellow Spurs, the camaraderie, the humour. A place to celebrate and commiserate. In off-topic sections members discover what else they have in common with like-minded individuals. The board generates traditional fan discourse as people meet up socially face-to-face.

Messageboards began the infamous online phenomenon called ITK, short for 'in the know', where individuals share inside knowledge of transfers. Nothing in the online community causes more excitement and more anger than ITK. Information about players and comings and goings has always been a staple of pre- and post-match pub debate. One of the authors can recall being told for certain that Matt Le Tissier was joining Spurs and on another occasion a rumour circulating round the Paxton Road that Barry Ferguson was signing for Spurs from Rangers that very week. Neither happened.

ITK is the same thing writ large. Much of it is bogus. Some is culled from media rumours then swiftly appropriated by the author. Occasionally it is real. One member of a messageboard was a north London estate agent who happened to field an enquiry from Freddie Kanoute's wife – they are moving, could they put the house on the market? A few days later, Kanoute's surprise move to Seville was in the papers. Another poster was roundly derided late one night when he said Harry Redknapp was the new Spurs manager. It was announced the following morning.

ITK makes intelligent people totally credulous. Twitter posters who purport to be ITK have tens of thousands of followers without any proof whatsoever that their source is anything other than Google and their imagination. Being ITK brings status. It is profitable – for monetised sites the number of hits generates substantial advertising revenue. To demonstrate this, one blogger fabricated a rumour that Carlos Tevez, at the time on peak form in Italy, was signing for Spurs. He received over 20,000 hits in a matter of hours even though the rumour appeared nowhere else. Other sites began to run with it. It was still being discussed on one site days after he admitted he had made it up.

Yet ITK reflects the same fundamental desires that supporters have always had, to know about what goes on behind the scenes. Football clubs remain secret places, where only a few insiders know what is really going on inside the inner sanctum. In an age when players and fans are distant from each other, this desire just increases.

Blogging is hugely popular – the appetite for Spurs news and comment is insatiable. At the time of writing, there are around 30 active blogs, not including the sites that recycle news. Lumping them all under the same category is not strictly accurate. Many sites are close to traditional blogs, small in scale with one or two authors. Others are more commercial, with a stream of articles from several contributors and aggregating news stories. Some have been taken over by multi-national internet entrepreneurs and rebranded under a corporate banner. Some specialise in one aspect of Spurs, like young players or tactics.

New sites pop up all the time. Last year *The Spurs Report* appeared. The author may be fresh to blogging but his motivation is the same as every blogger or fanzine writer in the last 25 years: "I'd taken some time out of work and I needed something to fill the void. I found myself thinking about Spurs, and following them online and in the media, more intensely than I ever had done previously. I submitted articles and generally engaged in the discussion below the line, but I felt frustrated when things didn't get published or seen, so I started posting my thoughts up on my own site.

"The more I wrote, the more I felt I had to say about Spurs. Clearly, it was a time of extraordinary change within the club. From the outside, you could see the ship slowly being turned around, and for the first time in a long time, a manager in Mauricio Pochettino who was able to change the culture of the club…

"To start with, blogging is a little bit like talking to yourself -- hours spent writing things that, if you are lucky, a dozen people may see. But social media gives everyone a chance to get their writing seen, and slowly – a retweet here, an upvote there – the readership grows. I love writing, so there is a simple pleasure that I always take from producing work. But even more, I just love talking about Spurs. When I write things, the research and thought process is just a starting point to a conversation. I spend hours on Twitter or email – knowing that there is always someone else out there who will want to shoot the breeze about transfer targets, tactics, Spurs players we either rate or don't rate, finances, the football industry… There is no limit to the discussion about Spurs. Conversations move from one topic to the next seamlessly, and when you finally return to the starting point you've forgotten what it was and can go again. It is an infinite loop."

Readers come to blogs and fansites for a variety of reasons. Most want news, others discussion, others to read opinion pieces. Fans feel that someone who is a supporter as opposed to a journalist brings a perspective absent from mainstream football coverage. For many, reading blogs is part of their experience of being a fan, checking out what other fans are saying, joining in the debate or, in some cases, enhancing their understanding of the game.

Most Spurs sites are written by fans in their spare time who do so for the love of the club and they feel they have something to say. It's something they just want to do, but blogging leaves authors exposed. Supporters always want to know how their young players are progressing. Are they close to the first team, will they make it?

'Home-grown' has become an anachronistic concept given that Premier League clubs recruit their youth teams from all over the world but supporters continue to feel close to 'one of their own' if they come into first-team contention. Tottenham have a reputation among their fans for recruiting young men who at 16 are the next big thing but who at 21 play for Swindon reserves.

Some fans take this interest further than others. For many years Ray Lo has written detailed, unassuming youth-team reports for *Spurs Odyssey* and travels across Britain and Europe to watch the under-18s and the under-21s. Chris Miller and his site *windycoys.com* is known primarily for his interest in youth players. He shares information, including his own observations from watching matches. Not everyone appreciates his efforts. "I am just a supporter who likes to write, and I have opinions," he says. "I don't see myself as more knowledgeable than anyone else – in fact, quite the opposite. I have the world's worst memory, and so I actually see myself as less knowledgeable than a lot of Spurs fans!

"I have made a few enemies, it seems. There are a group of people who seem to really dislike me; my friends tell me it's because they're jealous, whereas I think the 'haters' (for want of a better phrase) would tell you it's because they feel I have set myself up as some sort of 'spokesperson' or knowledge centre for Spurs. I have had parody accounts set up, I've had some fairly abusive messages… I generally try to rise above a lot of the spite and nastiness but sometimes I will defend myself if people are being particularly nasty, or are saying something that's untrue."

Dear Mr Levy is a well-visited established Spurs blog. It's run by Spooky, who has opted to remain anonymous. He's received his share of plaudits and poison but remains sanguine about his online presence. He tends towards the view that blogging and social media reflect an existing spectrum of perceptions and responses including the anger, rather than create anything new: "Social media, especially Twitter, gives uncensored access to our raw emotions. Especially as many of us live commentate on games, meaning that little things appear far bigger and critical than they would be if you were at the game. There's simply no filter. It's words that can also be lost with ambiguous context and tone – as the person reading them will often misunderstand. It's a mess but it's good fun, most of the time.

"The same conversations in real life, in a pub or face to face anywhere would be a far more composed conversation (heated too) but you've got the person staring right back at you. Meaning you engage in the best possible way you can. The biggest issue with say Twitter and most blogs/forums is that people want to be right and sometimes refuse to accept when they're wrong because of the sheer investment in ego that plagues the internet. Blogs are great because, well, it's more introspective. They allow people to consume the content, think about it at a slower rate than fast-paced 140-character responses. Again, it says more about people's general mentality in life than it says for football."

It's addictive, for writers and readers alike. Spurs may be an ideal club to write about – there's history, glory and failure to consider. The constant churn of managers and cultures in recent times mean nothing is certain, it's all about opinion and there is currently no shortage in that respect. *The Spurs Report* again: "Is this a sensible, productive way to spend my time? Certainly not. I will never make any money or be able to do this in a professional way. These are hours that I could be spending acquiring new skills, getting fit or fixing the world. In fact, I am embarrassed by the amount of time I spend blogging about Spurs, to the extent that I have kept my hobby secret even from my family...

"I love the anonymity of the Internet – I write under a pseudonym, and live a sort of Spurs double life. Maybe it appeals to some inner identity crisis or previously untapped capacity for duplicity. I have regular conversations with equally anonymous people on Twitter, and none of us know who we are talking to. It is wonderfully egalitarian: all that matters is that we love talking about Spurs and find what the other person has to say interesting. We could be in the same room and be none the wiser. If this sounds mildly insane, it's because it is. There is nothing about football that is logical. Us fans aren't consumers, we are addicts. Spurs are a particularly powerful drug: the highs have been high, but we always crash back down in brutal fashion. And yet, we all keep coming back for more."

In the space of 25 years football supporters had developed a voice and written a history that had gone largely unnoticed and unrecorded for the 100 years preceding. At Spurs, as at other clubs, it developed in its own unique way – reflecting what was happening elsewhere but retaining a distinctive character. And with the development of that voice came the development of organisation – organisation of a type that increasingly challenged those who ran the club and demanded a more meaningful stake in the decision-making process.

9

Protest in the boardroom

JUST as Spurs fans, along with supporters of other clubs, were articulating their own experiences in order to create a people's history to challenge the narrative previously written for and about them, the whole experience of being a football fan was undergoing profound change. The fact that there were improvements to the traditional experience was acknowledged, but the sense that something valuable was also being lost caused frustration, anger and regret in equal measure. And so the mood moved from articulating experience to trying to influence it.

It's important not to overestimate the impact of organised supporter movements, especially at the more established clubs. As Stuart Mutler said of the fanzines, most fans steadfastly ignored what was going on. But the new breed of organised supporters often punched above their weight, and by steadfastly refusing to accept they should just pay up and shut up, they began to build influence.

Football clubs exist to, obviously, play football and provide entertainment for their supporters. For the new generation owners of clubs there was another dimension – generating a return on investment. Spurs chairman Alan Sugar approached the club with a hard business head, something that he argues with some justification saved the club. And so he grew increasingly impatient with supporters who grumbled and protested. His attitude seemed to be that finishing in the top half of the table was perfectly acceptable. Supporters were suggesting that not only should we aspire to something more but also that Sugar had no apparent idea of how to improve matters.

It was in the doldrums of the 1990s and early noughties that the identity of the modern Spurs fan was formed. Supporters felt increasingly disillusioned, their loyalty pressured from all sides. Their own club afforded little protection. Supporters knew that the club was at best indifferent to them, at worst uncaring.

More than that, the experience of terrace life, of being supporters, had changed beyond recognition. The simple idea of meeting friends and family, having a drink and watching the game became surprisingly and unnecessarily hard. This culture offered many things – friendship, a sense of belonging, fun, a social life. It was also a counter-balance to what was happening with the club or the team. The club may treat supporters badly, the team may not have been doing well but the terraces were ours. We created the atmosphere, sang what we wanted, stood where we wanted, misbehaved, laughed, swore, drank too much but we got behind the team and it was ours. All gone. Supporters began to feel the loss keenly. "At least you had Ricky Villa dad. What have I got to look back on?" said season ticket holder Tom Fisher, 28.

This took place in a context of a conspicuous lack of success on the field. An entire generation of Spurs fans grew up deprived of the nourishment of trophies. As Spurs went through yet another season of rebuilding, older generations could at least wallow in nostalgia.

To make matters worse, this mediocrity stood in stark contrast to the achievements of Spurs' two greatest rivals, Arsenal and Chelsea. For supporters, however intense the rivalry on the pitch it pales into insignificance compared with rivalry in the playground and workplace. Television coverage means access to every side in England. It has become legitimate to follow teams from anywhere in the country. With such a wide variety of options, why choose Spurs?

In the resulting struggle, a distinct identity for the modern era has emerged. Spurs fans want to mark themselves as different and placed greater value on heritage and continuity rather than on-field success to sustain it. It's a culture and identity built to last.

Foremost, the club has always inspired profound devotion and continues to do so. There are official branches of the Supporters' Club in all corners of the British Isles and, more recently, worldwide. The Spurs tradition of going away continues also with away trips in Britain and Europe generating the best atmosphere.

Also, supporters are conscious of their heritage not as dormant nostalgia but as a guide to how they should show their support, which is not defined in terms of league position. The Spurs Way has become an inextricable part of identity. Flowing, attacking football is no mere wistful longing for better times or for that matter a stick to beat the current team, it is an aspiration that defines the Spurs fan. It is not success at any price, rather success by playing the right way.

Tottenham have never played a home match further than 600 yards from the current pitch. It represents a powerful unifying strand of continuity in an ever-changing world. The venerable old ground may be creaking a bit. Certainly it is small, old-fashioned almost, compared with the Emirates, Old Trafford and Stamford Bridge. That difference has become a virtue. Many drifted away, never to return. However, diminished though their experience is compared with the glory days of the Shelf, a new generation were brought up knowing the atmosphere an old-style football ground could create. The steepling stands tight to the pitch and enclosed by a wrap-around roof retained the essence of White Hart Lane. Any noise stayed where it was, amplified by the roof and echoing around the stands.

You can't see out. For 90 minutes, the Lane is your world, there's nothing else. Under lights, the effect is inspiring. Supporters are close to the players and even the fans in the back row have a decent view. Fans feel connected, to each other and to the action. The Lane is not a venue for a leisure activity. There are no distractions. You are part of the entertainment.

If there's any doubt, take the word of Arsenal fan journalist John Cross: "A north London derby at White Hart Lane is definitely my favourite London derby because Tottenham's home ground is tight, full of atmosphere on a night match and it's really fired up for the visit of Arsenal." Or Samir Nasri, an Arsenal player, when he said, "I probably shouldn't say this, but the atmosphere at White Hart Lane is very, very good."

Writing in 2007 Bolton fan Neil Bonnar praised White Hart Lane: "It's not the biggest ground in the Premiership, but it's by far the best stage. It's got a lot to do with the fact that it is one of the oldest, and, while it has been modernised, it has never lost its traditional feel. Spurs say they have to move to a bigger ground to accommodate their many fans who cannot be a part of their guaranteed capacity crowds. If they do, they'll lose more than they'll gain. Gone will be the unrelenting buzz and hair-raising atmosphere whipped up in an instant, and instead will be the hollow feel of every new ground. Watching a game at White Hart Lane is like taking a step back in time in a good way."

Another element of the Spurs identity had also been formed in adversity. Spurs fans embraced the idea of being 'Yids' as a term of belonging, turning the abuse from rival fans back at them. In use since the 1970s, the Y word was used more commonly into the start of the 21st century by the younger generation because it was another sign of a distinct identity that resisted the insults of rival supporters. These Spurs fans were Yids and proud.

Finally, years of failure led to a healthy fatalism. Something was bound to go wrong. The euphemistic so-called 'transitional season' became a term of derision to describe the lack of progress.

The reality is more prosaic. Chronic mismanagement off the pitch and inconsistency on it created those false dawns. Supporters reacted with pessimism and gloom knowing that as soon as expectations rose it would be the moment they were to be dashed. Latterly the term 'spursy' was coined to describe this process. First used by fans, it has become used so frequently that in 2016 it won a place in the *Oxford English Dictionary*, meaning 'to constantly fail to live up to expectations'.

It was amidst this sense of drift, of loss of identity and increasing disillusionment with the game, that Sugar finally sold up in 2001 to the English National Investment Company (ENIC), admittedly a company with strong personal links to Spurs in that the main financier Joe Lewis and chairman Daniel Levy were lifelong supporters. But its business plan was to acquire a portfolio of European clubs where value could be added to the original investment before being sold on. Sugar is reported to have made around £25m personal profit although he maintains taking over the club was the biggest mistake he ever made. That's a £25m mistake most wouldn't mind making.

If the goal of a football club is to generate wealth for its owners, then profit must be maximised. One effect of this process was to alter the relationship between the club and its supporters. As income from television, sponsorship and merchandising increased, so the income from the gate became less important. Supporters the length and breadth of the country would justify their right to witness a better performance by shouting 'we pay your wages'. Not any more they didn't, but Spurs fans have never sat on their hands and kept quiet, and they did not let the club have it all their own way.

What Sugar failed to grasp was that fans wanted some idea that the people running the club knew what they were doing in terms of their key role, picking the right manager and buying the right players. Sugar thought it would appease the fans if he bought a few star names and appeared aloof and bewildered at the complaints. Fans suspected that as well as lacking the knowledge to put together a winning football team; he did not want to overly invest in the transfer market because it did not make economic sense. In other words, the interests of Tottenham Hotspur plc would not be best served by spending too much money with no guarantee of success on the field. The Champions League was not the cash cow that it is today and Sugar, so the fans believed, thought he was better off sitting safe in mid-table with the chance of a cup run.

But loyal Spurs fans continued to fill the seats week in, week out. Sugar applied market principles, exploiting the fact that fan loyalty distorts market relations – the product can deteriorate in quality and become more expensive yet demand stays constant.

An all-seater stadium led to changes more far-reaching than any hooliganism or politician could ever have achieved. The vast majority of tickets were bought in advance. There were 22,000 season ticket holders, then membership was now required to gain priority over the 14,000 or so that remained. For big games these would sell out within hours. Access to tickets was therefore restricted. You needed a bank account and usually some form of credit, plus for big games the time to call the club or, later, time to sit in front of a computer screen waiting for hours for your turn to come around.

Spontaneity disappeared. Plans had to be made at least four weeks in advance, or in the case of season ticket holders, nine months ahead in order to justify the spiralling expense. Later, when dates were moved because of the over-riding demands of Sky Television, organisational and planning skills became almost as important as having cash to pay for the tickets in the first place. Seats meant the pleasure of sitting with friends and family was restricted. Should the Bloke Behind You be a loud-mouthed idiot, you were trapped. If you had a season ticket, you were in for a long season.

A supporter culture that had existed since the club first played on the marshes was gone. Football, the most social of interactions, became anti-social because friends and family were excluded.

Being a Spurs supporter would never be the same. This was not immediately apparent at the time, although supporters bemoaned the biggest change, the comparative lack of atmosphere now the Shelf was no more. Prices excluded an increasing number of working-class fans, football's traditional bedrock, for whom the cost became an intolerable burden. Gradually local people were priced out too. The local area is one of the most deprived wards in London and yet, as David Goldblatt observes in *The Game of Our Lives*, by 2007 30% of Spurs fans earned over £50,000.

In the face of change, Spurs fans refused to roll over. The Tottenham Independent Supporters' Association was one of the first supporters' groups to challenge clubs when they did not have the interests of the fans in the forefront of their planning. Building on the experience of Left on the Shelf and with many of the same figures involved, they realised that public protest outside and inside the ground was vital but it was also imperative to establish a profile in the media. TISA was the forerunner of modern protest because it opened a third front – protest in the boardroom or as close as it was possible to reach. Boots on the ground or trainers on the pitch went only so far – TISA brought sophisticated financial and business acumen to bear. Small shareholders may not have much influence but they were entitled to see the books and ask questions in public at the Annual General Meeting.

One of TISA's aims was to collect as many small shareholder votes together as possible in the form of a single block – just as Irving Scholar had done when building his takeover, an irony not lost on many involved. TISA hoped to represent as much as 20% of the total shareholdings. Anyone who has ever been to an AGM knows most business is nodded through before a swift adjournment to the finger buffet and a glass of warm, cheap wine. If this was the club board's hope for the 1991 AGM it was to be sorely disappointed.

According to journalist Chris Horrie's entertaining account, 700 supporters turned up at the Annual General Meeting in 1991, much to the bemusement of an uncomprehending board. TISA banners caught the eye of supporters and the media: "£22m Debt – It's Hummel –iating"; "Where's the money gone?"; "Board Out!" One banner displayed photos of Paul Gascoigne and Scholar, with the words: "Should Tottenham dispose of its assets or its liabilities?'"

Horrie describes a chaotic scene: "Inside the room there was a mood of supressed hysteria as fans wearing scarves and supporter gear crushed up against pinstriped investment brokers. So many people turned up that the meeting started 20 minutes late, after Nat Solomon [plc chairman] imposed some order on events. He was joined on the platform by Terry Venables and what seemed to the fans to be a huge number of anonymous Men in Suits who nervously shuffled their papers."

As the meeting got going, fans challenged statement after statement. The board's claim that they had maintained secrecy over their plans *because* they had the fans' interests at heart was roundly condemned from the floor.

The reaction to the rumoured sale of Paul Gascoigne illustrated a fundamental gulf between the perception of football directors and that of football supporters. Solomon confirmed the rumours were true. The board did not want to sell but "if someone came in we would obviously have to think about it". The language was measured, devoid of emotion. The logic and language of business up against the passion of fans. If this were intended to mollify supporters, it failed. Uproar ensued.

TISA then took the initiative through Steve Davies, a lawyer who was active in national supporters' movements too. He had prepared a list of 20 separate questions, all related to finance and company procedure. What was the total amount of debt? Were the subsidiary companies making money? Another TISA member asked why under the board re-election item no provision had been made for the resignation of directors – nobody was apparently taking responsibility for this mess.

Those present voted against the re-appointment of the two directors standing for re-election but the majority of proxy votes from board cronies carried the day. The meeting ended with a standing ovation for one man who sat stoically silent throughout proceedings. Bill Nicholson represented everything the fans wanted but were not getting.

This episode was an early illustration of the limits to supporter-led change in the modern game. The club is a business and the board has the ultimate power to take decisions. It is accountable to shareholders. In theory, small shareholders can band together, in practice this is virtually impossible to achieve to any extent that challenges the board, as TISA found out. The small shareholders bought shares for romantic reasons, not to make money or to be active participants.

Supporters have the power of not handing over their hard-earned cash if they disagree with the club's actions. The fact is, supporters want to support. Football is recreation, relief from the daily grind, a chance to meet old friends. They don't want to not go, and Spurs like other clubs take this loyalty into account when responding to objections.

Nevertheless, these limits and boundaries did not silence supporter protest at Spurs. Far from it: after this episode, the Tottenham Hotspur plc board would never again have things all their own way. The voice of supporters raised in protest would always be heard. TISA's intervention became the blueprint for fan protest in this country. It mobilised both fan support and the skills of fans who knew the legal and business world as well as any board member. And it provided the media with a succession of newsworthy stories.

TISA asked awkward questions and demanded the board be accountable as the Scholar regime crumbled and the club stumbled through financial crises of its own making. As Scholar prepared to sell, TISA demanded assurances about the terms of the sale and the identity and ambition of any new owner. It had absolutely no power or right to do any of this. Not in legal terms anyway. But it claimed its right to question and to hold to account from the fact that it represented supporters, the people whose passion the club was built on and whose loyalty and devotion had shaped it. That gave it heft with fans and the media, because they could see a very simple tale of heroes and villains.

"TISA was one of the first to take on a major issue, get national publicity and become a major influencer of the issues it sought to address, something we say a lot of clubs' fans emulate," says Steve Davies. "So it is something I think we should be proud of." Annelise Jespersen agrees, saying: "I think TISA did incredibly well to mobilise so much support and to be so credible in the media, especially at a time when there were no real alternative outlets to the mainstream media."

With Scholar prepared to sell up, TISA strongly favoured a bid from a consortium fronted by manager Terry Venables and support was mobilised through *The Spur*, the main Tottenham fanzine, and contacts in the press.

During one game fans held up three-foot-high boards with letters spelling SCHOLAR OUT and VENABLES IN. Applause rippled around the ground each time – although as always there were differing views. One of the authors, holding the letter L aloft in the Paxton Road stand, was told to "Take the fucking thing down or I'll shove it up your arse" by one fan. The L stayed up. Leaflets had circulated pre-match urging supporters to remain behind in peaceful protest after the final whistle. Venables emerged to acknowledge the crowd and the event generated considerable publicity. Spurs ownership was a big back-page story.

The club made little or no effort to silence the protestors. Stewards must have waved the placards through – you couldn't have sneaked those in under a coat – while the police officer in charge, Chief Inspector Barry Keenan, was a sympathiser, telling TISA that he had wanted to buy his daughter a season ticket but after the price rises could not now afford it.

In 1993 TISA organised another fan protest involving Terry Venables, this time against Alan Sugar's decision to sack his manager, who the chairman increasingly saw as a threat. In an enterprising move, they circumvented the restrictions around protest at White Hart Lane by protesting at a testimonial match at nearby non-league Enfield. Fans protested before the kick-off and took to the pitch at half-time with 'Sugar Out' posters. TISA's Bernie Kingsley spoke to *The Independent* about the season ticket boycott that was being called in response to the move to oust Venables. "The language Mr Sugar seems to understand is money and this is worth about £4m to him," said Kingsley. "The fact that no one has said why this decision has been made is the most astonishing and disgusting thing about it. We think Mr Sugar has a duty to tell the shareholders of the company and the thousands of Spurs supporters."

The Independent found fans in bitter mood. David Cawdron, a supporter for 25 years, said: "There will be a hell of a reaction from Tottenham supporters. I don't see many season tickets being bought again until Terry is reinstated." Reporter Mike Rowbottom interviewed a militant Lee Moore, aged 20. He made the decision not to renew his season ticket as soon as he heard the news. "I went straight to the ground. There were about 400 other supporters there, and there was a feeling of disbelief. There were a few shouts for Venables and a few shouts for Sugar that were not nice. I won't be buying another season ticket as things stand. You can't support a club that is going to get rid of its best people. I mean, I still support them. They become part of your life. But whether I'll turn up to watch them, I don't know."

Sugar did not grasp the extent of supporters' concerns nor did he care. It is impossible to know just how many did not renew, but the proposed boycott, loudly endorsed at a packed meeting called by TISA in Tottenham Sports Centre and addressed by the great Bill Nicholson himself, who spoke in favour of retaining Venables, crumbled in the face of Sugar's intransigence and what many supporters see as the thing that defines them as supporters – the need to go and see your team regularly.

TISA remained active for the next decade, but the limits of what it could achieve had been exposed. An intransigent chairman saw no role for fans in the running of a club. To hit the club financially, fans had to stop, as they saw it, being fans. And as the court battle between Venables and Sugar revealed more details of how the club had been run, many began to question whether the fan groups had backed the right horse in any case. There's no doubt the overwhelming mood of the fans originally was to back Venables as the football man.

But, many began to ask, what did fans really know about boardrooms? TISA may have asked the right questions, but did it come up with the right answers?

The fact is that asking the right questions was in itself an achievement. Often when the achievements of fan groups are derided, the critics forget how low the bar was set. Merely by asserting the right to ask, to challenge, fan groups such as TISA embedded the idea that fans were not just there as a backdrop or a cash cow. They were part of the club itself, an assertion that took the club back to its roots and those first meetings under the lamppost on the High Road.

TISA refused to go away, and Sugar refused to have much to do with them. Fan organisation withered. There were sporadic attempts by new groups to restart the fire. Some were sparked by the latest mini-crisis or setback as the club entered an extended period of drift, at other times the fact that Spurs seemed to feature among its support an unusually high number of people who were convinced that they and only they could run the club better than anyone else threw up yet another splinter group.

But this in itself showed fans bought into the idea of fan involvement in clubs they still saw as theirs. And as we've observed in this book, Spurs fans have never been slow to voice their opinions or to assert their sense of ownership. What was at times little more than sheer bloody-mindedness was having an effect. Whether it was Spurs fans questioning the board of a leading club, albeit one becalmed, or the fans at more modest Northampton Town not only rescuing their club from financial ruin but also taking it over and running it, the idea of more formal supporter involvement was gaining traction in political circles.

The election of a Labour government in 1997 led to the setting up of a Football Taskforce, and that Taskforce produced a report called Investing in the Community that led to the establishment of the Supporters' Trust movement and of Supporters Direct, a national body funded and backed to promote the idea of Trusts. The report said: "Supporters have shown they have an important role to play in maintaining a strong relationship between clubs and the community. Fans' organisations are being asked to play an increasing consultative role and financial support should be available to them."

It was a sea change in the way fan organisations were viewed. Supporters Direct began its work in 2000, and in 2001 the Tottenham Hotspur Supporters' Trust was formed. That came about after long and at times heated negotiations between various protest groups, fanzines, websites and individuals, and a number of the individuals who were involved in previous organisations. A Trust, backed by a national initiative such as Supporters Direct, seemed to have a chance to be an organisation of a new type at Spurs, but it needed to be a unified voice for fans. Agreement was eventually reached and the existing organisations agreed to back a new Supporters' Trust, with TISA donating its substantial remaining funds to the new organisation before formerly disbanding.

The Trust was formed as new owners ENIC arrived on the scene, and there seemed to be a thawing of relations between the club and its organised fans. ENIC agreed to meet with the new Trust. But that started a whole new set of problems.

The terms of reference for the new relationship were vague. The idea of a Trust was a classic example of Blairite Third Way politics, but like much Blairism the substance and detail seemed to be lacking once the surface shine had been scratched. At Spurs, the Trust's decision not to begin building a shareholding in the club to give it a real stake at board level was to prove misguided, ceding the last chance of fans gaining any real power at boardroom level because of the financial changes that were about to happen. On top of that, for the best of reasons, the focus was on building a working relationship at board level arguably at the expense of nurturing a link with the grass roots. It was more technocratic than democratic, and the club seemed to play the situation cleverly – allowing the Trust recognition but conceding very little information. Prices rose steeply, the issue that was most obvious to most fans; ENIC consolidated control and shunned any public discussion or examination of its affairs, even delaying the publication of heavily edited accounts of its meetings with the Trust for so long they became irrelevant. All of this, despite the best efforts of a good number of people over a good number of years, led to a waning of confidence in an organisation that seemed to be a good idea, but ineffective and too close to the club's board in practice.

Then, in October 2008, Tottenham chairman Daniel Levy formally announced plans to build a new stadium on land immediately to the north of White Hart Lane. It was to be the centrepiece of an ambitious urban regeneration scheme called the Northumberland Development Project that included social and private housing, leisure and educational facilities for the community and improved travel links. Plans for a new ground had been in the air for more than a decade but expanding White Hart Lane had effectively been ruled out because the ground was so cramped by surrounding housing and a school bordering Worcester Avenue to the east. A design to extend the East Stand by building over the road proved to be impractical, while proposals to move to a new site in Pickett's Lock, several miles to the north, had long since faded from view.

Most supporters accepted with a tinge of regret that change was inevitable. The Premier League saw an unprecedented concentration of wealth, and wealth meant success. By the end of the noughties, the Premier League imperceptibly split into a series of leagues within a league with the wealthiest clubs rising to the top and staying there. Chelsea and later Manchester City created that elite through a change in ownership with foreign owners with bottomless pockets.

Manchester United and Liverpool attracted another class of investor, foreign owners who sought profit as well as trophies.

Spurs were in a small trailing group of hopefuls, hovering between fifth and seventh with two fourth place finishes. For a club of their size, they punched above their weight, although many supporters complained at a perceived lack of investment in players. Spurs regularly pitched up around 14th or 15th in a league table of European clubs ranked by income, an achievement of a kind given that White Hart Lane has the smallest capacity of any in the top 20, and relative lack of success. In comparison, Arsenal allegedly earned £1m more than Tottenham *per home match*. To compete, Spurs ticket prices were among the highest in the country, with only the 2008 League Cup to show for it. The table of club wages mirrored the league table almost exactly and Spurs had to generate more income over an extended period or risk falling behind.

In the past Spurs have been innovators. With the new ground, they benefitted from lagging behind. They learned what worked and what didn't from the experiences of other clubs who had already developed their grounds. The night before Levy's announcement, Spurs came from 4-1 down at the Emirates to draw 4-4 in injury time. The delirium in the away section contrasted with the sedate atmosphere in the antiseptic curves of the Arsenal ground. The Gunners had improbably found a site in London a few hundred yards from Highbury to build a 60,000-capacity bowl that looked beautiful but which distanced fans from the action as well as demolishing the redoubtable North Bank, thus detracting from the atmosphere.

Unbeknownst to fans, Tottenham Hotspur had a long-term strategy to buy land and property around White Hart Lane, just as it did when constructing the East Stand in the early 1930s. This time it focussed on the former factory on the High Road that was now a trading estate for small businesses. Spurs could stay local.

Levy talked enthusiastically about making the new ground a special place for supporters and appeared to have put the board's money where his mouth was. The stands were close to the pitch and rose high rather than leaning back, as if recoiling from the action, while the tidemark of corporate boxes around the ubiquitous stadium bowl was broken by a 17,000-capacity single tier 'end', the largest of its kind in Europe. Thus the demands of City finance could be met without detracting from the interests of supporters. All this a goal kick away from where the schoolboys gathered in 1882. Trumpeted as the largest private sector stadium build in Europe, it was an ambitious and brave balancing act.

Broadly the development was welcomed both locally and by supporters. It seemed a good fit, balancing the needs of the football club with those of the community. The Northumberland ward where the club is situated is among the five per cent most deprived wards in England, while in Tottenham as a whole 80.3 per cent of children live in low-income homes. The community approach also allowed the club to access pools of funding earmarked for development in London.

Local dignitaries gushed their appreciation. George Meehan, leader of Haringey Council, praised the economic benefits of Spurs remaining in the community, adding: "But more than anything, Spurs have played an integral role in giving a sense of identity to the area it calls home. Tottenham would not be Tottenham without its football club." Tottenham MP David Lammy did not hold back either. "The club is a fundamental part of the lifeblood of the community and its continued presence and vision will inspire new generations of young people well into this century."

The mood was infectious. Daniel Levy was moved to express his delight at being able to put forward "a viable option which we know to be the fans' favourite – remaining at the club's spiritual home." Planning permission was not granted until the end of September 2010, two years almost to the day. It was frustrating but no surprise. These things take time. The news that emerged the following day therefore came as even more of a shock. Tottenham Hotspur announced their intention to bid for the Olympic Stadium site in Stratford, east London, after the 2012 Games.

205

This bolt from the blue took a few days and some inflammatory comments from rival bidders West Ham (chairman David Sullivan: "If it happens, there will be real problems that could easily lead to civil unrest. I think there could be riots") before the full implications sunk in.

Although the papers cranked up the story, most supporters greeted it either with disbelief or accepted that Spurs were merely covering themselves in case of a last-minute slip-up with the Tottenham planning process. 'Expression of interest' isn't saying very much. Then, the management of our 'partners', American company AEG, were bullishly quoted in the press. *The Guardian* was unequivocal, in the headline at least: 'Olympic Stadium Now First Choice for Tottenham'.

Shrouded in secrecy and rumour, Spurs' plans gradually seeped into the public domain. It became abundantly clear that the club had invested heavily in designs and preparation. This was no back-up plan, this was deadly serious. Amongst supporters, astonishment turned to outrage. It was the most momentous decision in the history of the club, yet the fans were the last to know. In stark contrast, during the Northumberland Development Project preparation, the club had been falling over themselves to involve fans because they needed support in the planning process. Fans were encouraged to contact Haringey Council. Local people and businesses were roped in, plus an online consultation exercise.

The Olympic site is in Stratford, east London, about five miles from Tottenham as the crow flies. Football in London weaves a complex web of allegiances that combine geography, family links and patterns of success. What everyone would agree on is that Stratford is West Ham territory, with due respect to Leyton Orient who lie in between.

Tottenham planned to knock down the Olympic Stadium itself and build from scratch. The Games were intended to provide London with a legacy, although demolishing the stadium was probably not what the public had in mind. Estimates suggested the cost could be less than half the price of staying in Tottenham and without the hassles of planning permission. The site was spacious with plenty of amenities in the nearby shopping centre and, crucially, getting there was relatively straightforward, ten minutes by Tube or Javelin train from central London.

The battle to remain in Tottenham was on and the campaign it spawned appealed directly to the club's history. Significantly this wasn't about self-interest. Growing concerns about exorbitant ticket prices and the perceived lack of investment in the team provoked frustration whenever Spurs fans started talking to each other but did not lead to concerted protest against the board. Modern football supporters are characterised as being consumed by egocentricity and inflated expectations, yet at Spurs only this threat to the club's heritage and identity could create sufficient anger to ignite open conflict.

The supporters' campaign against the move to Stratford was started by Darren Alexander, a lifelong fan who sadly died in 2014. He was a board member of the Tottenham Hotspur Supporters' Trust, the long-established link between fans and club. He tried and failed to persuade the Trust to take a position on Stratford, but the Trust – illustrating the situation into which it had allowed itself to fall – decided it could not take a stance because some fans opposed the move while others supported it. Alexander resigned to set up a protest group called We Are N17, this being the White Hart Lane postcode.

Season ticket holder Katrina Law recalled her reason for morally supporting the campaign: "Stratford was the easiest, cheapest and quickest option but didn't take into account the emotion and how you feel about Tottenham and you can't do that, you can't strip it out into an economic argument. Football isn't rational. Football isn't like that. So for me it was just sacrilege. I don't buy the cold-headed businessman's argument. There is no Tottenham Hotspur without Tottenham."

A conflict over where a football club should play is in fact about the supporters, their profound emotional attachment to their team and the meaning they ascribe to that loyalty, a meaning that goes far beyond the balance sheet or trophy room. This was fundamentally about identity, a commonly-held understanding that being a Tottenham Hotspur fan meant something, something deeper than the pursuit of trophies and profit. Every single Spurs home match had been played no further than 600 yards from the corner where the club was formed in 1882. The club had always been buoyed by loyal support both home and away. Those supporters wanted Spurs to do it the right way, to play good football and look after the fans and not to jeopardise those aims in rash pursuit of fame or victory through any other means. The Hotspur were inseparable from Tottenham.

From the outset this was to be a very modern campaign. Kat Law adds: "Darren pulled together a small group of people with the right attitude and skill set to make an impact – a seasoned campaigner and lobbyist, a strategist, a website builder, a graphic designer, those with political contacts and nous. They came up with a visual identity for the campaign, built a website and got the message out there. Around White Hart Lane before matches there was a petition, they organised a march…

"The *Evening Standard* gave it a lot of coverage, and BBC local news," says Law. "I recall Darren saying how there was some debate about whether We Are N17 should contact the club directly. Darren was resolute that they push on with the campaign and that Spurs would be in touch sooner rather than later. And he was right. Sure enough they were summoned to a meeting opened up by Daniel Levy asking Darren why he was trying to kill the club. Fair to say this was a tense meeting!"

In many ways the campaign defied logic. The number of supporters who attend White Hart Lane regularly and live in N17 is virtually nil. Frankly, most supporters do not *want* to live there. Also, We Are N17 were not a bunch of luddites wallowing in a quicksand of nostalgia. They and their supporters recognised that competition in the modern world required increased revenue – Spurs needed to expand.

For many supporters, and certainly the We Are N17 group, success was not something to be achieved at any price. Moving to Stratford stripped away what made Spurs unique. The memories could never be erased but it felt as if the Hotspur was to become a franchise, to be bought, sold and moved around in pursuit of profit. There's nothing wrong with profit but not as the primary goal of a football club with Tottenham's proud history.

The importance of White Hart Lane as the focus uniting the fanbase in Britain and abroad cannot be over-estimated. The passion remains the same but the nature of support changes over time, and changes have never been more rapid and far-reaching than in the years since the Premier League was formed. One constant has been the Lane itself. Supporters live all over London, the south-east and further afield, in Britain and worldwide. Television has made games more accessible than ever before and with the money has come astronomical wealth. But the Lane represents what we have in common. More than a matchday focus, it brings a sense of place, of feeling at home, of belonging. It embodies a refreshing consistency and continuity in a fast-changing world over which supporters have little control and where fans feel increasingly distanced and alienated from the game they love. Never has this sense of place been a more cogent symbol and signifier of support. The Lane is ours and we are the Lane. It was worth fighting for.

Not every supporter felt the same way, however. The debate around 'should we stay or should we go?' revealed divisions in the fanbase about how to define the best interests of the club and supporter. Accusations flew both ways as groups struggled for the moral and tactical high ground of being the 'real' fans.

Those in favour started with the balance sheet. Increased revenue from the stadium without accruing huge debts from construction costs meant money to invest in the team and to compete with the best in England and Europe, or to use the phrase with popular currency, 'move to the next level'. This was the best way of securing the future of the club as a major force in English football, a vision that recognises the primacy of finance and income in an increasingly wealth-driven football environment.

Also, runs the argument, we should not be ashamed of better facilities and getting to and from White Hart Lane is a trek and a half. Anyway, Spurs fans don't live in Tottenham and actively avoid it if the football's not on. Finally, the proud heritage of the one and only Hotspur was strong enough to withstand a short hop across London.

More than a battle between heart and head, the battle around Spurs' new stadium exemplified a conflict between modern football and a concept of the club that goes deeper than money or success and recognises the powerful hold the club has on supporters throughout the world. Football was changing and so was the way in which fans followed their club, and not every supporter saw things the same way.

But events have a habit of producing the most unexpected consequences. That the campaign for Spurs to stay in Tottenham gained so much support was one – something that showed that more traditional values of place and identity had not been swept aside by the commercial tide. But the battle over Stratford also gave supporter organisation a shot in the arm and arguably forced the club to concede it had to work in a more genuinely collegiate way with its fans. Spurs would eventually lose out on Stratford when the stadium was awarded to West Ham. How much the fan campaign contributed to that will be argued about for a long time, but what the campaign did succeed in doing was reinvigorating the idea that supporters could have influence at the highest level.

When the battle over Stratford was won, We Are N17 had no reason to exist. But the energy it had generated remained, and fans had been reminded that their active involvement was necessary to preserve their sense of their club. As the dust settled, some fans began to look ahead. Was a new organisation needed? Or could the machinery already there be revived? It was a discussion Alexander had with Law, who he knew from matchdays at White Hart Lane.

"The old trust had lost control of membership data," says Law. "There was no new blood, three of the five-person board had to step down because of the 12-year rule. It would have been sad to see it go. Darren wanted to give it a last shot at breathing some life into it, so he got in touch with We Are N17 reps Tracey Mottram, Ellie Kershaw, Graham Wilkinson, Scott Hammerton and me to float his ideas for resurrecting the Trust. It was about putting a skill set together, not just being a Tottenham fan. We stood for election at the AGM and joined the remaining two members of the old Trust board in February 2013.

"The easy option would have been to set up an Independent Supporters' Association with no legacy issues, no history and credibility issues," says Law. "We thought the right thing to do was to try and revive the Trust because it is a formal democratic organisation that was already recognised by the club.

"Trusts are recognised as the structure to drive dialogue between supporters and clubs, the fact that the club had bought into this offered the chance of face-to-face dialogue. I bought into the democratic element of it as well. Anyone can join, anyone can stand for election. If you didn't like what we're doing, stand and change it. ISA don't have that democratic accountability."

Discussions did not always go smoothly, but enough of the old board recognised a new approach was needed. There were some partings of the way, while others stepped sideways to be more involved with the Tottenham Tribute Trust, another fan organisation set up to work with the club to help raise money for former players in difficulty. "With the old Trust, I think it's fair to say they didn't push things as far as they could," says Law. "It wasn't particularly active in terms of lobbying."

THST was revamped, the membership reconnected with, and a proper branding and communication strategy put into place, helping the organisation raise its profile with fans. A more outward-looking stance was adopted as the Trust contacted national fan organisations Supporters Direct and the Football Supporters'

Federation and other club Trusts to work together on campaigns around ticket pricing and the policing of fans. As well as dealing with the club board, THST also aimed to deal with fans at a grass roots level, handling significant amounts of casework around issues such as ticketing and legal problems.

"The challenge is to retain our independence and it's a tightrope at all times," says Law, who is now Trust co-chair along, we should point out, with one of the authors of this book. "There are situations where we will be a critical friend to the club, others where we will be in outright opposition, and others where we will work alongside them. It's done on a case-by-case basis. The relationship we have means we know who to speak with at the club to get a response to a specific matter. We do a lot of case work, go into bat for fans who are banned for ticketing offences or for persistent standing or for pitch invasion… We can only do that because of the position we hold as a trust."

The Trust also worked openly with grass roots initiatives such as the 1882 group, a loose collection of fans that came together to encourage better expressions of support at games. Similar groups were springing up at other clubs too, but the two fans who got things going at Spurs were a prolific blogger and ran the popular blog *Dear Mr Levy*, and Flav Bateman.

"We'd been emailing back and forth vaguely throwing about ideas with no particular aim," says Flav. From those discussions *The Fighting Cock* podcast was born "because we considered some of the existing podcasts to be overly negative" he explains. The Love The Shirt and 1882 initiatives quickly bubbled up.

A notice went up on *The Fighting Cock* website. It said: "On the 16th February 2012 Tottenham's youth side take on Charlton at the Valley in the fifth round of the FA Youth Cup. We want them to have a taste of what it might feel like to play for the Spurs first team. We want you to join The Fighting Cock in creating an atmosphere on this night that these players will never ever forget. We want to create something that will go down in Tottenham folklore. And all you have to do is turn up and sing your heart out. Bring flags, scarves, anything you can swing around! For one night, be one of the Tottenham Ultras."

Some 600 turned up that night. "It was pay on the door so there was no need to contact Tottenham," says Flav. "Our support on the evening was mentioned on the official site's commentary and post-match articles." But some were uneasy about the use of the term Ultras. That original calling notice had talked of Ultras as "fans renowned for their fanatical support and elaborate displays", mentioning banners, tifo choreography, flares and vocal support in large groups as distinguishing characteristics. But for many fans, Ultras also meant 'hooligans'. So to avoid a diversionary debate about the name, the Tottenham Ultras became 1882. And that also meant the group could open up a dialogue with the club.

"The first contact with the club came when we wanted to do a game at White Hart Lane," says Flav. "Because the Charlton game went without a hitch I think it was pretty straightforward. We were playing Barcelona in the NextGen Series and the club allocated us two blocks, 600 tickets in total, and we sold them out."

One fan who was there, Glen Stanbury, wrote: "The best bit of the night was the reaction from my Dad. For 70 fantastic minutes I saw him become the young boy who used to sing his heart out from the Shelf every weekend in his glory days." Clearly, some mojos were being rediscovered.

The evening had taken most by surprise – including the club, and there was some tension between the fans and the stewards over what is now termed "persistent standing". Flav explains: "Given that the 1882 is at its core an anti-modern football movement, the issue of standing was always going to be at the forefront of any issues with the club. I'd rather not go into the conversations with the club during the days after the Barca game, but it's safe to say that they were a little wary of what 1882 was actually about."

That wariness became apparent when 1882 began organising for the Europa League group game against Maribor. These early stage games in UEFA's 'other' European tournament were rarely sold out – it's a sign of the times when a European night at the Lane is not the attraction it once was – and so it seemed an ideal opportunity. The call went out to buy tickets and congregate in particular blocks but, says Flav, "the club reacted by suspending ticket sales in that block of the stadium. Then they called us to White Hart Lane for a meeting to outline the intentions of the group."

Back in 1963, the president of the SSC had moved to quickly disassociate the organisation from more robust expressions of support. But times had changed. THST worked with 1882 to help them secure blocks of tickets and, in a move that sums up much about the modern game, to reassure the club that the people who wanted to turn up and vociferously support it really were OK.

It all sounds a long way from the days of Sack The Board. "It's very easy to bang your fist on the table and demand someone goes but not come up with a credible alternative," says Law. "The long-term aim of any supporters' trust is to own your own club but let's be realistic, it's not going to happen at Spurs or any Premier League club.

"I think our fans will get behind an issue when it matters to them. They are fairly well measured to be honest. I can't think of any issues that have been big enough to provoke a call to get the whole board out. Maybe Stratford would have been! The walkout at Liverpool over ticket pricing took balls. They have a history of a particular kind of activism and even then their fan union Spirit of Shankly were not sure it was going to work. I think we have tremendously passionate fans at Tottenham but they wouldn't necessarily express their dissatisfaction in the same way as fans at Liverpool. I think we have a different kind of support."

Fans began to see an active organisation run by people like them, but one that was also willing and able to get stuck into the more sedate business of boardroom discussions. THST insisted regular meetings with the club board were regular, and that report backs from those meetings should be published within 72 hours. In short, THST asserted itself. And the club realised it had to deal seriously with the Trust, rather than just pay lip service to the idea of supporter consultation. Although, as some would no doubt observe, getting support from the fans for the stadium project in Tottenham the club now had to revive served its purpose.

Of course, not every fan is supportive of the Trust. No fan organisation can represent every strand of opinion, and there's a significant minority who think it's their responsibility to knock off any heads that appear above the parapet. And as with any organisation that sits down and talks across a table, there's always the suspicion that it might get too close to the other side. The balancing act between being independent and being constructively engaged is always delicate.

It's probably still too early to say that fan organisation at Spurs has gone from outsider to insider status. The balance of power is still overwhelmingly with the club. But THST is established as a recognised voice that has achieved practical success, whether that be in securing ticket price freezes and reductions, defending fans in court, securing improvements in the stewarding and policing of away fans or helping with atmosphere initiatives such as crowd surfers and flags.

"The club do give us a lot of their time," says Law. "They answer more of our points and they consult with us more than virtually any other Premier League club does with their fan organisations. We'd like to be in the loop more and like them to listen sometimes rather just hear and we also need them to be far more transparent than they are. They are getting better at understanding their audience but sometimes they genuinely think they have communicated something when in fact it was at the bottom of a statement six months ago in a language that no one understood."

One of the many challenges it faces, especially around those atmosphere initiatives, is ensuring that the experience of supporting the team does not become overorganised, corporatised. Fans are very conscious of the fact that the game often tries to sell what they created back to them, and so the irony of having to organise what looks unorganised is thrown up.

And the fact remains that most fans still simply go to the game, they go to get away from the pressures of working life and politics and finance. Where fan organisations succeed now is where they recognise their limitations as well as their potential. What most fans want is to see a winning team at a reasonable price in decent surroundings. That enough now recognise that getting this means some fans have to do something is a step forward, and something that has been acheived at Spurs by every fan who has ever stood up and tried to change something – all the way back to those protesters in Trafalgar Square in 1961 asking for more FA Cup Final tickets or even back further to the volunteers who helped find and fund the first enclosed ground.

After a long journey, the fact of a supporters' organisation having a genuine voice at board level of the club is an established one. But modern football clubs are such big and complex beasts that this raises its own tensions. The roots of this book lie in the view that clubs are not businesses like any other, but cultural institutions created over a long period by ordinary people coming together. The success and influence of clubs has taken them away from their roots. Fans still feel they are the club in the same way the boys who formed the Hotspur under a lamppost did in 1882, but they are far removed from it in any meaningful way. And while that's a source of disquiet and resentment, the fact is that most fans simply want to consume the product rather than be involved in it.

The problem is that that emotional attachment, combined with the money the thing we are attached to demands, creates a tension in most fans. We know we are stupid for being so devoted, but it also means something to us. We feel entitled to complain vociferously and assert our sense of ownership, but we don't really want to take it much further. 'It's only a game' is a phrase guaranteed to annoy, but we also know it's true. Being a fan is a mug's game. Being a fan activist is even more of one. The conundrum facing the modern fan is just how much to care, how much to be involved.

In this, Tottenham fans are no different to any other fans. The distance between the people and the people's game is the key tension of modern times. That's because the fans shaped what the club is. The connection is still there. But everyone is working out what it means now.

10

Does your rabbi
know you're here?

"WE fucking hate Tottenham and we hate Tottenham." The spirit of hospitality extended to both
home and away supporters hadn't spread to a gaggle
of Sheffield United supporters as they spilled out of a popular pre-
match venue before the League Cup semi-final in 2013.

One of them shouts "The Jews…" and laughs. We were leaving
the Irish Centre but the irony passed her by. Yet this inconsequential
incident captures two major elements of being a Spurs supporter.
To fans of other clubs, Tottenham Hotspur is a Jewish club: we are
the Yids. Second, when fans of other clubs use the word, it's always
a term of abuse.

The rest of the group left it there and decided instead to express
in song their apparent distain for Cockneys. Yorkshire rivals Leeds
were known for many years as a Jewish club – another city with a
large Jewish population, football mad and owned in their golden
years by a Jewish family. But not Yids.

A few months before this incident the police had become so
concerned about anti-Semitism that they were arresting people,

218

including Spurs fans, who used the word in the street or the ground. These were troubled times. Supporters, regardless of their faith, were vulnerable in the aftermath of heightened security following the terrorist murders in a Paris Jewish supermarket a fortnight before.

When one of the authors texted his wife to tell her about the delayed kick-off, she immediately assumed there had been an incident related to this. A Jewish club and a streetful of potential victims? Where better to strike? In fact, the Sheffield team coach had been stuck on the North Circular but the ultimate implications of this strand of identity are inescapable.

Like most myths there is a kernel of truth. A proportion of Spurs' support has long been drawn from the large London Jewish community and the three chairmen since 1982 have all been Jewish businessmen with pre-existing degrees of allegiance to the club. Yet the proportion of fans who are Jewish, impossible to know precisely, is likely to be small. The best estimate is a maximum of 5% of the crowd. Arsenal have at least as many Jewish fans. But they are not Yids.

Spurs supporters did not grow up as Yids, they became Yids in adversity through a complex and contested process of identity formation. Forced to respond to pejorative, abusive taunts from rival supporters, many in the crowd embraced the term in order to render the abuse impotent. But the word yid remains highly controversial within the Jewish community, many of whom abhor the use of the word in any context. Many Jewish Spurs fans support their club despite the word not because of it.

The Jewish community in Tottenham began to grow in the early 20th century. Eastern European Jews fleeing pogroms in Russia came to Britain from 1880 onwards, with a surge in 1905/06 as their persecution intensified. Many settled in the East End amidst its long-established Jewish community. Others then moved further north, taking advantage of the good transport links and employment prospects in the Tottenham area. The Jewish Dispersion Committee encouraged the move from overcrowded Whitechapel and Brick Lane.

Unskilled work was plentiful in the fast-growing industrial sites around Tottenham Hale. Several large businesses were Jewish-owned. Lebus furniture, at one time the largest furniture manufacturer in the country, moved to the area in 1899. Most famous for its cheap and cheerful post-war utility furniture, it also made parts for the Mosquito bombers and Horsa gliders used on D-Day. Gestetner became a world leader in duplicating machines, the forerunner of modern copiers. The Eagle Pencil works, later known as Berol, and Flateau Shoes employed thousands.

Over the next 30 to 40 years, Tottenham Hotspur became part of the lives of these predominantly working-class Jewish men living in the crowded streets between the Hale and Landsdowne Road. Strictly speaking we are talking about a series of Jewish communities here rather than a single entity. For example, the ultra-orthodox Hasidic community in Stamford Hill retain a distinctive identity to this day. And for all Jews the holy Sabbath rules out Saturday football, in theory at least.

However, for many Jews settling in this country, the drive for assimilation has been an over-riding imperative and football has been instrumental in that process. Writing about this powerful anglicisation, Anthony Clavane says football is: "A space where ethnic identity has connected, even become intertwined, with national identity; an arena where Jews have fought the notion that they were invaders who needed to be fended off, newcomers who did not belong."

Many Jews, especially the second generation who were born here and called Tottenham home, sought belonging and identity on the terraces at White Hart Lane. They weren't the only ones: the history of Tottenham Hotspur is linked inextricably with the lives of the newcomers, the displaced, the ambitious, the hungry who came to Tottenham in search of work and a better life. Generations have found comfort and comradeship in the swaying masses who follow the navy blue and white. Through their club are expressed hopes and aspirations, of being part of something, of being somebody. The Hotspur *was* Tottenham.

This assimilation was particularly important in the Tottenham community that faced hostility, often violent, after the so-called 'Tottenham Outrage' in 1909, when a botched armed robbery by two Russian immigrants led to a police chase involving hundreds of officers from Tottenham to Chingford that ended with a policeman and a child caught in the crossfire dead and 24 injured. This case attracted unprecedented national interest and provoked a period of anti-alien feeling, which in Tottenham meant 'anti-Jewish'.

In 1911, Algernon Lesser, well-known as a youth worker amongst the Jewish community, spoke of how he tried to help young men anglicise, with football providing one of the main avenues: "The results of the games in the football leagues that afternoon are most keenly discussed, and loud is the wailing and great the distress among the supporters of the Spurs if Tottenham Hotspur have had to lower their colours."

Jewish attendance at football matches rose after the First World War, especially among second generation young men. Partly this reflected changes in social patterns as, in the East End, Saturday became a day for leisure rather than strict religious observance. The British-born generation forged their own identity in this fast-changing urban world. Proud of their heritage and faith, people adopted football as another element of this new anglicised Jewish culture alongside the old customs. So in the words of a correspondent to the *Jewish Chronicle*, for a Saturday kick-off at 2.30, "it was possible to be in synagogue until the end of *musaf*, to nip home for a plate of *lokshen* soup and then board a tram from Aldgate to White Hart Lane."

One creative interpretation of religious law claimed that the *Shabbos* tradition could be maintained by purchasing a ticket on the Friday morning and going by an electric tram, not a combustion-engined bus, although we suspect not every rabbi agreed. However they travelled, the good transport links made the journey straightforward.

Jewish support was not without its tensions within the community. The older generation, the immigrants, abhorred the idea of going to football, with the *goyim* and on *Shabbos* at that. Yet the game had taken hold among the younger generation. Clavane quotes a young Ralph Finn, author and Spurs historian, whose eastern European grandfather spat at him in the 1920s "*Footbollick* – grown men running around like *meshuga*, nothing with nothing."

Few Jews avidly followed their local team, West Ham, with its origins in the docks as part of the leisure activities granted to the Thames Ironworks workforce by an employer keen to keep them happy and minimise industrial unrest. Not many Jews in the docks. Also, as we have seen, Tottenham Hotspur appealed to all sections in society with a history of welcome and independence. Arsenal's Jewish support grew later, in the 1930s, from the more affluent north London community. They were the team for the Jewish émigrés, the intellectuals attracted by the splendour of the ground and the team's dominance under Herbert Chapman.

Spurs were by far the most popular team within the community at the time. The *Jewish Chronicle* confidently stated that in the 1920s almost all Jews who followed the game were Spurs supporters and the Jewish fanbase continued to grow in the 1930s. A reporter from the *Daily Express* writing in 1934 said he was surrounded by Jewish fans on the terrace. The following year, several papers quoted a figure of as many as 10,000 Jews in the crowd, a third of the total.

These figures became newsworthy in December 1935 when White Hart Lane was chosen by the FA as the venue for an international between England and Germany. The Nazis saw this as a propaganda opportunity. As well as giving their side clear instructions as to the imperative of winning, 10,000 Germans were transported to London, ostensibly to watch the game but they were escorted round the capital in orderly, happy throngs, their every move captured in print and in the newsreels.

Playing at Tottenham was seen at the time as an affront to the Jewish community, demonstrating that in the mid-1930s Spurs were widely perceived as a club with a large Jewish support. Opposition was organised. "The Jews have been the best supporters of the Tottenham club ever since its formation, and we shall adopt every means in our power to stop the match," one of the protest organisers told the *Star*, London's paper. "We regard the visit of the German team as an effrontery, not only to the Jewish race but to all lovers of freedom."

4 December 1935 was the day the swastika flew over White Hart Lane. It was also the day when trade unionists and political groups stood in solidarity alongside the Jews of Tottenham. Protests that had begun several weeks before continued on the day but the game went ahead peacefully. The German team gave a wincingly sinister Nazi salute to the crowd before kick-off but England did not. The flag didn't last too long – a fan climbed onto the roof of the West Stand and pulled it down. Neither did German notions of natural superiority – they lost 3-0.

The following year, the British Union of Fascists led by Oswald Mosley used the Tottenham crowd to attack the "Jewish sporting mentality" which was at odds with the upstanding principles of the "Nordic race". They alleged that a supposed increase in barracking on the terraces emanated from Jewish supporters unable to comprehend the decency and fair play that characterised British sportsmanship.

The club was reluctant to reciprocate this dedication that spanned generations. Mickey Dulin played for Spurs in the late 1940s and kept quiet about his heritage. "They didn't know I was Jewish, Turkish or Greek, we didn't talk about it. We all just kept schtum," he says. Spurs 'superfan', businessman Morris Keston, was given five shares in the pre-plc days but the club refused to register him. "People used to say to me: 'They [the board] don't like you because you're Jewish.' They didn't want any outsiders," he told Anthony Clavane. Another writer, Mihir Bose, says that before

Irving Scholar took over in the early 1980s there was "unofficial apartheid" between Jewish supporters and Gentile directors.

Arsenal, on the other hand, openly acknowledged the connection. In the mid-1960s for example their programme wished supporters well over Yom Kippur, the holiest day of the Jewish calendar. Spurs did not follow suit until 1973. When Chapman died in 1934 his *Jewish Chronicle* obituary praised him as a 'friend of the Jewish people'.

Despite the club's attitude, Jewish Spurs fans continued to feel they belonged in the stands and on the terraces at White Hart Lane. Changing patterns of class and affluence meant that by the 1960s, the local community had shrunk considerably but family allegiance remained strong in the large Jewish communities in north London and south Essex. Many moved from terrace to the seats but they still felt safe and secure.

Jewishness then became more inextricably intertwined with the identity of being a Spurs fan as Tottenham became the Yids, an aspect of supporter identity that persists to this day and remains intensely controversial and contested.

Jews have always been called Yids. From the *goyim* it is an insult. Fellow Jews have come to use the term amongst themselves as slang self-description, as appropriating the word nullifies its abuse. Many Jews however would never use it because it is the ultimate, foulest form of the anti-Semitic abuse that they have endured all their lives. To them Yid can never be used in any other context.

David John's family, Tottenham locals for three generations, did not recognise the image of Spurs as a Jewish club. They never heard that label. Neither did Peter Levene, who moved to the area as a boy in the late 1940s when his father bought a pub, but as a Jew he knew that anti-Semitism was never far away and he was prepared to defend himself on the streets of Tottenham: "My father came out the army in 1947, he said you've got to learn to protect yourself. First thing you do, get a couple of pieces of wood and shape them, one in that pocket, one in that pocket. If you ever get into a fight, just put them in your fists, they'll be much harder. Then when you punch them, aim between the eyes. I only got into one fight because I then started going to boxing, the Chingford boxing club then later on the Stoke Newington boxing club, and once people learned that I went to a boxing club, everything stopped. Everything. No one said a word.

"It was part and parcel of life. My grandmother, during the war she was out shopping and one of the neighbours was going on about how these Jews were sitting at home doing nothing and our boys are over there fighting for them... Grandmother blew her top, she said 'I've got one son in the tanks, one son in Burma, one son flying Lancaster bombers and whaddya you got? None of your talk' and she whacked her! They picked the wrong one with my grandmother, that's for sure.

"My father, died in 1982, he didn't talk about the war at all but I managed to get hold of his war record. Very sparse, he was a tank commander. He was a sergeant, then was made down to corporal, then put back up to sergeant again. Turns out one of the officers called him 'a Jew bastard' and he whacked him and knocked him out!"

At some point from the late 1960s onwards, opposition fans began to chant abuse at Spurs supporters using the word. It's impossible to date exactly when this began. Most Jewish supporters of that era are convinced they know when it began but probably are recounting the first time they heard it. One told us with certainty that it was started by Charlton fans in the early 1960s. Another saw Spurs win the 1967 FA Cup Final from the Chelsea end and was appalled by the anti-Semitic abuse.

Others blame the popular 1960s and 1970s sitcom *Til Death Do Us Part* and its central character, the bigoted West Ham-supporting Alf Garnett, played with gusto by Spurs season ticket holder Warren Mitchell, who referred to Spurs supporters as Yids. However, it's more likely this came from writer Johnny Speight's sharp ear for the East End vernacular.

Through the 1970s abuse from opposition fans referring to Spurs fans as Jews was commonplace, especially when going away. The chant "does your rabbi know you're here?" was mild and amusing compared with the rest. "I've never felt more like gassing the Jews...", "one man went to gas, went to gas a yiddo...", "Spurs are on their way to Auschwitz, Hitler's gonna gas 'em again", Nazi salutes and, perhaps most insidious of all, the hiss of escaping gas. Supporters of Tottenham Hotspur, Jew and Gentile alike, have heard it all.

Spurs supporters have not been the only British fans on the receiving end. A milder variant of the same abuse could be heard at Leeds at the same time, another club with a large Jewish support at the time and a Jewish chairman. However, there has been nothing that remotely compares with the vitriol and persistence of the abuse directed at Tottenham fans. And to the authors' knowledge it has never been directed at Arsenal fans.

In response, something remarkable happened. Instead of repudiating the long history of Jewish support and the Jews who stood amongst them, fans embraced it. In response to the abuse, fans danced up and down on the terraces singing "We are the yids, we are the yids, we are we are we are the yids!", appropriating a chant "We are the Mods!" from an existing subculture and providing yet another example of the swirling soup that is London culture. Supporters wore skullcaps to games. The Israeli flag flew from the terraces. The Star of David was incorporated into home-made banners or the decorated white butchers' coats that were popular at the time.

Using the word as a term of endearment and comradeship nullified the negativity before the words left the mouths of abusers. Context is key to meaning: Spurs fans do not use the word in a derogatory way. They refuse to be demeaned or controlled by the abuse.

There is, of course, a danger in making too much of this. There was, no doubt, an element of the simple 'sod you' mentality on terraces not known as a hotbed of political activity – something different and unusual happened to fashion our response in this particular form. But the fact remains that it would have been easy, in the face of the abuse, to blame the Jews – after all people have for the last 3,000 years – and turn on them. Instead, the response was acceptance, as it always has been on the White Hart Lane terraces. Tottenham resisted the casual racism endemic in 1970s football. During the many troughs in our fortunes over the last 35 years, there have been few hints of anti-Semitic feeling towards any of the three Jewish owners. The thread of a heritage of independence and inclusivity runs through the fabric of support to this day.

To label this awareness of the process of discrimination as political consciousness would be to overstate the case, but supporters are conscious of the process of discrimination and they refuse to accept it.

While the term has been in regular currency for decades now, over the past ten years it has been used more readily in chants and in social media to define loyalty, continuity and heritage, perhaps in part because Spurs supporters have become more conscious than ever before of their history and identity in response to outside forces such as the consistent success of rivals Chelsea and Arsenal and the heated debate about the decisive break with our roots to the Olympic site in Stratford, east London. What makes Spurs fans unique has become extremely important in an homogenised, money-dominated Premier League and many choose to express this through using the word Yid about themselves and their team.

It has become so embedded, the recent re-igniting of the debate about the word showed that many younger supporters had no idea about the origins, it was just part of being a Spur. Yet the term remains the subject of intense, sometimes bitter controversy from both within the Spurs community and outside it.

Mark Damazer, born and brought up in a north London Jewish family and a supporter since 1961, eloquently explains the case against the word from within the community: "I first came across the chant in the mid-1990s. I was with my two small children. I thought the crowd was shouting 'yeast'. I asked a neighbour and was shocked when he told me. I am still shocked when I hear it.

"Well-meaning non-Jewish Tottenham fans may think of it as a defence mechanism to employ against anti-Semites among opposing supporters. But this is a word that for centuries has not merely been used to convey ignorance, suspicion and prejudice. It has also been a way of identifying people who subsequently were marked out for servitude and death.

"I don't want to claim that, in all circumstances, only Jews can use the word 'Yid' but I am very doubtful that most of those who chant it know the word's history and potency."

This view, that context is rendered insignificant compared with the prejudice and abuse intrinsic to the word, is supported not only by representatives of Jewish organisations but also by a substantial number of Jewish Spurs supporters, who tolerate its use rather than embrace it. One of the authors of this book is Jewish and wholeheartedly defends its use by Spurs supporters while at the same time never using it to describe himself or other fans, because deep down it does not feel right.

The most voluble critic of Spurs supporters' use of the word from outside the club is David Baddiel, the Jewish comedian and author. His view is that Tottenham fans should stop using the word completely. The tribalism that bedevils contemporary fandom means many reject his arguments purely on the basis that he is a Chelsea fan. In fact, his campaign began when he admonished Chelsea fans chanting anti-Semitic abuse in a match against Spurs.

In a widely circulated short film and subsequent discussions around the subject, Baddiel not only says the word has no place in football grounds or anywhere else for that matter, he also contradicts the process of reclamation, saying that as non-Jews, Spurs fans have no right to the word in the first place.

While Baddiel's viewpoint is a serious attempt to address the complexities of reappropriation of language, he ends up in the contorted position of requiring Spurs fans to stop, regardless apparently of anything sung or done by the opposition, thus denying the context of decades of abuse and implying that rival fans are justified in their use of Yid for as long as Spurs fans use the word. His argument sounds suspiciously as if it is their own fault.

That contorted logic emerged in a different and surprising context in 2013 when the debate went national, involving the police, the FA and the Prime Minister, David Cameron.

It's highly unlikely Cameron has the interests of football fans anywhere near the top of his agenda. When in early September 2013 he pronounced his verdict on the long-running debate, his intended audience was those involved in the free speech debate. Yet he struck a chord with the majority of Spurs fans. "There's a difference between Spurs fans self-describing themselves as Yids and someone calling someone a Yid as an insult," he said. "You have to be motivated by hate. Hate speech should be prosecuted – but only when it's motivated by hate."

No doubt sensitive to issues around discriminatory and abusive language in the light of other cases such as the prosecution of England captain John Terry for alleged racist language, the FA took it upon themselves to address what it termed the Y word debate. In their carefully worded statement, the organisation outlined both sides of the argument and, significantly, reached a conclusion: "The FA considers that the use of the term 'yid' is likely to be considered offensive by the reasonable observer."

Having acknowledged the complexity of the debate, the FA reached the conclusion that "rules on acceptable behaviour and language need to be simple, understandable and applicable to all people at all levels of the game".

This definition was endorsed by the Metropolitan Police, who declared before the home match against West Ham in September 2013 that all fans who use the word, including Tottenham supporters, could be committing an offence under section 5 of the Public Order Act. A year previously, the Met had stated that fans would not face prosecution in these circumstances because there was "no deliberate intention to cause offence".

Context had been removed. There was now no apparent distinction between opposing fans giving Nazi salutes and singing about gassing the Jews, and Spurs supporters getting behind their team. And the argument had moved from one about prejudice to one about offence, a much broader and very different debate and one which raised uncomfortable questions about the limits of free speech.

At the game against West Ham, songs about Hitler and gas chambers were clearly audible from the away section. Nazi salutes were also seen. A fan was arrested, a supporter of Tottenham Hotspur who had used the word Yid in a chant. In the following weeks, two more Spurs fans were arrested for racially aggravated public order offences. Unusually, their names were released by the police. Publicly named as racists, the fans had bail conditions imposed that did not allow them within 2,500 yards of any stadium where Spurs were playing from four hours before until four hours after a game. The club banned the fans from its ground and withdrew their memberships and season tickets. The presumption of innocence until proof of guilt had apparently been cast aside.

After months in which the three fans remained publicly labelled as racists and during which time the case was repeatedly postponed, the Crown Prosecution Service announced that the charges were to be dropped because there was "insufficient evidence to provide a realistic prospect of conviction". The club rescinded its ban, reinstated memberships and refunded money for games missed.

The fans had been backed throughout by the Tottenham Hotspur Supporters' Trust, the membership of which had itself debated whether or not to back the fans. The Trust put the fans in touch with a legal team which, once the case was dropped, issued a strongly worded statement criticising a "misguided and over-zealous approach by the Crown Prosecution Service and the Metropolitan Police". The defence team went on to support the refusal to concede the word yid to the fascists and bigots, and concluded: "Any organisation or individual that sets out to brand Spurs fans' use of the word Yid as being racist runs a high risk of being perceived as pursuing other self-serving agendas. We urge them to focus their attention on those who are clearly using threatening or abusive words or behaviour towards others based on hostility or hate towards others' race or religion."

The episode raised challenging questions about the decision-making processes of public bodies such as the police and the CPS, and about whether football was subjected to a different set of laws and judgements to other citizens. It sparked debate over free speech, and further muddied the waters for those attempting to challenge out and out bigotry. Most ironically of all, it popularised the use of the word Yid among Spurs fans after a period when use of the word seemed to be falling away. It cemented it as an expression of pride in being a Spurs fan, and in so doing removed it still further from its original roots. Something that could be seen as the ultimate irony.

What the whole episode did was underline once more the complex identity of the Spurs crowd, the network of references and experiences that are woven together to create identity. It is arguably one of the most complex cultural constructs in football, quite some achievement in the world of football fandom where the appetite for and imagination deployed creating cultural realities is particularly strong.

11

More than customers

IN 2010 Tottenham Hotspur announced not one but two new shirt sponsorship deals, one for the league and another for cup matches. Unlike past sponsors such as Holsten, Hewlett Packard and Thomson Holidays, Autonomy and Investec were hardly household names and, frankly, most supporters don't pay much attention, aside that is from complaining when Thomson included a red logo.

Chairman Daniel Levy was delighted however; "delighted to have Autonomy as our new global partner" and "delighted to have Investec as our new club sponsor and partner. Investec is a well-respected international specialist bank and asset management company and we shall be working with them to grow their brand internationally."

Football was changing and Spurs were going global. The Premier League has a worldwide audience. Every match is televised live outside Britain – the overseas television rights alone for 2016–19 will bring in over £2bn. Shirt sales and other merchandise generated increasingly significant income streams for teams such as Manchester United, Liverpool, Arsenal and latterly Chelsea. Spurs, lagging behind because a comparative lack of success on the field led to a lower profile, wanted their share. But what would this mean for the traditional, domestic support, a support which had, for so many years, shaped the club?

In 2013 the club put a lot of energy into raising its profile in the United States. The club toured, Gareth Bale's image was up large in Times Square – there was a huge push. The Supporters' Trust raised it with the club, putting the view held by many fans that their club seemed to be putting more effort into communicating with potential fans overseas than with existing fans at home. They were told 'it's a market we need to break'. The Trust warned the club about the risks of alienating home supporters in the scramble for new markets. There was a balance to be found.

Two years later, THFC director Donna Cullen gave an interview to the website sportsmedia.com in the middle of Spurs' pre-season American tour. Spurs were by then sponsored by AIA, a finance and insurance company with strong interests in the Far East (and with a red logo). Tottenham's post- and pre-season friendlies used to be a cobbled-together stroll against Scandinavian sides and English lower-league teams, plus the occasional big game versus Rangers or Celtic. Now, the planning process is very different. "We obviously have our key territories that are important to us as a club and at the moment they happen to be Asia and the US in equal parts," said Cullen.

The extent of interest in Spurs in these areas is remarkable, given the club's lack of success on the field, a testimony to the enduring attraction of the Hotspur. In Australia in 2015, 70,000 people attended a friendly, 5,000 an open training session and the queue for a store signing went round three blocks. In the US Spurs have 43 affiliated supporters' groups.

Creating a supporter base is a meticulously planned operation, as Cullen enthusiastically explained. "After our 2014 tour we saw a 48% uplift in our figures for social media engagement… We have a growth appeal out there because we are a challenger club and the Americans have really got behind that aspect of us and enjoy the style of play as well. Our global coaching guys go out at least a week before the first team travel, so they have already done a lot of grassroots football. So what we are looking to do is engage with the younger fan base out there. We have 'Super Clubs' in the US which is a new initiative by the club which is embedding our academies' philosophy and style… and all of that working its way through to where you see increased sales. We are doing extremely well there at the moment in terms of having fans engaged with us."

The growth in global support, itself rooted in the increased familiarity fans across the globe had with Premier League teams due to saturation TV coverage, was creating a new strand of fan culture – something that was a challenge for both the club and traditional domestic supporters to get to grips with. The American journalist and Spurs fan Aaron Wolfe wrote an evocative account of matchday in America for *The Fighting Cock* website. Spurs were away at Manchester City in February 2016 and dreams of a title challenge were beginning to take shape.

"It was -16°C in New York City on Sunday morning but Flannery's Bar was packed with Spurs supporters. I wrestled my way towards the back to a few square feet of floor space with an uninterrupted view of one of the screens. I had been at the Billy Nic in Tottenham a few months ago to watch us play Woolwich away and it hadn't been half as crowded as Flannery's was this past Sunday. Fifteen minutes to kick-off and there was barely room to breathe…

"Tottenham is a dream. It's a fugue-state induced by the slow emerging patterns and the push and pull of attack and defence. When we're losing it's a meditation on the impermanence of life. When we're winning it's an affirmation…

"This feeling right now that you're feeling? The feeling you felt when Lamela's perfectly-weighted pass split the legs of Otamendi and found Eriksen? That's the process of winning. That moment that Eriksen coolly took a first touch and you knew that the next touch was going to put the ball in the back of the net?

"The ball hops over Hart's leg. The ball ripples the net. The scream emerges. The theatre of celebration begins. I scream, I jump, I hug strangers, I hug Jonah, Jonah grins ear to ear, I'm singing. I'm singing. I'm singing… That's the best feeling in the world… the moment of potential. The moment that the scream is building in your throat…"

Wolfe and his fellow supporters felt that win, sharing their delirious delight with the ecstatic away end at the Etihad Stadium even though they were 3,000 miles and an ocean apart. Tottenham Hotspur have long since had supporters' groups in all parts of Britain and abroad. A long history of signing star players from the United Kingdom and Ireland has cemented links with Wales, Scotland and Ireland, where Spurs were especially popular in the sixties and seventies. Groups from Belgium and Scandinavia regularly fly over for home matches. In America, Spurs have really taken off.

Graham Rolfe started the LA Spurs in 2005. It's the oldest Spurs supporters' club in the US. "My own history with Tottenham started in the early 1970s when I was a lad back in the UK," he says. "Back in the early 1990s when I moved to California, I did not really know any other Spurs fans in LA. Occasionally I would run into one or two but that was about it. On 14 January 1998 at my sister's birthday party in Pasadena, via a work colleague, I got to meet Spurs fan legend Graeme Rudge and that in itself was quite an experience. Imagine meeting someone for the first time and them telling you how many times they had been arrested for supporting Spurs. But that was the beginning.

"Graeme invited me to his wedding and we ended up going to quite a few games together, but it was just the two of us. This continued for quite a while and was sometimes quite difficult as wherever we went we seemed to be the only Spurs fans… until we started an e-mail list. And things have blown up since then."

Now, up to 200 LA-based fans meet for every Spurs match at their adopted home, the Greyhound Bar and Grill. For big games, they've had to close the doors, leaving fans locked out. It's a mixed crowd, mostly Americans with a sprinkling of ex-pats and stars like Eddie Marsan and Marina Sirtis. The atmosphere is raucous and positive.

"I think the newer Yank fans have a more positive take on things Spurs (and things generally in life), still singing at the end of games we're getting tonked in and I think us ex-pats pick up on that." The ex-pat speaking is Ashley Collie, a Los Angeles-based writer with several strings to his bow including interviewing film and sports stars for glossy profiles. It's a far cry from Newport, Wales where he was brought up and became a Spurs fan because his mother, noted for her style and good taste, saw the magic in the dazzling all-white of Tottenham's European kits under the lights.

"The ones who do come over to the Lilywhite side — not the dark, other north London side — have done their due diligence," he says. "They've been supporting US teams in other sports all their lives, so they know about winners and losers and dynasties: like Yankees, Red Sox, Giants and Dodgers in MLB, and Steelers, Packers, Patriots, 49ers and Cowboys in NFL. So they know sport. They don't want to bandwagon and just pick a traditional top-four or top-five team.

"Yet, they've wanted a team with potential. And most importantly a team with a story. There are a lot of Uniteds, Cities and Reals in the world but only one Spurs — as newbie US fan Scott Shapiro said to me, 'This crazy club with a crazy name was the one that finally roped me in.' And the cockerel with fighting spurs on the crest is also a big attraction. And so is our history from Blanchflower's quotes about 'style' to more recently the exploits of Gareth Bale and now of Harry Kane.

"It's a unique and expanding phenomenon, this coming into the Spurs fold. As Spurs pushed Leicester for the title during this season, guys at my Hollywood YMCA were asking all sorts of questions: why do teams play a different amount of games; explain promotion and relegation; how much of a fairy tale is it to have teams like Leicester and Spurs competing?"

Everyone has a story to tell about how they became a Spurs supporter. British fans cite family, geography, friends perhaps or being enthralled by the magic of watching a big game. None have told us that logic was involved in any way. Not so in America, where supporters know their history because they have researched it meticulously, and it is precisely that heritage that they have fallen in love with. Here's Ken Saxton, who contributes to the *Hotspur America* podcast out of Dallas, Texas, speaking on *The Spurs Show* in May 2015: "Supporting Spurs, it was something I did a lot of research on. I took about a year to actually figure out which club that I wanted to support because I knew it was going to be a big deal. A lot of fans, just like over here [England], they're very impatient so they jump on United, Chelsea or Arsenal, the ones that you hear about. It would have been very easy to jump on that bandwagon but you know, I said, I'm going to look at this objectively. I wanted it to be a club that belonged in a city that I could go visit and enjoy my visit there, so London was a big deal, and a team that wouldn't soon be relegated. I chose Spurs, or they chose me – it fell in line with all the other teams I root for. They are just about good enough but just not quite there… they're going to break your heart every time."

And should there be any doubt, Ken's concluding remarks show he completely gets it: "This is Tottenham Hotspur, you have to take the good with the bad, because there's going to be a lot of bad, there just is, and you accept that once you decide to become a fan."

There's no questioning the passion and loyalty of Tottenham supporters in the US. Nor in the Far East, where large groups gather in cities in India and Thailand – to take just two examples of the territories into which the Premier League club brands are pushing – to watch games and swap stories. What's interesting about these newer fan groups is the hunger with which they devour the history and traditions of the club. There's a palpable sense of a search for something real and rooted, not just for another brand to consume. And so again we are reminded of the special nature of the football business and its relationship with its consumers.

Add the newer territories to places such as Australia, with its many thousand strong chapters of Spurs fans in major cities, and Scandinavia, where fans not only congregate in great number to watch Spurs on TV, but travel in great number regularly to White Hart Lane. One of the authors was struck, when visiting the London AGM of Norway Spurs, how many Norwegian-based fans had home season tickets. Norway to White Hart Lane puts the transport problems on the North London Line into perspective.

As the supporter base grows, so the interests of supporters diverge. What concerns the fan in Johannesburg or Mumbai may not concern the fan from Essex or north London, and vice versa. And so in modern times, that divergence of interests is what is shaping how supporters shape their club.

Tottenham's ticket prices are amongst the highest in the country. This impacts upon any fan wanting to see the team live, but more upon the fans who go regularly. The BBC Price of Football survey published in October 2015 showed that the cheapest season ticket at White Hart Lane cost £765, the most expensive £1,895. The cheapest matchday seat was £32, the most expensive £81. Underlying these figures is a tiered system categorising matches according to the popularity of the opponent so the same seat for the Arsenal match, category A, could be up to £20 more expensive than for the visit of, say, Stoke.

On top of this was the cost of membership, around £40 per year, which for the big games and/or if Spurs were doing well was the only way non-season ticket holders could gain priority to buy a ticket.

This gave Spurs the dubious honour of having the second most expensive season tickets in the country. In fact, probably match for match it is the most expensive as the club in top spot, Arsenal, include Champions League matches as part of the cost whereas Spurs season ticket holders are entitled only to the first two home cup ties. The cheapest season ticket is 49% higher than the league average, the most expensive 114% higher, prices that represent a rise of almost 700% in the last 15 years, which leaves the inflation rate trailing in its wake.

These prices are at best a deterrent to supporters, at worst serve to exclude them. A family of four attending a mid-price match would pay a minimum of £120 for tickets, more if the children were not members and therefore not entitled to concessions. That's not including transport costs or food – in 2015 a Spurs pie cost £3.50, a cup of tea £2.20. Hardly the best way to 'engage with the younger fan base'.

That's supposing you can buy a ticket in the first place. Spurs were one of the first clubs to introduce a system where tickets could be bought online. Since this was outsourced to Ticketmaster, the symbol of progress once logged, either a purple bar or circle, has become an image of dread for fans as they watch it slowly moving, or not. What infuriates fans is not so much the delay but the lack of available information. It feels like the club are not making the effort.

It projects an image of a club who are keen to call their fans 'consumers' or 'customers' – every season ticket holder is known by their customer number – without providing the level of service that this relationship implies. Resolving problems with the ticket office or administration was extremely difficult. Until 2013 the club had no meaningful dialogue with supporters' representatives and chose to consult only when it deemed it necessary, as the decision to bid for the Stratford stadium site amply demonstrated. The Tottenham On My Mind blog wrote: "I like to think we are something more than customers or consumers. In reality, the plc defines that relationship as it chooses according to the circumstances. The fans are great when they get behind the lads, travel all over England and Europe, but these same loyalists are dismissed if they dare to grumble, see Adebayor this year and AVB last. As 'customers' the ticket money disappears remarkably quickly from our accounts yet you can't get through on the site to buy the tickets in the first place.

"All clubs including Spurs exploit the loyalty they profess to admire and value. Shoppers and shareholders who moan about Tesco's recent performance and prices can go to Sainsbury's if they wish but we're not going to the Emirates and that distorts the 'customer' relationship right out of shape. And don't mention a boycott because one, not enough people will; two, someone else will just sit in my seat if I give it up; three, the TV deal means the club have massive income from other sources and could play in front of empty seats as league sides in Italy do; and four, I've loved this club for a lifetime so why the bloody hell should I give up now?"

The truth is that a growing number of fans feel marginalised, precisely by the forces that mean football has more coverage than ever before. Yet the percentage of seats sold in Premier League grounds has never been higher. It's a tension that shows itself in the different and changing ways Spurs fans view their team.

In the last decade, the average crowd at White Hart Lane for league matches has never dropped below 98.4% of capacity. It's a sign of enduring loyalty. Anywhere up to 40,000 patiently stand by on the season ticket waiting list.

Yet the composition of the crowd bears further scrutiny. The club itself will not release full statistics but the average age of season ticket holders is around 43 and rising. The family section in the Paxton Road encourages young fans but it is now virtually unheard of for groups of two or more young people coming to the game without adults, whereas in the past groups of young fans were commonplace. Partly this is a function of a safety-conscious society – both the authors of this book used to travel alone across London to Spurs matches in their early teens but this would be discouraged these days.

There can be no doubt that the price of tickets is the main factor however. As Spurs fan Alex Bottomley says, it's a matter of priorities: "Not that I couldn't afford a £60 ticket, but we're extending the house and the wife's pregnant. I can't justify that expense." Children and young people do want to come, as demonstrated by the numbers and enthusiasm of families attending cup games where the club reduce prices. However, it has become a treat, once or twice a season, rather than a fortnightly habit.

Matt Bigg has a story to tell about how supporting Spurs has changed across three generations: "My parents lived in White Hart Lane and my whole family is Spurs. They got married on a non-matchday and everything. When I first started going, early 1980s this was, we used to get all our tickets through the person who washed the kit. I went to loads of games…

"Now I live in St Albans. I currently have four seats at Watford. It surprises people because I'm a Spurs fan and I make sure my kids are Spurs, we try to go to as many Spurs games as possible. A few years ago my boys wanted to go to more and more games. They love football, playing it and going to stadiums. We've been to Barca, Malaga, all over.

"I had started my own business and just couldn't afford to buy four seats at Tottenham, not that they were available. I am a bronze member, 7,000 on the waiting list or whatever, but even if a ticket became available, my boys are 8 and 13 so I would want to go with them and that was never going to happen.

"So we go to Watford. My four seats cost a total of £600, which equates to about £7 or £8 a game per person. One of the tickets, because my boy is under 10, it's something like £30 a year. They do early bird offers, freeze ticket prices, encourage families to go…

"Thing about the Championship is, anyone can win, anyone can get relegated, you feel closer to the club and players. The other thing I really liked about the Championship was Saturday 3pm kick-offs – for me that's football. I watch St Albans too, leave the house at 2.30pm, have a pint on the way home…

"My kids can't not be Spurs, my dad would kill them. My youngest, his favourite player is Harry Kane and I want Kane to be his hero, not Troy Deeney. The deals for the Europa League games, under lights, the kids love that. With all the money coming into the game [from the TV deal], why do they have to charge £60 a ticket?

241

Fact is, it's cheaper for me to take them to watch Dortmund play... I went to Tottenham more when I had no money as a student because I could still afford it and that's what supporters did.

"If I could get four seats in the new stadium, that would be a dream if I could, my dad could take the kids if I can't go."

Isolating the difference between 'fan' and 'supporter' has never been straightforward. In this book they are used interchangeably. However, the defining characteristic in both everyday usage and academic analysis has been attendance at matches. 'Supporters' attended most if not all home matches with extra status conferred on those who go away. This argument assumes that supporters' bond with their club is therefore tighter than that of fans, who come to some matches, may pick and choose according to the opposition, and follow their team via the media. There is an implied hierarchy here with supporters claiming true authenticity. This definition cannot hold. In the age of the Premier League, large numbers of willing spectators simply cannot afford to go. We've moved a long way from the people's game, the full impact of which may not be felt until the next generation become adults. They have learned that being a supporter and attending matches do not necessarily have to go together and they may choose to stay at home.

If access to the stadium restricts opportunities to watch Spurs, then modern media offers more opportunities than ever before. Tottenham feature heavily on satellite television and every league match is easily accessible on the internet. The flow of information about the club is incessant. Traditional media outlets offer wall-to-wall coverage while blogs, message boards and social media offer the chance to talk with fellow fans, any time of the day or night from anywhere in the world. The 'rite of passage' now comes not through personal participation on the terraces but mediated through television and social media. It is a modern paradox that the connected world we live in atomises at the same time. We are at the same time connected but separated from each other, and that paradox increasingly shapes the relationship between fans and club.

Fans use social media in different ways. Twitter and the messageboards can be a way of augmenting experience at the match, before and after. Many now use social media as their primary source of interaction to replicate the terrace experience, the camaraderie of being part of something. Through social media, watching football on television has become a communal rather than isolating experience. It's easy to chat with fellow supporters. You can moan, cheer, share the joy and pain. Keep up to date with all the information and gossip about your club. It's educational – you are socialised into learning what your club stands for, how loyal fans behave.

Another variant is those who through choice or necessity watch Spurs in the pub, where fans can reproduce to some extent the heady, overwhelming experience of being part of the crowd. The pub has not just become a way to see your team, it's arguably the best way. Meet friends, mingle and have a few drinks. You don't have to plan months in advance, fork out a substantial proportion of your weekly wages and you're not immobile in your seat.

Being a Spurs fan on Twitter is a disconcerting experience. Debates with like-minded fellow supporters can lift the spirits in victory or be comforting in defeat. At the same time, the level of vitriol can be astonishing, the nature of discussion abominable. Perhaps Spurs Twitter accurately represents the broad spectrum of supporter perspectives, the difference being only that you would not have access to such a range of opinion in the normal course of things. Matchday Twitter only reflects the view of the fan you dread being trapped in front of during the game or the one you sidle away from in the pub. Writer and Spurs fan Seb Stafford-Bloor agrees: "I think it was always there. Social media allows people a stage for their opinions and permits them to be bolder and braver than they would be in person. It's exaggerated, of course, because I think more rational and considered voices often get lost in the noise, but I see Twitter/blogs etc as a facilitator for pre-existing issues."

Extreme views are a new element of contemporary fandom. Modern support is increasingly tribal. Loyalty is demonstrated by blind faith in your team. Holding strong, entrenched views is a badge of honour among some groups, particularly younger fans. The stronger the abuse, so this argument runs, the greater the loyalty. It has become a way of showing your fellow fans just how big a fan you are, a quality which in the past was defined by the number of matches you went to or the extent of your knowledge about your team. In March last year a supporter of a rival team tweeted this: "Would be fucking unreal if White Hart Lane collapsed, would remind me of the holocaust with a hint of Hillsborough unreal hybrid".

Posted at 7.21am, it feels like the author has thought about this quite carefully and risen early to celebrate the possibility, however remote, that thousands of football fans might be killed. The reference to the holocaust links to the image of Spurs as a Jewish club, a common trope for anti-Tottenham online insults.

In no way does it represent the real views of rival fans but it was popular on the Tweeter's timeline, receiving 52 retweets and favourited 23 times. It is an example of two trends of modern football support, a tribalism that extends to vicious threats of violence against fans of other teams and that such threats enhance the status of the author.

Spurs' social media itself is riddled with internecine argument leading to aggression (in tweets and messageboard posts at least) between Spurs fans. This may seem odd – after all, we support the same team and that's why we are tweeting in the first place. Some of it seems like an argument for argument's sake. However, beneath the disagreements lie alternative notions of identity and what being an authentic Tottenham fan means.

The 1882 movement is frequently derided by other Spurs fans. It has been portrayed as something that is exclusive, which other fans cannot take part in. Regardless of a structure that deliberately has no leaders and no membership, some fans feel excluded. This relates to different ideas about how to support Spurs. What these and other comments remind us is that traditional Spurs support has not been organised in any way. The terraces of the Shelf and the

Park Lane were anarchic, chaotic, friendly and sometimes violent, but for many fans this represents authenticity, the way things should be. In reality there is little difference between this view and that of the 1882 movement whose aims stretch to making some noise and having fun, no further. To some older fans it clearly feels very different.

It is perhaps the subject of expectation that provides the strongest example of how modern support impacts upon the club and shapes the way it is supported. In 2016 a young, inexperienced side mounted their strongest title challenge for at least three decades and the club finished in its highest ever position in the Premier League. This was the most enjoyable season in years for the majority of supporters who revelled in exciting, attacking football in the very best tradition of the Spurs Way. Even then, disagreement on social media was rife, with criticism of what is characterised as an over-optimistic view of how well Spurs have done. Supporters, true supporters that is, are not to be happy with failure and to be satisfied with anything less implies a lack of authenticity.

Paul Johnson, who saw his first match in April 1978, is one older fan who is critical of the younger fans who he says are "too young to have experienced the 1990s/00s of really average middling junk. They're spoilt by the last six years of European qualification and becoming a fixture on the edge of the top four. There's an unpleasant sense of entitlement and a shallow knowledge of what it takes to really do something special when there are eight clubs trying to do the same, four with far greater resources/experience. This sub-set of fans will grow significantly with the new stadium in my opinion."

This dissonance is not confined to social media. Ken Saxton contributes to the *Hotspur America* podcast. Speaking on the *Spurs Show* podcast, he described his first match in England: "Stoke away, 2015 May, we lost 3-0. Big fight on the concourse between younger fans singing 'we're shit and we know we are' and the older thugs... Not the proudest thing to witness on your very first trip to England to see your club. We went down at half-time, grabbing a few beers and at Stoke they let you outside which is very unusual. It was a little bit crowded and you could see some scuffling going on. All of a sudden stewards were going down into the concourse and then the next thing you know we had, what, 40–50 people singing how shit we were and another 40 or 50 who were taking extreme offence at that. You had two sets of fans almost at war with each other, bottles flying, alcohol flying, coins flying. It was not pretty…"

The culture of the Premier League distorts what is realistically possible. It creates a culture of expectation and instant gratification where anything less than finishing fourth constitutes failure regardless of at what point the team's development has reached or the resources consumed compared with other clubs. Winning trophies is less important than finishing in the top four and thus qualifying for the Champions League. In 2015 the *Spurs In The Blood* site ran a poll – given the choice between 'Cup Glory' and 'Top Four', 57% preferred the latter. The irony is that these fans do not expect Spurs to win the competition. But qualification generates more income to mount a better challenge for the top four come the following season where Spurs can qualify again with no hope of winning, and so on.

Writer Seb Stafford-Bloor is a Spurs fan in his early thirties. He finds common ground with Spurs fans of all ages but worries that this will change: "I grew up in Oxford, and so before I was old enough to travel to Spurs games alone, me and my friends (Arsenal, Chelsea, West Ham and even Man United and Liverpool supporters) would go to see live football at the Manor Ground. It was £6 for U12s, it was terraced and, even in the early 1990s, it offered a distinctly 1980s experience. As a consequence, I haven't suffered that 1992 divide that many in my generation do and I cherish the kind of matchday experience that was typically more common before my time.

"However, I think this is going to become a much bigger problem. My generation is perhaps the last to experience football in something vaguely reminiscent of its original form and those Spurs fans who are only now approaching adulthood are far more indoctrinated by Sky Sports' presentation of the game. They have less tolerance for failure and, I fear, will ultimately treat Tottenham as a character within a television programme. They'll cheer and they'll boo, certainly, but I worry that they'll never enjoy the depth of experience that I have or develop that distinctive 'Tottenham identity' as a supporter."

Perhaps the greatest irony of all is that, in 2016, with the club arguably projecting as strong a sense of personality or brand as it ever has, it's the supporters who have shaped it who are questioning exactly what it is that they support. Being a Spurs fan is a much bigger thing than it was when you supported the Flower of the South, the rising team of the suburbs, the push and run masters or Bill Nicholson's Super Spurs. The common experience is still Spurs, but it's the way fans come to that and what they take from it that has spun off into myriad avenues. What's interesting is the continued hunger to know the history and traditions of the club, to have a sense that this most modern of things is rooted properly, that it's not just a creation of the connected consumer age. And during the 2015/16 season, the connection between fans – who had not long before felt little connection with their club – and Tottenham Hotspur was drawn on to fuel the title challenge.

This has been a people's history of Tottenham Hotspur. History should be learnt from in order to make better decisions about the future. And that is something that percolates in the present.

Epilogue

By Alan Fisher

OUR lives are full of our stories, our stories are full of our
lives. We tell stories about ourselves, about what we do,
what makes us laugh and cry, happy or sad, what makes
our heart beat faster. It's how we make sense of our world and our
place in it. We tell stories about our lives to other people so they
know who we are, to our children so they understand what's truly
important. We tell ourselves those stories because sometimes we
are the only ones who listen. In those tales we find out who we are,
what it means to be us, our identity. We shape those stories, the
stories shape us. So it goes.

Football fans have told stories ever since people first gathered on
a muddy touchline to watch other people kick a ball around. As if
kicking a ball around isn't trivial enough, we turn up to just watch.
Our football stories are about meaning, a reason to be, reasons to
believe, reasons to be cheerful, to turn up next week and the week
after. They're an expression of what we feel when we see the game,
feelings that cause a stir deep down and we're not sure quite why.
Stories about why football is more than a game, why we come back
not just to watch any team but this team, our team. The team in
white shirts and navy blue shorts.

All good stories are a mixture of fantasy and reality. Myths and legends create excitement and mystery, an aura around the ordinary, but myths don't survive unless at their core lies meaning. Sometimes fantasy is the easiest way of expressing reality.

Spurs fans tell each other stories. About the Spurs Way, attacking football, fleet of foot, pass and move. In an age when the gap between club and fan threatens to become an abyss, Spurs supporters turn to a past captain, Danny Blanchflower, who spoke of how the 'game is about glory, doing things in style', and former manager, Bill Nicholson, to express our aspirations. Bill Nick said: "It is better to fail aiming high than to succeed aiming low. And we of Spurs have set our sights very high, so high in fact that even failure will have in it an echo of glory."

There may be myth-making at play here. Veteran Fleet Street football writer Norman Giller knew Danny and Bill well and suggests that if Bill said those words, it was undoubtedly Danny who put them in his mouth. No matter: they will always be precious for supporters, who hold the heritage dear and pass it on down the generations. About how doing things the right way comes first, before the trophies. How winning cups is not just to do with silverware but the thrill, the atmosphere, the supporters. How frustration and disappointment is always just around the corner. Above all else, about loyalty.

We tell our stories to fellow Spurs fans so we can have a laugh over a pre-match beer. To our children so they will follow in our footsteps and if not, at least they will understand and take pity. To friends and colleagues – it doesn't matter if they don't get it, it's so they know who we are. To complete strangers, who will never see us again but see as we pass the proud cockerel on the ball, the navy blue and white, and know who we are. To ourselves, during interminable journeys to and from the ground, when we bash the credit card once again, for comfort during restless nights worrying about a result or moments, and we all have them, where we doubt our faith, 'this is why I do it, this is who I am'.

Being a Spurs fan means something, something deeper and more profound than just wearing a shirt. Trace that right back through our history to the very origins, it's the golden thread that runs through the bad times, the good times and hardest of all, the ordinary times. It's also about the future, and woe betide the club or its supporters if we lose it.

Our People's History demonstrates the constants rather than the differences between then and now. Supporters down the ages have had the same preoccupations – getting there, getting in and getting behind the team. Transport to and from the ground or to away games led fans to come together, first in informal travel groups by train and coach, then through the organisation of the Supporters' Club, Aubrey Morris or the Trust negotiating a special train or plane. When they arrive, is there enough room for them to get in or get a ticket? The prawn sandwich brigade and corporate entertainment at the expense of the true fan seems a very modern and unwelcome development but complaints date back to the fur coat brigade in the fifties and early sixties.

If somehow a contemporary fan could meet a 'bobber' from the terraces in the 1930s or another who crowded the touchline before Tottenham were a league club, they would speak a common language, tell the same stories. Of how Spurs fans have always been loyal, on the marshes and gathering round the Hotspur pitch in preference to Park or Latymer, turning up week in week out in the 1920s and 1930s despite the Arsenal arrivistes up the road, home and away, whether it be New Brompton, Old Trafford or Rotterdam. Of independence and self-reliance, the schoolboys forming the club, Left on the Shelf and 1882. How the bobber and Spurite would enjoy tales of Greaves, Mackay, White and Bale, of Rowe and Nicholson. Of how those fans cheer good football and barrack players who don't try their hardest. Of the noise, whether it be the Tottenham Roar or Spurs 2 Arsenal 1 in 2015.

Above all, there is Tottenham. The Hotspur have never played a home match more than 600 yards from the second lamppost on the right down the High Road. World War Two friendlies aside, ever. Consider that for a moment. Every single Spurs fan has walked in the same streets to watch the team.

In a time of what seems like significant change in the game, it has remarkable resonance. It's the sense of place that unites us. The first fans walked to see their local team, then the easy transport links in this growing London suburb made the journey convenient. Now it's very different. Spurs fans come from far and wide, from different places, backgrounds and cultures, but come to a run-down part of north London they do, for magic, passion and the history. That place is the one thing that unites us, with each other and our heritage. Unlike, say, Liverpool or Newcastle, we're not part of the culture of the city. That's why staying there is so significant. If we had moved to Stratford, of course the club would carry on but it would never have been quite the same. That heritage is who we are.

Now it is time to create stories of our own. The new ground is a watershed moment in the history of Spurs fandom. The club could do irrevocable harm to their relationship with the supporters unless they pay due attention to our heritage. Due to be complete in time for the start of the 2018/19 season, it looks like it won't be the generic modern stadium with its cool, sterile lines and atmosphere to match. There's a skywalk, hotel and a retractable pitch for NFL. Frankly, so what? Get behind the team, so the stands rise close to the pitch and we have an 'end', at 17,000 capacity we can make it ours and make some noise.

However, at the Trust meetings we hear feedback about the bank wanting guaranteed income streams and maximising revenue to justify the loans. Money, in other words. If it is the people's game, this opportunity will be wasted if ticket prices exclude vast swathes of the fanbase.

At the end of the 2014/15 season, talk turned to season ticket renewal. It's a ritual, part of the cycle of support, but never before had I sensed such a questioning of the effort and expense. Not marching-down-the-street protest but heartfelt, almost furtive conversations among diehards as if Pandora's Box would burst open should the unmentionable be overheard let alone said out loud – 'I'm thinking about not renewing.'

Spurs had made themselves hard to love. It was not so much the lack of trophies but the absence of any coherent plan. Never mind 'aiming high', we weren't aiming at anything, as well as having spent big on a striker who apparently wasn't aiming at anything much either. At the time, planning permission for the new stadium had not been agreed so that was looking like a white and navy blue elephant. Yet we were being asked to pay some of the highest prices in the country despite the club responding to the Trust's plea for a price freeze.

This is modern football: the prices, dates and kick-off times for the convenience of a largely uncommitted television audience not the paying supporter, late changes too and football potentially every day of the week so no chance of planning anything else in advance. Travel problems: dodgy trains, nearest tube 20 minutes away, car-parking almost as distant. Spurs have a flourishing corporate section but the body of fans are not day-trippers or flash geezers. For many the expense is harder and harder to justify. The game, the merchandise, the seats, the fans, treated like a commodity. Wears down even the most dedicated. The club have even usurped Bill Nick and Danny Blanchflower's inspiring words, turning them into a marketing ploy, embossed in shirts, emblazoned on advertising. Last year shirt sponsors Under Armour created a fans' gallery of photos in the tunnel. Fine – but the idea was sold as, 'show you are a real fan – send in your photo.' Real fans send in photos and wear the sponsor's gear, you don't have to be there any more. Everything becomes a commodity in the end and they can't even clean the pigeon shit off my seat.

And what about Matt Bigg and his family? He wants to take his football-mad boys to watch his team. Hardly a lofty aspiration yet impossible unless the price is reasonable.

If you build it, we will come but the temporary fans, the South Korean tourists, the curious, they may be filling the spare seats and Stubhub's profits now but they'll go elsewhere in a flash. Spurs are about loyalty and longevity. Gloryhunters and football hipsters don't come to N17.

Culture runs deep. It's embedded in the way Spurs supporters think, feel and act. Like any culture it flexes with the times. A generation brought up in the doldrums of the nineties and noughties value commitment and the Spurs Way over and above hubristic expectation and instant gratification. Supporter unrest at Spurs has come not in protest at 'only' being in the top six or for that matter high prices in themselves but when loyalty has been exploited and our heritage of support betrayed, and in part our People's History is about this action and reaction, fans organising when being wronged by the club. When the East Stand was built in 1934, the club was praised for looking after the ordinary fan. The Shelf became the support of legend, then was destroyed by executive boxes. Left on the Shelf, further fan protest, the move to Stratford, all about support and our history. It's no coincidence that the 1882 movement of predominantly younger fans take their name from our year of origin and want not to take the club over but simply, vitally, to get behind the team and support the shirt to the hilt. They get it. Now the club need to get it too.

2015/16 ended with feelings of frustration and disappointment, but for very different reasons. A young, inexperienced but ferociously committed Spurs team built up a head of steam over the season, mounting the first serious title challenge in a generation. Frustration because we fell away in the final four or five games.

Superficially, this seems the same old Spurs, never delivering. That could not be more wrong. This was a Spurs team over-achieving, performing above expectations, better to aim high and fail. More importantly there was a sea-change in the relationship between the supporters and the players. This group gave everything and were as committed as the fans. Such was their intensity, you could warm your hands on the heat of their ambition and effort. Manager Mauricio Pochettino's grasp of what the club means to the fans exceeds his command of English. And they play the Spurs Way, fast, flowing football, anxious to get the ball forward.

The distance between players and fans diminished. Goal celebrations weren't some choreographed in-joke, rather an outpouring of togetherness and exuberance shared with the fans, especially at away games where the 90-minute noise from our packed enclosure has been praised by supporters across the country. The 'one of our own' Harry Kane song became a totemic anthem, player and fans together. Against Norwich on Boxing Day, the players were reluctant to leave the field at the conclusion of an outstanding performance as if they didn't want the thrill to end. Supporters delayed their cold turkey and ham to applaud every step of an impromptu half-lap of honour.

This is the way Tottenham Hotspur has been in the past and should be in the future. Playing the Spurs Way, in Tottenham, supporters close to the pitch. Football's changed but some things stay the same. Now it is over to Daniel Levy and the board to make Tottenham football accessible. Not cheap, football sadly never will be, but affordable. Short-term income gains must not outweigh the long-term benefits of making supporters feel welcome.

This is one People's History. There are many others, because every supporter has their own story. There are some we didn't have time to tell. Chris and Dan bonding as father and son through Spurs. Arthur and Steve flanked by their children and grandchildren. The collectors, the obsessives, the comedians. Others whose lives have been disrupted by tragedy, who lost themselves in the crowd and found comfort. Now is the time for new stories to be created as we pass on the flame. There's only one Hotspur.

• *Since we completed this book, we have heard that Tottenham Arthur, who we mention in the text, has indeed died. Nobody knew where he lived or if he had any family, but he always had Spurs and the fans took care of him. Rest in peace.*

Bibliography

Clavane, A. (2012). *Does Your Rabbi Know You're Here?* London: Quercus.

Cloake, M. (2013). *Sound of the Crowd* – Spurs fan culture and the fight for future football (Ebook ed.) Amazon.

Cloake, M. (2014). *Taking Our Ball Back – English football's culture wars.* London: CreateSpace Independent Publishing Platform on Amazon.

Cloake, M & Powley, A (2004) *We Are Tottenham*, Mainstream

Finn, R. L. (1972). *Tottenham Hotspur F.C. :The Official History.* London: Robert Hale.

Goodwin, B. (2007). *Tottenham Hotspur: The Complete Record.* Derby: Breedon Books.

Hough, I (2007) *Perry Boys;* Milo Books

Holland, J. (1957). *Spurs: A History of Tottenham Hotspur Football Club.* London: The Sportsman's Book Club.

Horrie, C. (1992). *Sick as A Parrot – the inside story of the Spurs fiasco.* London: Virgin Publishing.

Inwood, S. (1998). *A History of London.* London: MacMillan.

King, A. (2002). *The End of the Terraces: The transformation of english football in the 1990s* (Revised paperback edition ed.). London: Leicester University Press.

Lupson, P. (2006). *Thank God for Football!.* London: Society for Promoting Christian Knowledge.

Mason, T. (1980). *Association Football and English Society 1863-1915*. Sussex: Harvester Press.

Protz, C. (2009). *Tottenham: A History*. Chichester: Phillimore.

Russell, D. (1997). *Football and the English – A social history of association football in England, 1863-1995*. Preston: Carnegie Publishing.

Soar, P. (1996). *Tottenham Hotspur – the Official Illustrated History*. London: Hamlyn.

Taylor, M. (2013). *The Association Game – A history of British football*. Oxon: Routledge.

Wagstaffe Simmons, G. (1947). *Tottenham Hotspur Football Club: Its birth and progress 1882-1946*. Tottenham, London: Tottenham Hotspur Football and Athletic Company Ltd.

Ward, A., & Williams, J. (2009). *Football Nation – sixty years of the beautiful game*. London: Bloomsbury.

Weekly Herald. (1921). *A romance of football: The history of the Tottenham Hotspur F.C. Tottenham*, London: Tottenham and Edmonton Weekly Herald.

Welch, J. (2012). *The Biography of Tottenham Hotspur*. Kingston-upon-Thames: Vision Sports.

Wilson, J, (2014) *Inverting the Pyramid*, Orion

Wombell, P, (1978) *Tottenham Boys We Are Here*, Independent publication